The Wirksworth Branch

by
Howard Sprenger

THE OAKWOOD PRESS

© Oakwood Press & Howard Sprenger 2004

First Edition 1987
Second Edition 2004

British Library Cataloguing in Publication Data
A Record for this book is available from the British Library
ISBN 0 85361 625 6

Typeset by Oakwood Graphics.
Repro by Ford Graphics, Ringwood, Hants.
Printed by Pims Print, Yeovil, Somerset.

Title page: The evening train to Wirksworth is seen at speed near Shottle hauled by Ivatt 2-6-2T No. 1205 on 15th May, 1947, a month before withdrawal of passenger services.
J.C. Flemons, H.C. Casserley Collection

Front cover: A Derby-built diesel multiple unit 4-car suburban set (later class '127') on test at Wirksworth when new in May 1959. Thirty of these sets were built, spending most of their working lives on Bedford to St Pancras services. *Ray Oakley/Colour-Rail*

Rear cover: Stoneycroft Quarry on 26th December, 1969 (by then also referred to as Middlepeak Quarry Lower Level). The tracks are coming in from under Middleton Road on the right, and the huge lime-kilns dominate the quarry floor. *R.G. Cash*

Published by The Oakwood Press (Usk), P.O. Box 13, Usk, Mon., NP15 1YS.
E-mail: oakwood-press@dial.pipex.com
Website: www.oakwood-press.dial.pipex.com

Contents

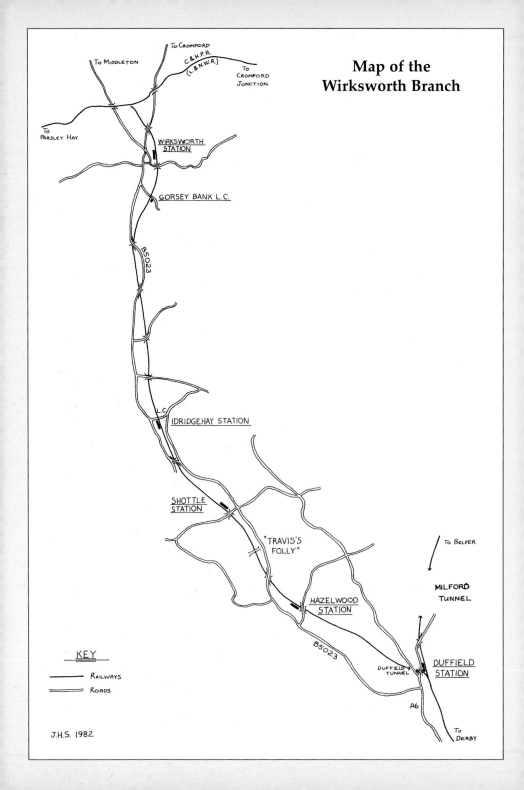

Map of the
Wirksworth Branch

Chapter One

Historical Background

The market town of Wirksworth lies at the head of the Ecclesbourne valley surrounded by hills on three sides. Locked beneath these hills is the lead ore on which, physically and metaphorically, Wirksworth was founded. This hidden wealth attracted the Romans to the settlement which had existed from Ancient British times and lead mining was to be the staple industry of the town until the 19th century.

The town had grown slowly but steadily and in 1801, with a population of 2,978, was the fourth largest town in Derbyshire. The 19th century was a time of great expansion but the growth of other centres of population due to the Industrial Revolution was not reflected in Wirksworth, and by 1901 the population had grown by about 900.

Industry in the town prospered, notably limestone quarrying and tape weaving. This growth of new industry, however, almost exactly mirrored the decline of lead mining which may account for the relatively stable size of the town.

The coming of a railway usually results in the rapid growth of a community, but although the quarrying certainly benefited from this development, Wirksworth did not follow the standard pattern. This is partly due to the fact that, compared with other similar towns, Wirksworth had always enjoyed good communications with the outside world.

It was well served by toll roads, notably Duffield to Wirksworth (1757) known as 'Top Road', Ashbourne to Oakerthorpe (1761) and Wirksworth to Hulland Ward (1792). In 1812 a road was opened through the Ecclesbourne valley from Duffield to Idridgehay where it joined the road from Hulland Ward.

Travel on these roads was tiring and uncomfortable so communications were greatly improved by the opening of the Cromford Canal in 1793. Farm produce and coal could now be carried to and from the canal less than three miles away.

The next major development was the opening of the Cromford and High Peak Railway in 1830. This very well documented line figures prominently in the history of the Wirksworth branch as will become evident later. At the time of its opening, only five years after the Stockton & Darlington Railway (and in the same year as the opening of the Liverpool & Manchester), it must have caused a minor revolution in the area. Wirksworth was not on the line of the railway but was within a mile. Indeed, Middle Peak Wharf at Middleton was much nearer to Wirksworth than many later stations were to the settlements which they professed to serve. Despite early experiments in passenger carrying, this was truly a goods line so travellers still depended on the turnpikes.

In 1846, there were carriers, omnibuses and mail-gigs operating to and from Alfreton, Ashbourne, Belper, Chesterfield, Cromford, Derby, Nottingham and Matlock. In 1852, carriers and omnibuses operated to and from Alfreton,

Ashbourne, Bakewell (via a connection at Cromford), Brassington, Chesterfield, Cromford, Derby, Matlock, Nottingham and Winster.

Between these two years (on 4th June, 1849) a new railway had opened between Ambergate and Rowsley; the 'little line with the long name', of which this was part, was ostentatiously called the Manchester, Buxton, Matlock & Midlands Junction Railway (MBM&MJR). The latter part of the title was at least correct as the line joined the erstwhile North Midland Railway (NMR) at Ambergate which had opened in 1840.

The Matlock line by-passed Wirksworth but, as with the Cromford Canal, was only some three miles away in the Derwent valley. Access from Wirksworth was quite easy, Cromford being the nearest station on the line. The Midland Railway timetable dated 1st June, 1860 carried the note: 'WIRKSWORTH - A conveyance for Wirksworth meets all Down Trains at Cromford Station on Weekdays'. There were in fact six down trains a day; this note did not appear in the timetable for 1854.

Whatstandwell station was almost as near, the original station (slightly to the north of the present station) having been opened at some time between June 1852 and January 1854. The January 1854 timetable shows trains stopping but fares are not shown. In those days fares were always shown against established stations. There is a possibility that there was some sort of connection between Wirksworth and Whatstandwell from the time of its opening.

At about this time, there were three proposals for lines which would have placed Wirksworth directly on the railway map. The first, dating from 1845 was known as the Staffordshire & North Midland Junction Railway and consisted of three proposals:

(a) A line between Stafford and the North Midland Railway at Ambergate via Ashbourne, Bradbourne and Kirk Ireton.
(b) An alternative line to Belper.
(c) A branch to Wirksworth.

On the plan, the branch peters out just short of Wirksworth at a distance of 3 miles, 6 furlongs and 1 chain from the proposed junction at Kirk Ireton.

The second, dated 1852, was the South Derbyshire Railway and had two sections:

(a) A line from the Midland Railway at Duffield to Ashbourne via Shottle, Biggin, Atlow and Sturston.
(b) A branch from Turnditch to the Cromford and High Peak Railway at Wirksworth.

The distance from Duffield to the junction at Turnditch measured 4 miles and 8 chains and the length of the branch was 5 miles, 9 chains and 70 links. To reach the High Peak line there would have been an incline similar to that eventually built by the Midland Railway (MR). The gradients were to be equally formidable, and would have been worked by a stationary engine.

Proposed Gradients from Wirksworth to the
Cromford and High Peak Railway (South Derbyshire Railway)

Approximate distance (furlongs)	Gradient
2	1 in 120
2½	1 in 64.6
1	1 in 20
1½	1 in 15
1⅓	1 in 9
⅓	1 in 3.2
⅓	level

The junction with the High Peak line would have been at about the same place as the eventual junction but facing towards Cromford instead of Whaley Bridge. At the Duffield end of the line a triangular junction would have been formed between the station and Milford tunnel. The line to Wirksworth would have been similar to that which was, ultimately, built.

The plans of both these railways can be studied in the Derbyshire Record Office and, like many other schemes of this era, are the only tangible relics of what might have been.

On 9th November, 1846 notice was given of a Bill to be brought to Parliament, part of which was to provide for a branch from the MBM&MJR at Cromford to Wirksworth. Care has to be exercised here, however, as very often Parliamentary Bills quoted the names of the relevant parishes, so that a branch from the Parish of Cromford to the Parish of Wirksworth, might have simply referred to a deviation around Lea Woods, rather than a branch between the two places. Whatever the intention, the Bill was passed on 22nd July, 1847 but, like the other two proposals, this third one came to nothing.

From the middle of the 19th century, therefore, Wirksworth enjoyed railway facilities which many similar towns would have envied. Although without a railway of its own, it had easy access to two major systems: the Midland Railway and the London & North Western (LNWR) (which had taken over the Cromford and High Peak in 1862).

To establish the *raison d'etre* of the Wirksworth branch, it is necessary to look, not just at the local pressure for a connection to the main line, but also at other happenings which occurred between Derby and Manchester in the mid-19th century. Certainly, public clamour played a large part in the story but inter-company rivalry was the deciding factor, for the branch was a ruse, a £40,000 gamble by one company to thwart another. In that, it succeeded, and in doing so became an expensive luxury almost as soon as it had been completed.

As mentioned, 1849 saw the opening of the Manchester, Buxton, Matlock and Midlands Junction Railway from Ambergate to Rowsley. This line was jointly promoted by the Manchester & Birmingham Railway (M&BR) and the Midland Railway, the idea being that the Midland would gain access to Manchester via its partner's line near Stockport. The Manchester and Birmingham was to subscribe £190,000 and the Midland £285,000, giving the Midland 14,000 shares to the M&B's 9,500. The Midland was to work the line for 19 years on payment of rent equal to 2½ per cent on £421,300 of called-up capital.

Fate decreed, however, that on the very day that the MBM&MJR Act was obtained, the Manchester & Birmingham became a founder constituent of the LNWR. The resulting unholy alliance between the MR and the LNWR caused the truncation of the Matlock line due to pressure by the LNWR which saw the partnership as a means of clipping the Wyvern's wings. A new joint lease of the Matlock line was drawn up on 1st July, 1852 between the two rival companies which, again, was to last for 19 years. Shortly after the lease was agreed, on 30th August, 1852, the MBM&MJR purchased the Cromford Canal for £103,500.

On 21st February, 1853 the Cromford & High Peak Railway (C&HPR) opened its junction with the MBM&MJR at High Peak Junction and thus ended 23 years of splendid isolation.

The scene then moved to the Manchester end of the line. In 1854, the Stockport, Disley & Whaley Bridge Railway Act was passed by Parliament with strong opposition from the Manchester, Sheffield & Lincolnshire Railway (MS&LR) which had its own plans for the area. Heavily supported by the LNWR, the Stockport, Disley & Whaley Bridge Railway (SD&WBR) gained a second Act a year later enabling it to join the C&HPR at Whaley Bridge, and in 1857, powers were obtained to extend to Buxton. Thus, the LNWR was preventing the Midland from progressing north from Rowsley and the MS&LR from moving south into Buxton where it might eventually meet the Midland.

Meanwhile, back in Wirksworth, the local worthies were becoming increasingly agitated at the decline of their town compared with others in the area. One of the most vociferous was a prominent solicitor by the name of Philip Hubbersty. As a would-be promoter of railways, he had a first-class pedigree, and had received a letter from George Stephenson as long ago as 1835 offering to promote a railway from Duffield on the yet to be opened North Midland Railway if the people of the town would give it their support.

So it was that a public meeting was held in the Moot Hall at Wirksworth to look again at the possibility of securing a railway line to the town. About 300 people attended, and they appointed a committee (the first of many) to look into the surveying and costing of the line. The meeting was held on 8th October, 1858, and those present seem to have been blissfully unaware of the events taking place around them. If they had been, they might have approached one of the rival railway companies straight away. As it was, they funded the feasibility study (as it would be called today) themselves.

At a meeting of landowners and townspeople in the Moot Hall on 8th June, 1859, it was reported that the committee had met with landowners two weeks previously to discuss a railway from Wirksworth to Duffield and from Idridgehay to Ashbourne. W. Cantrell had been appointed Secretary, and although the Midland and North Staffordshire railways had been invited to attend the meeting, Cantrell was disappointed to report that no representatives had been sent. Conversely, The C&HPR was believed to be enthusiastic, but unfortunately, it was also penniless. Another committee appears to have been created at this time, consisting of Captain F.G. Goodwin, Mr James Milnes (Alton Manor), Mr Cantrell, Mr Wm Wheatcroft (Middleton), Mr B.S. Currey (representative of the Duke of Devonshire, elected Chairman), Mr Abbott, Mr R. Wall, Mr W. Marsh, Mr T. Newton and Mr D. Wilson. The meeting ended with the following resolution being passed: 'That it is desirable there should be a railway communication between the town of Wirksworth and Duffield so as to connect it with Derby and the South, South-east and South-west of England'. It is interesting that the North of England was not mentioned, and perhaps it was simply felt that the biggest market for Wirksworth's exports lay to the south.

In late June 1859, a letter was received from a Mr John Leonard of 9 Mortimer Road, St Johns Wood, London. He mentioned that he had lived for many years in Wirksworth, and had been following 'with pleasure the present renewed movements for obtaining . . . a line of railway between Wirksworth and Duffield'. His apparently unsolicited letter included his own estimate for the cost of building such a line, based solely on his knowledge of the locality and 'founded chiefly on recollection and without reference to plans and sections, other than an ordinary country map on a small scale'. Accordingly, he acknowledged that there might be some inaccuracy in his estimate, which amounted to £25,000 for a single line. Leonard admitted that a junction with the C&HPR would require a very steep gradient, and it is likely that his estimate did not include this. He finished by offering his services without charging any fees.

It seems inconceivable that the Committee should have given this estimate any credence given the rather flimsy basis on which it had been drawn up, but perhaps the offer of Leonard's services for nothing was too tempting to ignore. So it was that an encouraging reply was sent to Leonard on 2nd July, in which it was noted that a junction with the C&HPR would provide a great source of traffic for the line, particularly as the white limestone of Hopton and Middle Peak was much sought after by the iron masters of South Staffordshire. With this in mind, and with the observation that the heavily loaded wagons would be descending the line from the High Peak line, Leonard was encouraged to come up with a scheme that included a junction with the C&HPR, and was invited to Wirksworth to present his ideas.

The committee met Leonard on 3rd August at the Reading Room of the Mechanics Institute in Wirksworth, and were shown a survey for a the first two to three miles from the proposed junction with the C&HPR at Steeplehouse. Based on what they saw, they instructed Leonard, together with a local surveyor, Parkin, to survey the rest of the line to Duffield, and their report was presented to the committee on 26th August. Evidently, Leonard's original thought had been for a railway starting at Steeplehouse on the C&HPR and ending at Duffield, keeping to the contours similar to the way that some early canals had been built. This would have resulted in a very circuitous route at the Wirksworth end, with the town served by a station a considerable distance away and up a very steep hill. Even then, the gradients involved would have been at the very limit of those that could be negotiated by the locomotives of the time, so he settled on a proposal that was very close to that which was eventually built, with a self-acting incline from the High Peak line down to Wirksworth, and then a single line to Duffield. Even the short tunnel at the southern end was predicted, and he envisaged stations 'at Wallstone for Ashleyhay and Kirk Ireton, at Shottle Gate for Idridgehay and Shottle, at Cow House Lane for Turnditch, and at the Puss in Boots for Hazlewood [sic] and Windley'. His estimate for the line was a more realistic £45,000.

There followed some discussion, the Chairman being of the view that Leonard's estimate of 50,000 passengers annually was over-optimistic, to which it was pointed out that if the proposed fare of 6*d*. was doubled to a shilling, half that number would generate the same revenue. The Chairman then expressed the hope that the landowners would accept the agricultural value of their land, which Milnes (as one of the larger landowners) confirmed. As we shall see in Chapter Three, Milnes assurances turned out to be somewhat hollow. Parkin then revealed that the Midland Railway was thinking of closing the station at Duffield, but had now decided to wait and see whether the plans for the Wirksworth line were carried out. Dr Webb claimed that an 'eminent engineer' had offered to build the line and work it himself, whereupon Parkin revealed that he had received a similar offer from a contractor. The end result was the formation of another committee to oversee the building of the line, with Milnes as Chairman and Joseph Kingdon as Secretary. Parkin was appointed Surveyor and Leonard, Resident Engineer. Inexplicably, despite the momentum built up in the previous year, everything then went very quiet.

In July 1862, Hubbersty's partner, the aforementioned Joseph Kingdon, called another public meeting at the 'Red Lion' to revive interest in the railway. There is no doubt that he was prompted to do so by the takeover of the C&HPR by the LNWR a couple of months earlier. After all, if the new owners were as keen on the idea as the C&HPR Directors had been, there might be a possibility of extracting the necessary cash. One interested party at the meeting, Capt. Goodwin, was still pushing for an independent railway, and claimed to have a contact who would be prepared to meet most of the cost of the line if the local committee provided the rest. There was some support for the idea, and one of the members of the committee asked what the LNWR would do when it met the MR at Duffield if it supported the scheme. Kingdon, with some naivety it has to be said, stated that they should confine themselves 'to our local requirements and leave the LNW or any other company to do as they choose'. And so it was agreed that a deputation should go to the LNWR to invite its support.

As a response to all this, the *Wirksworth Advertiser* of 21st July carried a letter from John Leonard. He had received the paper reporting this new meeting, and believed that the scheme would fail like its predecessors, citing apathy as the main cause. Despite offering his services for free in 1859, he claimed that his expenses had still not been fully settled. The paper published another letter from him the following week, adding more detail about his claim. Altogether it amounted to a little over £30, and of the 11 committee members at the time, two had declined to pay as they were not at the meetings, a third had declined without giving a reason and a fourth had not paid because 'he was a miner'. The remaining seven, Messrs Fryer, Milnes, Currey, Cantrell, Wright, Wheatcroft and Aldern had each paid £3 6s. 8d., leaving him short to the tune of £7 8s. 0d. 'I have only to add that if the sum is an object to those whom the "cap may fit" they are heartily welcome to it, I am sick of the subject, and having had my say, willingly bid farewell to it.'

Throughout all this, the Midland was not letting the grass grow under its feet. Although it did not have sole ownership of the Matlock line, there was nothing to prevent it from building a line from Rowsley to Buxton. Having obtained an

Act in 1860, the line was opened on 1st June, 1863 two weeks before the SD&WBR reached the town. In order to reach Manchester, the Midland joined the MS&LR in promoting a line from Blackwell Mill, near Buxton, to the latter company's metals at New Mills. Completed in 1867, the line allowed the Midland to run trains into Manchester, but much depended on the attitude of the LNWR when the lease of the Matlock line expired in 1871.

Quite what happened at this point is not clear. It is possible that an approach was made to the LNWR, but within three months of the meeting at the 'Red Lion', the Midland had decided that a branch to Wirksworth could be extended to Rowsley thus bypassing the MBM&MJR if necessary. On 24th October, 1862, the *Wirksworth Advertiser* carried an optimistic piece about the line:

> A new railway to this place is now confidently talked of, and we have it on good authority that the Midland Railway have at length taken the project into consideration and intend making a line from Wirksworth to Duffield. Such a line, when completed, cannot fail to be a great convenience and benefit to the town and neighbourhood, and it is earnestly hoped that nothing may arise that will in any way mar or interfere with the undertaking and that, although all previous schemes have fallen through, the proposal of the Midland Railway will be attended with a different result and the line will ere long be commenced and carried to a successful issue.

On 6th November, the paper reported that Midland Railway Company surveyors were surveying the line, and a week later it reported that the Midland was to put a Bill into the next session of Parliament for the new railway. The same issue reported that lead mining was in a depression. It is believed that the MR survey very closely followed that done by Leonard and Parkin in 1859.

The building of the branch will be described in the next chapter but we can leap ahead a few years to 1869 when the joint lease with the LNWR had only two years left to run. At this point, the Directors of the MR ordered that '. . . the extension from Wirksworth to Rowsley be surveyed and the necessary measures taken to deposit the Parliamentary plans for the next session'.

The LNWR, realising that the Midland fully intended to build an alternative line to Rowsley and seeing the folly of maintaining a line quite separate from its own system, decided to abandon its interest in the MBM&MJR. Although, by now, it had acquired the C&HPR, in no way could this line be sufficiently upgraded to provide a passenger through-route from the Midlands to the North.

The Directors of the MR announced in a report dated February 1870 that they had 'negotiated the heads of an agreement with the Matlock Directors for vesting the undertaking in the Midland company alone'. The Midland was also to take over the 'Ambergate (Cromford) Canal with all liability and obligations thereon, and pay the shareholders of the Matlock company at par in a 5 per cent stock, with the option of converting it into Midland ordinary stock at any time within twelve months from the expiration of the lease'. The Midland subsequently took sole possession of the line from 1st July, 1871.

So now the people of Wirksworth had their own railway and the Midland had realised its ambition of running trains to Manchester. Unfortunately, it also had a line which it neither wanted nor needed. It had proved its point and gained a victory over the LNWR but at what price?

Chapter Two

Planning the Line

On 14th October, 1862 the Midland ordered its Engineer, Crossley, to make the necessary surveys and plans for the branch to Wirksworth. Notice of the Parliamentary Bill for the line appeared together with the plans in November of that year. This proposed:

A railway to commence in the township and parish of Duffield . . . by a junction with the Midland Railway at a point ten chains or thereabouts southward of the booking office of the Duffield Station . . . and to terminate in the township and parish of Wirksworth . . . in or near a certain field called the 'Round Meadow' belonging to Thomas Newton.

The link with the C&HPR from Wirksworth station was dealt with in the same Bill but as a separate undertaking:

A Railway to commence by a junction with the said last mentioned intended Railway . . . and to terminate by a junction with the Cromford and High Peak Railway at a point eleven chains or thereabouts eastwards of a certain bridge carrying the turnpike road leading from Wirksworth to Middleton . . .

Understandably, the main opponent was the LNWR but it received certain safeguards and withdrew its objections. It is also known that another opponent was Mr John Shaw, one of the founders of Bowne & Shaw, who had a large interest in limestone quarrying in the area and feared that the line would result in limestone entering the district from quarries around Leicester. It is ironic that his fears, far from being unfounded, were quickly confounded when the line opened and limestone production rapidly increased.

On 21st July, 1863 the Midland Railway (New Lines and Additional Powers) Act (26 & 27 Vict. Cap. 183) received Royal Assent and gave powers in Section 7 for:

1. A New Railway from a junction with the Midland Railway in Duffield to Wirksworth.
   and:
2. A Railway from a junction with the last mentioned intended Railway in Wirksworth to terminate at a junction with the Cromford and High Peak Railway.

Section 41 of the Act stated that:

The junction with the Cromford and High Peak Railway (leased by the London and North Western Railway) shall be made by means of a siding at such place within the limit of deviation defined on the said plans as the London and North Western Company and the Company shall agree upon.

If the companies could not agree there was provision in the Act for arbitration and, if this failed, the Board of Trade could be approached to smooth the way.

Further concessions to the LNWR were that its Engineer should both approve the plans for the junction and supervise its construction. Furthermore, it was given the responsibility for the maintenance of any 'signals and conveniences' provided at the junction and also of the junction itself, for which the Midland was to pay half-yearly.

Two level crossings were allowed where bridges would usually have been required. That at Idridgehay was described as a minor farm access road and the other at Gorsey Bank was allowed because the building of a bridge embankment would have disrupted the water supply to Haarlem Mill. Finally, it was stipulated that if the line was not built within five years the Midland would be liable for severe financial penalties.

Incredibly, almost nine months were to pass before the Duffield and Wirksworth Construction Committee met for the first time on 2nd March, 1864. The meeting was chaired by Mr Hutchinson, the rest of the committee being Messrs Garbutt, Smith, Birkin and Jones, Sir Joseph Paxton MP and Sir Isaac Morley. So long was the delay that, in ignorance of this construction committee meeting, a public meeting was called at the Moot Hall. Having given vent to their feelings, the residents and landowners arranged for a deputation to meet the Directors of the Midland but, of course, by this time, things were beginning to happen.

At the first meeting of the committee it was resolved to offer the appointment of Land Valuer to Mr Charles Sanders at a payment of £30 per mile. This was accepted by Sanders and at the next meeting on 6th April he was duly appointed.

The Engineer was John Sydney Crossley who, in his post of Civil Engineer to the Midland Railway, supervised the construction of over 200 miles of new railway including the Settle and Carlisle line. At the April meeting, Crossley was ordered to stake out the line and '. . . prepare the necessary land plans for notices'. It was also reported that the MR had met the principal landowners on 23rd March (possibly the meeting referred to earlier) and extracted from them an agreement to accept a 'fair agricultural value for the land'.

On 16th April, the *Wirksworth Advertiser* reported that three sites at New Bridge were being considered for the terminus. These were described as being the bottom of Mr Hubbersty's field, part of Mr Wood's tanyard and the end of the Hannages.

By 31st August, seven miles of the route had been staked out, the section taken and the gradient settled. The plans were in the hands of the lithographer and copies would '. . . shortly be ready for the Land Agent to make what purchases he could effect by agreement'. The committee was also told that 'the line has been varied so as to cause the least possible severances in the large estates, forming for a considerable distance a boundary line between them'.

Staking out was nearly finished by 5th October by which time the sections and land plans were made for six miles and lithographed for three miles of the line. At the next meeting on 2nd November, it was ordered that the Engineer should obtain tenders for the construction of about six miles of the line from Duffield as soon as he was prepared to do so. Negotiations with landowners were progressing well, but the agents of the Duke of Devonshire insisted on the

diversion of the River Ecclesbourne for a length of nearly half a mile parallel to
the railway and the construction of an accommodation bridge 35 feet wide; '. . .
these requirements being most injudicious as regards the River diversion and
most extravagant as regards the bridge have been declined and the business
must wait for better counsel to prevail'.

Better counsel did not prevail, however, for this is the first reference to,
arguably, the most extraordinary and superfluous piece of civil engineering in
the history of railways. This was the massive 19-arch 'occupation viaduct'
between Hazelwood and Shottle which served no other purpose than to link
together two farms on either side of the line. Known locally as 'Travis's Folly',
its full story will be told later but it is clear that the MR was severely
embarrassed by having to build such a structure. No mention of it is made in
the minutes of the Construction Committee other than a couple of oblique
references, this being the first.

The MR was also experiencing some difficulty at Duffield where the
proposed route required the demolition of several buildings and the
re-alignment of certain roads. Agreement had to be reached with the Trustees
of Duffield Schools concerning the demolition of the Duffield Boys Endowed
School. This was not the first time that the school had had to be moved as a
result of railway expansion. In 1843, the Trustees of the Free Grammar School
(founded in 1565) were notified that, under its statutory powers, the North
Midland Railway was taking over the school premises. The new school was
completed in 1844 on King Street at a cost of £600. The purpose of this is not
clear as the NMR had only opened three years earlier and thoughts of the
Wirksworth branch were many years distant. Perhaps Philip Hubbersty's
contact with George Stephenson in 1835 was an indication that the North
Midland had been thinking seriously about a branch after all. Now, 20 years
after its construction, the new school was required by the railway.

'Travis's Folly', the 19-arch 'occupation viaduct' between Hazelwood and Shottle.
Author's Collection

The Trustees would only agree to the use of the school land on condition that the MR pay the cost of a new site and build (or provide money for) a new school house and school room. The railway was prepared to buy the land at a 'liberal price' and rebuild the school house on an adjoining piece of land. The Trustees objected to having the school so near the railway and preferred a site on the opposite side of the road. To meet the Trustees' requirements would have cost £2,150 so the conditions proposed by the Trustees were declined.

No further mention is made in the minutes but it is known that the school and grounds were bought for £1,600. The schoolmaster's house and part of the school room were demolished and, with the proceeds of the sale, a new school was built on Vicarage Lane and opened in 1869. The remains of the old school room in King Street were rented from the railway by the Parish Council as a Parish Room; only in recent years did it become unsafe and was demolished.

The Way and Works Committee minutes show an entry dated 18th February, 1868 referring to the fact that about 1,080 square yards of spare ground at Duffield were to be sold to the Trustees of Duffield School at 2s. 6d. per square yard. The school in question here may be the old National School, which was replaced in 1870 by a new school built on a site acquired from the MR next door to the new Parish Room in King Street.

The land on which this school was built was just north of the junction of Crown Street and King Street where the railway was built through a tunnel directly below the junction. An Inn called 'The Crown' was situated here and it too was sacrificed for the sake of the new line.

The Pennines, which over the years have presented almost insurmountable problems to railway engineers, begin their steady rise in this vicinity. Though geographers may argue about the precise point at which the 'backbone of England' has its base, the humble Duffield tunnel (all 52 yards of it) can claim some fame as being the southernmost tunnel through the range. Nearby, on the main line, Milford tunnel must be one of the earliest to breach the barrier, having been driven by October 1839.

Before the Wirksworth branch was built, the main road through Duffield passed close by the station. Known as Chapel Street, the road was severed by the new line, and a new route had to be made from the bottom of King Street to Milford Road. This crossed the branch by means of an iron bridge over the cutting just north of the Wirksworth platform.

Much land was being acquired in Duffield owing to the railway slicing right through the heart of the community. The minutes detail the buying of land near to the road diversion which '. . . could cause great injury to it'.

In December 1864, the *Wirksworth Advertiser* reported that there were to be three intermediate stations: Idridgehay, Cowers Lane and Puss in Boots. It had been decided to build the station in Wirksworth on Greenhough Croft (owned by Philip Hubbersty), and that access would be gained from New Bridge where the Turnpike Road would be raised to bridge the line. With an optimism only appreciated with hindsight, it predicted the completion of the line within a year of work starting.

At a meeting on 4th January, 1865 the committee ordered that the Engineer obtain tenders for a contract to build about nine miles of railway northwards

CUTTING THE FIRST SOD
OF THE

WIRKSWORTH & DUFFIELD
RAILWAY,
WEDNESDAY, APRIL 19th.

THE COMMTTEE appointed to make the necessary arrangements for a Public Demonstration on the cutting of the first sod of the above Railway, beg respectfully to intimate that the following is the programme proposed, and will be adhered to as far as practicable.

PROGRAMME.

PROCESSION, CONSISTING OF

THE WIRKSWORTH VOLUNTEERS,

ACCOMPANIED BY THE BAND,

(With Permission of Captain Hurt, the Commanding Officer.)

CLERGY, GENTRY, AND TRADESMEN

of the town and neighbourhood.

The various

FRIENDLY SOCIETIES
With their Banners.

Excavators, Miners, Quarrymen, and other Workmen.

The Procession to meet at the Market Place by 12 o'clock. Then to proceed from the Market Place to the place appointed where the Turning of the First Sod will be performed by MRS. PRICE WOOD, accompanied by the Ladies of the town and neighbourhood, at 1 o'clock. The Procession then to return to the Market Place.

At 2 o'clock, p.m., a Public Luncheon will be provided at the Red Lion Hotel, at a Moderate Charge.

The Committee and Contractors have invited the Directors, Engineers, and other officials of the Midland Railway Company to be present at the ceremony and partake of the luncheon.

Shortly after 4 o'clock, p.m., the Committee propose that all should adjourn to the Hannage, where, by permission of N. P. Wood, Esq., suitable amusements will be provided. The Bands will be in attendance.

It is understood that the Shops and other places of business will be closed at 12 o'clock at noon.

Cutting the First Sod. Extract from the *Matlock Advertiser* 15th April, 1865.

from Duffield. These tenders were to be received no later than 9 am on Tuesday 17th January and related to the building of the branch as far as Wirksworth station. The link with the C&HPR was to be dealt with separately on completion of the main section of the line. It appears that the earlier request concerning six miles of line was ignored and one wonders why this request was made.

On the appointed day the committee met to consider the following tenders:

	£	s.	d.
Messrs Tomlinson	50,727	13	2
Messrs Cope & Smart	42,518	10	10
Mr Miles Barber	40,177	4	10
Messrs Thompson and Co.	49,214	17	8
Messrs Benton & Woodiwiss	39,687	8	5

Not surprisingly, on 31st January, 1865, the contract was awarded to Benton & Woodiwiss. The most interesting feature about these tenders is the manner in which estimates were made to the nearest old penny. This must either reflect the immense value of a Victorian penny or the unswerving exactitude of Victorian quantity surveyors.

Benton & Woodiwiss had done a lot of work for the MR and some five years later were to be heavily involved with the construction of the Settle and Carlisle line. The firm was based in Derby and Shetford (Lancs.) and was awarded two out of the five contracts for this line. The Hawes branch was included in the total of 23 miles for which it was responsible out of a total of 79 miles.

On Tuesday 21st March work began at the Duffield end of the line where the proprietor of the 'King's Head', Mr Locker, cut the first sod. The *Wirksworth Advertiser* of 13th April carried another piece about the new railway line and, in particular, the seeming lack of celebrations to mark the beginning of the work at the Wirksworth end.

> . . . accordingly, a public meeting, which would have been better attended had a little more notice been given, was held in the Moot Hall, on Monday last . . . to determine what steps (if any) should be taken to commemorate this event.

The Chairman, Philip Hubbersty, noted that this was not the first time that he had had the pleasure of attending a meeting concerning the building of a railway to Duffield but that he had never been at one which was so poorly attended. Nevertheless, having made a decision to mark the cutting of the first sod, and having heard that the contractors would be prepared to subscribe £25 towards the event, a committee was formed to organise the proceedings. Among those on the committee were Messrs Hubbersty and Isaac Woodiwiss. It was noted that 19th April was a convenient day as far as the MR was concerned. It is interesting to note, in the light of subsequent events, that it was not the custom for the railway company to make any contribution at this time. Charles Sanders was present and told the meeting that the railway would support the festivities at the opening of the line, only.

The committee met at the Mechanics Institute the following day to organise the event, the *Advertiser* noting that:

We have not the slightest doubt that it will be a day of great pleasure and enjoyment for everyone that chooses to be present . . . We are pleased to learn that Mrs Price Wood has kindly undertaken to perform the ceremony . . . which will give additional éclat to the day's enjoyment.

On 19th April, 1865, nine days after the meeting, the first sod was cut at Wirksworth. That all the arrangements were made within those nine days is, indeed, a wonder and the occasion was duly recorded in the *Advertiser* as follows:

The triumphal arch opposite the Red Lion Hotel bore the following inscription: 'Success to the Wirksworth Railway - May the line be soon extended'. On the banner erected by Mr Beeson in Coldwell Street, we read, 'May our Railway increase our Commerce'.

At 11.30, the band of the Matlock Rifle Volunteers arrived and at about the same time so did the hastily-prepared ceremonial wheelbarrow and spade with which the first sod was to be dispatched. These implements were placed on a light dray and drawn into the Market Place to be viewed by the spectators.

The silver-plated spade was supplied by Mr W. Tomlinson, an ironmonger in the Market Place, and was described as being 'of the round-nosed shape'. The wheelbarrow, made by Mr George Frost, was 'larger in proportion than the spade, light and fanciful, and polished, the handles being covered with silk velvet'.

At approximately 12 noon, the procession started for Horse Pasture Field near the Hannages in the following order:

The Band of the Wirksworth Rifle Volunteers
The Wirksworth Rifle Volunteers
The Ladies
Directors and other Officials of the Midland Railway Committee, Clergy, Gentry and
    Contractors
Tradesmen
A light truck on which was placed the Wheelbarrow and Spade
The Matlock Rifle Band
The Hopton Stone Company's Workmen (about 60 in number) with models of their
    working implements
The Wirksworth Drum and Fife Band
The Wirksworth Lodge of Oddfellows and other Wirksworth Friendly Societies, and a
    portion of the Middleton Clubs

Several hundred members of the public joined in the procession and by one o'clock the stage was set. The wheelbarrow and spade were placed on the ground and the spade was then handed to Mrs Wood. The first sod was cut and placed on the wheelbarrow and Mrs Wood was requested to cut another. This she did before wheeling the barrow some 10 yards to empty the contents amidst enthusiastic cheers from the crowd and the strains of *God Save the Queen* from the Band. It is perhaps irreverent to think that Mrs Wood's labours may have saved the MR the odd 5d. on their bill from Benton & Woodiwiss, but her efforts were followed by an address to the assembled company. With a hearty 'three cheers' to the Midland Railway, the procession returned to the town for refreshments.

At about 2.30 pm, about 100 ladies and gentlemen attended a luncheon chaired by James Milnes at the 'Red Lion' in the presence of Josiah Lewis (Director of the Midland Railway), the engineers, Crossley and Underwood, and Charles Sanders. In a speech, Philip Hubbersty remarked that he had found a letter from George Stephenson, offering to promote a railway if the townspeople would give it their support. He and Dr Cantrell were the only survivors of those who had given the idea their support at the time. Lewis replied that the railway would put Wirksworth in connection with all the great cities of the empire, and Crossley and the contractor, Woodiwiss, both stated that construction was expected to take a year. Following the luncheon, 'amusements' were laid on for the young people in the Hannages, and so ended one of the biggest days in the history of Wirksworth.

The ceremonial spade is now kept in a glass case in Wirksworth Town Hall but the wheelbarrow has disappeared. The inscription on the spade reads:

Presented by
The Inhabitants of Wirksworth
to
Mrs. N. PRICE WOOD on the occasion of her turning of the first sod
of the
WIRKSWORTH DUFFIELD RAILWAY
April 19th. 1865

An interesting incident recently came to light concerning the ownership of land adjacent to the branch at Duffield. The MR purchased a considerable amount of land at Duffield so that, in the event of the Rowsley extension being required, sidings could be provided at the junction. In the 1960s, on the opposite side of the branch from the platform, a block of town-houses was built. In the late 1970s, however, British Rail discovered that it owned the land on which three and a half of these houses stood! Evidently, the owners of the orchard which occupied the area lost sight of this when they sold the land to the property developers, having continued to use the land when the MR failed to develop it. The Midland certainly does not seem to have fenced off all the land that it had bought.

The ceremonial spade with which the first sod was cut (and the second). Behind the spade is an envelope, which contains a letter from a relative of Mrs Price-Wood, dated 1935 thanking the council for their best wishes after his having donated the spade to the town. There are also the remains of a telegram dated 1938, the contents of which are not clear, but which mentions the Queen.

Cyril Sprenger

Gradient Profile

WIRKSWORTH — 192
GORSEY BANK — L.C. — 133
102
120
131
224
IDRIDGEHAY — L.C. — 246
100
122
126
170
SHOTTLE — 253
164
246
HAZELWOOD — L
308
177
132
DUFFIELD JUNCTION — L

Chapter Three

Building the Line

On 5th May, 1865 Crossley reported to the Construction Committee that the contractors had commenced work on many parts of the line including the cutting at Duffield. There was still a dispute over the diversion of the River Ecclesbourne and this had been referred to a Mr Cottingham.

As might be expected, the *Wirksworth Advertiser* followed the construction of the line closely. On 24th April it reported that it was struck with the rapid progress that was being made. At the Wirksworth end of the line the sub-contractors, Messrs Walker, were putting in culverts for the brooks which crossed the station site. Also involved in Wirksworth were Messrs G. & T. Hankinson and Messrs Slack & Buckley who were excavating the cutting through the Hannages. The paper noted that at this point the excavators had found coal, and it was thought that coal veins or beds were not far distant. It was also said that the specimen found contained petroleum or rock oil.

By June, work was progressing rapidly. The philanthropic nature of the Midland Railway was indicated in a minute which ordered that a cheque for the princely sum of £5 'be drawn and given to Mr Lewis to be added to a fund for providing a reading room for the navvies at Duffield'. In that same month, nearly £9,000 was paid out for land and construction costs.

In common with most, if not all, new lines, local materials were used. Referring to a bridge over the Ecclesbourne, the Engineer reported that 'the quality of stone is good Duffield stone . . . Of course the stone is not the same quality as the Dukes Quarry - but it is of the same quality as the Old Bridge'. There is a quarry near Whatstandwell called Dukes Quarry which might have supplied stone for the building of the North Midland Railway. The 'Old Bridge' referred to could be the bridge that carries the Makeney road from the A6 over the main line south of Duffield.

At Yew Tree Farm, Hazelwood, a certain John Ford had a brickworks which supplied bricks for the construction of the branch. Brickmaking had ceased by 1887 when Sir John Gay Newton Alleyne, 3rd Baronet, bought the property. He would not deserve a mention here were it not for the fact that as an engineer with the Butterley Company, he was responsible for the roof of St Pancras station.

Although there were no major natural obstacles to overcome, construction was not always free from problems. Despite the fact that landowners had been approached in connection with earlier schemes, numerous wrangles beset the progress of the line, not least one involving James Milnes of Alton Manor. As we have seen, he had served on (and been Chairman of) various committees looking into the possibility of building the line and had given assurances about the willingness of landowners to sell their land at agricultural value. He had even chaired the luncheon to mark the turning of the first sod at Wirksworth, and yet he claimed to have moved to Alton Manor from South Darley to escape the presence of the railway. Now he was demanding a private siding to be built

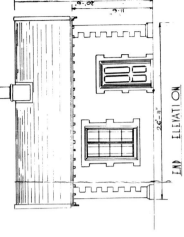

END ELEVATION

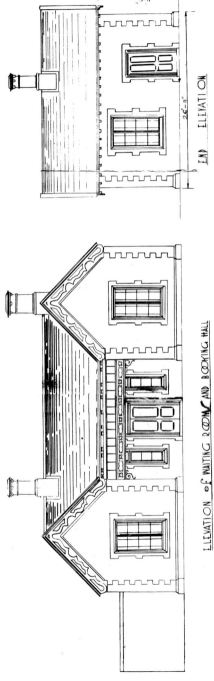

ELEVATION of WAITING ROOM and BOOKING HALL

Architect's drawing of Shottle station building
(typical of all the intermediate stations).

SHOTTLE
STATION BUILDINGS

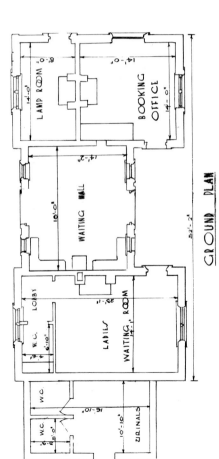

LAMP ROOM

BOOKING OFFICE

WAITING HALL

LOBBY

W.C.

LADIES WAITING ROOM

W.C.

W.C.

URINALS

GROUND PLAN

at the MR's expense, and as long as the Midland refused, his agent, Parkin (who had been the surveyor of the original independent line), insisted on dismissing the construction workers from the site.

This dispute, and that with the Duke of Devonshire, was soon resolved, however. The last we hear of Milnes is in the minutes of the Construction Committee meeting of 6th September. We are not told how agreement was reached and, as indicated before, the minutes are very circumspect about the Midland's capitulation to the Duke of Devonshire's demands.

According to the *Wirksworth Advertiser*, some cottages were being pulled down at the site of Wirksworth station, 'the inmates having had to procure dwellings elsewhere'. Messrs Hankinson had,

> . . . done a good stroke of the deep cutting, since the rails have been laid down, whilst Messrs Slack & Buckley are pushing on with their contract near the Haarlem Tape Works, where the Messrs Walker have just erected a substantial occupation bridge, and also a temporary bridge across the turnpike leading to Derby.

The paper also reported that a Sheffield contractor had begun to erect cast-iron fencing in the grounds belonging to Mr N.P. Wood. This innocuous comment elicited a response from a Mr J.N. Easton, Agent to J. Rowell, Great Queen Street, Westminster, who wrote:

> I beg to inform you that the patent stranded wire fencing now being erected on this line, through the lands of N.P. Wood is supplied by Mr Joseph Rowell, of St Paul's Street, Aberdeen and 4 Gt Queen Street, Westminster, London, and I shall be obliged by your correcting the error in your next impression.

In late September the *Advertiser* reported that in digging the foundations for the Wash Green bridge, 'a very old pack saddle bridge' had been found and Messrs Webster & Sons had pulled down a large batch of buildings belonging to Messrs Wall & Son. These buildings were 'stables, skin house, etc.' according to the Construction Committee minutes. Richard Wall had been given land in exchange and Websters were also charged with building new premises at the Midland's expense. On the Derby Road, railway engineers were setting out the skew bridge near Haarlem Mill.

At this stage, all but a small section of line in the middle of the branch had been subcontracted. Fine weather had allowed progress at Duffield to be particularly encouraging though this was less true at the terminus. As a result, the navvies were asked to work on Sundays but local protests put paid to this quite quickly.

Completely ignored by the minutes was the abandonment of their contracts by two of the sub-contractors. It is thought that one of these was Slack & Buckley and the *Advertiser* begged: '. . . is there no spirited contractor to take (the contract) or is the price such that it is worth nobody's attention?'

Notwithstanding this setback, on 1st November, Crossley reported that 'a good length of line is now formed to receive ballast and an engine is ready to be placed on the line'. In the following month the Engineer was requested to prepare plans of the station buildings and submit them to the committee.

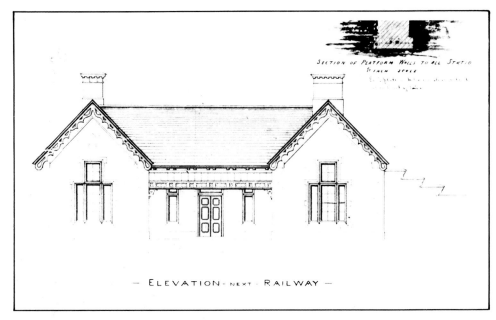

Elevation and plan of the station buildings at Wirksworth.

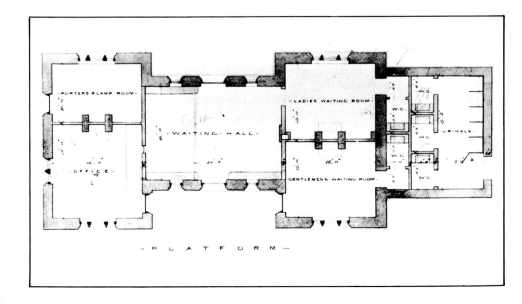

A further hold-up occurred in January 1866 due to a shortage of materials. As a result, 300 tons of rail was sent from the Otley line to enable tracklaying to be continued on the Wirksworth branch. This was all beginning to worry the *Advertiser*, which was predicting that the line would not be finished on time, and implied that the sub-contractors who had left had not been replaced. March 1867 was being suggested as a likely month for the completion of the line. On 28th February, at Wirksworth Petty Sessions, a labourer, James Bowland, attempted to sue Benton & Woodiwiss for the sum of 13s. 6d., which he alleged Woodiwiss had promised him after the sub-contractors had left. Out of sympathy to the men who had been abandoned by the sub-contractor, Benton & Woodiwiss had evidently made some *ex-gratia* payments, but the magistrates were not convinced that Bowland was owed any more.

At a General Meeting of the Wirksworth Gas Light & Coke Co. on 28th March, 1866 it was resolved 'that the Directors are hereby authorised to extend the main of the works to the Railway and where they may think necessary'.

Not until May did the weather relent sufficiently for real progress to be made and, in the same month, Crossley was ordered to obtain tenders for the construction of the station buildings and for a 'weighing machine' for each station. An engine turntable was required for Wirksworth, and two 13 ft wagon turntables were also needed. The *Derby Mercury* for 16th May carried a report of an accident near Wirksworth. John Booth was driving a horse when it kicked him on the cheek. He was knocked onto the wagon, and then fell to the ground senseless, the wheels fortunately just missing his head. 'The man is getting on as favourably as can be expected.'

Yet another setback occurred when the Board of Trade insisted on easier approaches to the various road bridges over the line, but, by June 1866, Crossley had produced plans for the stations. These were duly approved and the committee agreed that Benton & Woodiwiss be given the contract to construct the buildings.

On 23rd June, the *Wirksworth Advertiser* gave details of an accident which had taken place at Gorsey Bank though no mention was made of it in the Construction Committee's minutes. Thirteen men were building the crossing-keeper's house and were filling wagons in the cutting when three of them were buried by a landslip. One of them by the name of Belfield was heard to cry 'Oh dear, I'm killed' but lived to be proved wrong. The other two, Samuel Stone and John Heathcote, were not so lucky for they were both killed. Neither the men nor the contractors were found to be in any way responsible when the inquest was held.

Less than a month later, the works claimed another life, when James Hadfield, a 'tip driver' working at Postern, was running alongside a wagon, when he caught his toe against the end of a sleeper, stumbled and fell across the rails, whereupon the wagon ran him over.

In July, Crossley was ordered to arrange the construction of the telegraph on the branch. This was perhaps rather premature as for the next few months wet weather severely hampered the work ' . . . horses have been lost and much injury done'.

At Turnditch Bridge, Shottle, the railway was to be built on land owned by the Ashbourne to Belper Turnpike Trust and on which stood a toll house. A

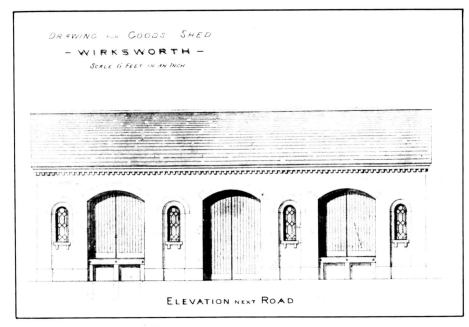

Drawings of the goods shed at Wirksworth.

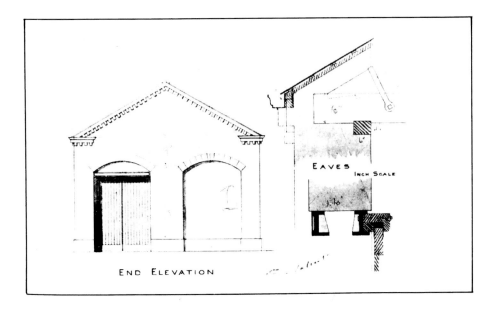

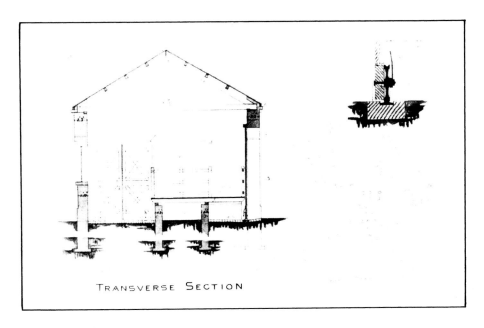

TRANSVERSE SECTION

Transverse section and ground plan of the goods shed at Wirksworth.

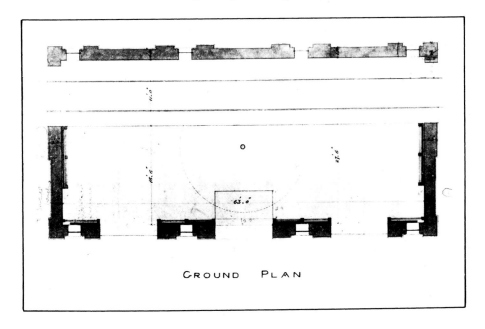

GROUND PLAN

meeting was held with the Turnpike Trustees at the 'Green Man', Ashbourne on 10th September, 1866 at which the MR agreed to build a new toll house and pay compensation. It was further arranged that the Midland would build a temporary 'box' on the other side of the road to the old toll house for the collector to use during the construction of the new one. Also, the railway was to provide rent-free accommodation for the collector during this period. Finally, the MR agreed to build the replacement within two months.

The junction at Duffield was put in during the early part of 1867 and the station buildings were in the course of construction by this time. An interesting insight into the planning of the line is given by a note in the minutes for February 1867. 'Necessary arrangements for the balancing the line have produced nearly a double line.' Balancing is the science (or art?) of excavating sufficient spoil from cuttings to form embankments along the route.

At the time the junction was put in, a new signal box was built by Edward Shenton on the up side of the main line opposite the junction, and a waiting room (presumably on the branch platform) was erected by Charles Humphries for £115. Duffield had been in an almost continuous state of reconstruction from the early 1860s. New sidings had been laid in 1862 together with a loading dock (or 'wharf' as it was called); new platforms had been put in, the approach road formed, existing platforms raised and new station buildings erected. Plan No. 114 in the Derbyshire Record Office (dated November 1862) shows the station building placed centrally on a platform about 230 ft long.

In early 1867, plans were put in hand for providing new stable buildings and platforms. The existing station building was to be converted into a pair of houses for pointsmen. It is at this time that the station was moved slightly south in readiness for the completion of the branch and it seems likely that the station building which stood until 1969 is the new one referred to here.

In March 1867 two tenders were received for the engine turntable which was to be fitted at Wirksworth. These were:

	£	s.	d.
Messrs Bray, Waddington & Co. Ltd	347	8	2
Messrs Thomas Swingler & Son	366	10	0

Bray, Waddington & Co. duly received the order but no more mention was made of the two wagon turntables. In the same month two weighbridges were ordered from H. Pooley and Son at a cost of £60 each. One was to go to Duffield and one to Wirksworth.

At this time work was proceeding well at all the stations except Idridgehay and it was predicted by the company that the line would be complete by July. Shottle station was still being referred to as Cowers Lane but Puss in Boots had become Hazelwood. The *Advertiser*, however, was confident that completion of the line was due within the next few weeks. So confident was the Editor, Joseph Buckley, that he wrote to the General Manager of the MR, James Allport, suggesting that the opening ceremony should coincide with the Well Dressing Festival. It was a good idea in theory. What better way to bring attention to the town and guarantee a large crowd? Allport was not so sure but he had a more realistic idea of the actual completion date.

Buckley was, evidently, a man of vision for he was always using the columns of his paper to extol the virtues of various schemes to improve the town. Sometimes he would wax positively lyrical, especially about the railway:

> With great pleasure everyone has watched the beautiful locomotive, which for some time has been running on the line, sending forth clouds of steam, rapidly flitting down the valley of the Ecclesbourne and disappearing in an elegant curvilinear form round the base of the hill while the shrill whistle is echoed from one side of the valley to the other.

He also wrote long sentences.

In early May, Allport was able to confirm that there was no hope of the line being ready for Whitsuntide. Undaunted, Buckley proposed postponing the Well Dressings a proposal which met with approval and was adopted. In June, while the Engineer was informing his committee that a great deal of work remained to be done, Buckley was informing his readers that only the Board of Trade inspection remained to be done.

On Saturday 22nd June, 1867 the *Wirksworth Advertiser* carried a report of an accident which had befallen some workmen on the railway a week previously. On Friday 14th June at about 6.30 am a party of 38 men was being propelled in an ordinary railway truck along the line. They were about 600 yards from 'the proposed station at Windley' (presumably Hazelwood) when one of them noticed a sleeper laid across the rails some 30 yards ahead. He managed to attract the attention of the driver who immediately began to stop the engine but it was too late. The truck was thrown off the line and, according to the report, was carried about 40 yards off the rails before being thrown on its end. Rails and sleepers were ploughed up, the axles of the wagon were broken and the 'underworks completely destroyed'.

Approximately 20 of the workmen were injured in the accident and these 'lay insensible and bleeding copiously from the wounds they had sustained'. Five men were dispatched to the Derbyshire Infirmary under the direction of Isaac Woodiwiss and, on arrival, one man had an arm amputated and another lost three fingers. These were the most serious injuries and none proved fatal.

The report concluded:

> It is conjectured that the sleeper was laid across the rails by some or other of the men previously employed upon the line, and who have been discharged. Information of the occurrence was conveyed to Mr Superintendent Shawe of the Derbyshire Constabulary, who at once proceeded to the scene of the accident, and who is pursuing every enquiry in order to discover the perpetrator of this dastardly deed. The men in the Infirmary are, we rejoice to say, progressing as favourably as could be wished.

Preparations were soon being made for the opening of the line and on 21st August, 1867 the first notice of this was sent to the Board of Trade. This initial notice was required to inform the Board of the intended opening and to request 'blank forms and documents required to be filled up and transmitted to the Board of Trade previous to the opening of the line in question'.

It was also reported that the Leeds Railway Plant Co. was to be paid £347 8s. 2d. for the supply and fixing of the turntable at Wirksworth. Water arrangements had not been completed, but it was possible to run from Derby to Wirksworth and back 'without water'.

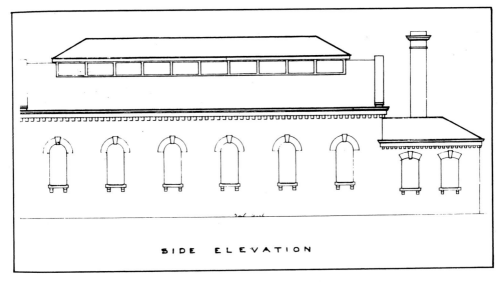

SIDE ELEVATION

The engine shed at Wirksworth.

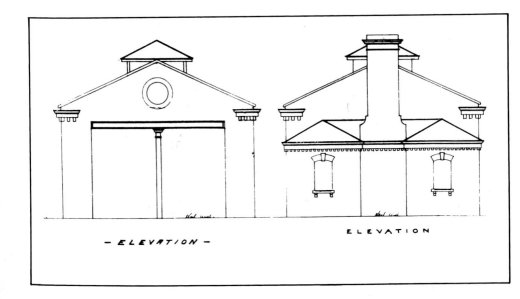

- ELEVATION -

ELEVATION

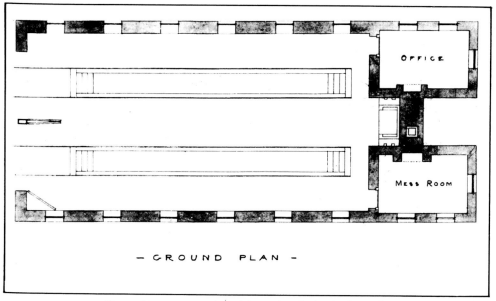

OFFICE

MESS ROOM

- GROUND   PLAN -

Plan and transverse section of the engine shed at Wirksworth.

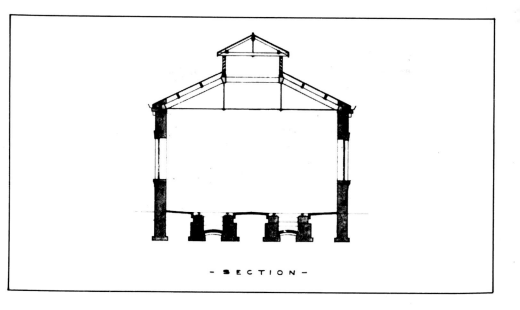

- SECTION -

On 13th September a second letter was sent to the Board of Trade informing them that 'after ten days from this notice, the new line of Railway from Duffield to Wirksworth . . . will, in the opinion of this Company, be . . . completed for the safe conveyance of passengers'.

Northern readers who bemoan the, alleged, 'southern' attitude that nothing exists north of Watford will be gratified by a note scribbled by D. McGregor of the Board of Trade which reads, 'Whereabouts is this line?'

'A few miles north of Derby', is the reply from one of his minions.

On 26th September the line was inspected by Col Rich who reported that 'land has been enclosed for a double line, and a great part of the works have been completed for a second line of rails'. Double-headed rail in 20ft lengths was laid throughout with a maximum gradient of 1 in 100 and a sharpest curve of 16 chains radius.

At Wirksworth the gradient was found to be 1 in 220 and Col Rich recommended that this 'should be changed to 1 in 300 if the line is ever carried forward'. It was noted that all passenger engines would be turned at Wirksworth and Derby. By now, Cowers Lane was being referred to as Shottle.

The Colonel was not very happy with the level crossing arrangements at Idridgehay and Gorsey Bank because the gates only closed to the railway on one side. He recommended that two more gates be installed at each crossing with crossbar signals and lamps mounted on them. Evidently, there were signals protecting the crossings but at Gorsey Bank they were out of sight of the crossing keeper and it was requested that they be moved. Catch points and stopblocks were not present at the various sidings and none of the points on the passenger lines had been supplied with 'indicators'. There were no clocks at the stations, gradient boards were not all present and there were several gaps in the fencing.

These and other minor omissions had been acknowledged by the MR which gave an undertaking that they would be completed within a week. Col Rich, however, had no indication from the MR as to the proposed method of working and he was not prepared to sanction the opening of the line until this had been received. On 28th September the MR replied that it would 'work the Wirksworth line with the Staff' and enclosed a copy of the rules for working the line.

This did not satisfy the Board of Trade who had always considered that such undertakings should be made under the seal of the company and signed by the Chairman and Secretary. This had been requested by the Board but all they had received had been a letter signed by Allport, the General Manager. Our friend McGregor was not sure about this. 'We have not always adhered rigidly to the Requirement. How shall we deal with this one?', he wrote. The reply came from Mr Herbert and is worth quoting in full:

> I do not think the Co. would repudiate the undertaking of their General Manager. If they would do this, they could not be trusted to an undertaking under their Seal. Until we have some power of enforcing compliance with such undertakings, their only practical effect is to relieve the Board of Trade from responsibility. I think Mr Allport will suffice for this.

This highlights the shortcomings which beset the regulation of railways in the 19th century as the Board of Trade had little power to enforce its recommendations. The Regulation of Railways Act of 1871 went some way towards rectifying this situation, but it was not until the Regulation of Railways Act of 1889 that the Board of Trade was given the power to make companies comply.

Thus on 1st October, 1867 the line opened to passengers but it was not until 6th August, 1872 that the Construction Committee resolved to hand responsibility over to the Way and Works Committee. The opening will be described in the next chapter but, needless to say, it was far too late for the Well Dressing Festival. As a result, no Well Dressings were held that year and it was to be 118 years before the railway made up for this disappointment.

It will be recalled that the main purpose of the line was to provide an alternative route to Rowsley, so Crossley was ordered to survey the route. A Prospectus was produced on 9th November, 1869 for a line 8 miles, 4 furlongs and 7 chains in length. It was to leave Wirksworth where the headshunt now is and go under the incline at Middle Peak. A 1,503 yds-long tunnel would have taken the line under the western slope of Bolehill followed by a 280 yds-long viaduct near Cromford. The line was then to go along the west bank of the River Derwent and under the Heights of Abraham through a 500 yard tunnel. Between here and Rowsley was another tunnel, 980 yards long and another viaduct, 300 yards in length. The Rowsley to Manchester line was to be joined to the north of the existing station by a trailing junction.

This was enough for the LNWR and, as we have seen, the MBM&MJR passed into the hands of the Midland Railway. The idea of extending to Rowsley was scrapped, the second line of rails was never laid to Wirksworth and the MR was left with an interesting but never-to-be-prosperous adjunct to its network.

```
          MIDLAND RAILWAY.
  OPENING OF THE DUFFIELD AND WIRKS-
               WORTH BRANCH.
   THIS RAILWAY was OPENED for PASSENGER
     TRAFFIC on TUESDAY, October 1st.  Trains
  will run between DERBY and WIRKSWORTH until
  further notice as under :—
                    1, 2, Gov.  1, 2 Class.  1, 2, Gov.
                      a.m.        a.m,        p.m.
  Derby, dep. -    -  8.5        11.50        4.30
  Wirksworth, arr. -  8.50       12.35        5.15

                    1, 2, Gov.  1, 2 Class.  1, 2, Gov.
                      a.m.        p.m.        p.m.
  Wirksworth, dep. -  9.5         1.5         5.40
  Derby, arr. -    -  9.50        1.50        6.25
     For intermediate Stations see Time Tables.
               JAMES ALLPORT,
                    General Manager.
```

Opening of the Duffield and Wirksworth branch as reported in the *Derby Mercury* for Wednesday 2nd October 1867.

RAILWAY TIME TABLES

For OCTOBER.

Midland Railway—Derby to Wirksworth.

	WEEK DAYS				SUNDAYS.		
	Gov.	1 2	..		Gov.	..	..
STATIONS.	a.m.	a.m.	..		p.m.	..	..
Derby ......dep.	8 5	11 50	..		4 30	..	..
Duffield	8 20	12 5	..		4 45	..	..
Hazlewood	8 26	12 11	..		4 51	..	..
Shottle	8 32	12 17	..		4 57	..	..
Idridgehay	8 38	12 23	..		5 3	..	..
Wirksworth....ar.	8 50	12 35	..		5 15	..	..

Wirksworth to Derby.

	WEEK DAYS				SUNDAYS.		
	Gov.	1 2	..		Gov.	..	..
STATIONS.	a.m.	p.m.	..		p.m.	..	..
Wirksworth ..dep.	9 5	1 5	..		5 40	..	..
Idridgehay	9 17	1 17	..		5 52	..	..
Shottle	9 23	1 23	..		5 58	..	..
Hazlewood	9 29	1 29	..		6 4	..	..
Duffield	9 35	1 35	..		6 10	..	..
Derby ....ar.	9 50	1 50	..		6 25	..	..

The first timetable published October 1867.

P. F. 70.

R 2.

Midland Railway.

WIRKSWORTH

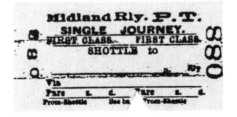

Chapter Four

Midland Railway Days: 1867 to 1922

On Wednesday 2nd October, 1867 the following article appeared in the *Derby Mercury*:

The Wirksworth and Duffield Railway

At last the line which pierces the district between Duffield and Wirksworth is open to the use of the public. Yesterday (Tuesday) the directors announced that the passenger traffic from which the inhabitants may win much convenience, even if the directors gain no profit, would be commenced; and henceforth the strange district through which this last effort has been made will be accessible to those who may wish to traverse it.

This rather dismissive attitude towards the new line was echoed by the Managing Director of the Midland who, at the opening, implied that the MR itself did not expect to make much profit from the line. The *Wirksworth and Matlock Advertiser* of 5th October was equally caustic in its report of the opening.

Contrary to the expectations of the public generally, this new branch of the Midland Railway was opened for passenger traffic on Tuesday last . . . For upwards of thirty years a railway to Duffield has been talked of: it is now a reality, and the inconvenience to which the inhabitants of Wirksworth have been put all their lives for the want of a railway . . . is now we trust forever removed. Considerably more time than was anticipated has been taken in the construction of the line, and the public mind had grown somewhat weary in waiting so long for the desired result.

These remarks might be thought to be a little bit 'rich' coming, as they do, from a newspaper which had done more than its fair share in raising 'the expectations of the public generally'. However, perhaps it can be excused for feeling a little less than happy with the way the town had been treated by the Midland. Not until Saturday 29th September was it informed that the line would open on the following Tuesday. Worse still (and despite Sanders' remarks prior to the cutting of the first sod), the Midland seemed to be wildly unenthusiastic about marking the opening with a ceremony of any kind. Nevertheless, there was 'a most enthusiastic greeting by many hundreds of the inhabitants who assembled upon the new railway bridge'.

The first train arrived at the appointed time (8.50 am) and was quickly prepared for its return trip.

The iron horse having been again attached, we (the writer being one of the passengers) started, for our first journey on the new line, amidst some cheering by many hundreds of spectators.

The writer returned by the 12.50 [*sic*] from Derby.

'Any more for Wirksworth?' sounded loud and well on the Derby platform, and we now began to feel that the old town just named was an important place after all.

On the opening day, there were about 160 passengers carried in each direction. The only celebratory event was organised by Mr Woodiwiss who invited about 20 of his friends to a meal in the afternoon.

The opening of the service was advertised in the *Derby Mercury* of 2nd and 9th October and in the *Chesterfield Reporter* of 4th and 11th October. This showed departures from Derby at 8.05 , 11.50 am and 4.30 pm and from Wirksworth at 9.05 am, 1.05 and 5.40 pm. The journey time in each direction was 45 minutes and each train stopped at all stations including Nottingham Road. There was no Sunday service at this time.

The line soon had an impact on local commerce for as early as November an advertisement offered 27 acres of limestone beds for sale 'near to the intended junction with the Duffield and Wirksworth Branch' adjacent to the C&HPR.

On 16th December, the goods service commenced with one train per day. Departing at 8.30 am from Derby, it crossed with the return passenger train at Duffield before arriving at Wirksworth at 10.30 am. Thirty minutes later it left Wirksworth and arrived at Derby at 1.00 pm having crossed with the second passenger train of the day on the main line near Little Eaton Junction.

At this time, the fares from Derby were:

	to Wirksworth		to Duffield	
	s.	d.	s.	d.
1st Single	2	8	1	2
2nd Single	2	0		10
'Gov' Single	1	1 ½		5
1st Return	4	6	2	0
2nd Return	3	6	1	5

The 'Extra Works' books of this period show a number of payments for work which must have been carried out immediately before (or even after) the opening of the branch. Hot air stoves for each station were supplied at a cost of £31 14s., platelayer's signals, lamps and flags cost £1 12s. 2d. and '3 repeaters and lights, indicators for Wirksworth, Belper and Hazelwood' amounted to £30. Signal lamps were supplied 'for signalling the new line' (£8 6s.) and nameboards at the stations were fixed, painted and lettered (£1 12s. 2d). The station master's house at Wirksworth was evidently found to be inadequate soon after the opening as additions had to be provided for £26 17s. 3d.

In 1867, tenders were invited for cleaning, painting and repairing the station master's house and station buildings at Duffield. They were received from:

	£	s.	d.
Joseph Bradbury	19	0	0
Thomas Skevington	19	10	0
George Wood	21	18	0

the successful applicant being Joseph Bradbury.

In 1868, at the request of the Traffic Committee, premises owned by the Midland that had been occupied as the 'Railway Inn' at Duffield were ordered to be converted into a private house. This is the end cottage in Station Row, nearest to the station. A year later, the *Derby Mercury* reported a revival of the earlier plan for a railway between Idridgehay and Ashbourne, which was proposed by Lucas & Wilkinson, engineers of London. The estimated cost would have been £42,000, but this was to be the last time the scheme was mentioned.

In 1871, another 'waiting shed' was provided at Duffield (probably on the island platform south of where the footbridge now is) by Edward Dusautoy for £87 3s. 6d. The sidings were rearranged in the same year, and two years later, a new lockup goods shed was provided. This building could be the one that still stands in the station yard and is, indeed, the only original building that is left. More sidings were added for coal traffic in 1875.

The first year for which receipts are available is 1872 with 17,619 passengers booked from Wirksworth, rising to 21,076 in 1884. From then until the Grouping the figures remained around 20,000 per year with a noticeable drop during World War I, followed by a postwar peak of 30,274 in 1920. This pattern was repeated at the other stations on the line with Idridgehay and Shottle having figures approximately half those of Wirksworth, and Hazelwood having about a third. Further details are given in *Appendix Two*.

The Royal Agricultural Society held its show at Osmaston, Derby in 1881 - the first time it had done so since 1843. To cope with the extra traffic, the Midland added an extra train from Derby to Wirksworth leaving at 7.30 pm on 15th, 16th and 17th July.

By 1885 there was a regular train in the evening which left Derby at 7.05 pm and arrived at Wirksworth at 7.45 pm. The return working was 7.55 pm ex-Wirksworth with an arrival time of 8.40 pm at Derby. All journey times were down to about 40 minutes. By now there was also a Sunday service from Derby at 4.10 pm arriving at Wirksworth at 4.45 pm and returning at 5.25 pm to arrive in Derby at 6.10 pm. This train did not stop at Nottingham Road in either direction nor did any Sunday train throughout the life of the branch.

The well dressings might have been a casualty of the late opening of the branch in 1867, but the festival drew considerable crowds to the town, and the Midland Railway naturally 'cashed in' as much as it could. In May 1886, a newspaper reported that, despite 'cloudy and threatening' weather, there were 'three or four long trains from Derby and specials from Nottingham, Sheffield and Burton'.

Carriage of 'Parcels, Horses, Carriages, Dogs etc.' was healthy and amounted to two-thirds of the value of the passenger receipts. Much of the parcels traffic was probably tape from the mills in the area. By the 1880s, Wirksworth was a main supplier of red tape to London for use in Government Departments. Work in the mills was the only large source of employment for women (apart from domestic work) but many women were regular commuters to Derby where they worked as shop-assistants and typists. Before World War I there were five mills in operation: Wheatcroft's Haarlem and Speedwell Mills, Thomas Webster's Willowbath Mill and Bowmer's North End and Providence Mills (the latter being at Gorsey Bank). After the war a sixth mill opened at Steeple Grange but this was put out of action by a fire in the 1930s.

Between the wars it was found to be cheaper to use roads rather than rail for bringing in the raw materials from Lancashire. Incidentally, the name 'Haarlem Mill' was transferred from a mill of that name in Derby that was owned by Wheatcroft's predecessors.

The earliest photograph found of the branch (and one of the earliest Midland Railway photographs) this is thought to have been taken in 1874, only seven years after the line was opened. It shows a Kirtley standard goods 0-6-0 locomotive No. 381, built by Robert Stephenson & Co., Newcastle in July 1856 standing in front of the goods shed at Wirksworth. The man in the centre of the group on the footplate is the station master at the time, Samuel Hodgkinson, and his wife, Emma, is standing in front of the tender. In January 1876, the locomotive was placed on the duplicate list as 381A, and it then became 338 in May 1878. It was withdrawn in 1903 having been shedded at Kettering and Burton-upon-Trent in the intervening years. *S. Hodgkinson*

By 1890 there were two goods trains each weekday in addition to the four passenger services. The early morning goods left Derby at 6.00 am and stopped only at Duffield before arriving at Wirksworth at 7.45 am. On Tuesdays and Fridays this train was stopped, if required, to leave cattle wagons at Idridgehay. On arrival at Wirksworth, it ran to Bowne and Shaw's quarry. The last train in the evening was a goods service leaving Wirksworth at 8.00 pm, probably with the daily load of limestone since it was not required to stop at Duffield to shunt. Arriving at 10.10 pm in Derby, it could stop at Idridgehay and Shottle to attach cattle wagons if required. The other services were a 9.45 am departure from Wirksworth and a 12 noon departure from Derby.

Another change at this time was that the final passenger train from Wirksworth was at 6.45 pm with no intervening service from Derby since the previous Wirksworth departure at 5.30 pm. There must, therefore, have been a spare engine at Wirksworth and this was undoubtedly provided by the last passenger train of the previous day which arrived in Wirksworth at 7.48 pm. At this period, it appears that the engine shed was used for its intended purpose, which was not the case in later years. This final round trip from Wirksworth and back only went as far as Duffield where the engine ran round for the return trip.

In 1897, plans were deposited for a line known as the North Staffordshire and Mid Derbyshire Railway. This was intended to run from the LNWR at Mapleton to the Great Central Railway at Williamthorpe via Atlow, Hognaston, Carsington, Wirksworth, Cromford, Tansley, Milltown and Clay Cross.

The line would have passed to the west and north of Wirksworth close to the town centre and would have crossed the MR's extension to the C&HPR by a bridge (arch: 26 ft, span: 14 ft 6 in.). Needless to say, this ambitious and, probably, needless proposal was mooted too late after the 'Mania' years for it to proceed any further than the planning stage.

This new scheme must have caused quite a stir in the area, and, when a landslip occurred on the Matlock line at Whatstandwell, the following article appeared in the *High Peak News* on 29th January, 1898:

THE RAILWAY SCHEME
SENSATIONAL DEVELOPMENTS
AN INSULT TO MATLOCK FORECASTED

We have been interviewing several of the most prominent residents of Wirksworth, upon the question of new railway developments, and find that they hold a strong opinion that the Midland Railway intend fully to carry out the proposed extension of the Wirksworth and Derby branch through to Rowsley owing to the Whatstandwell landslip. They even go so far as to assert that this last few days the Midland Company had been negotiating for the land in this district to secure the new route. One tradesman added caustically that when this extension was complete 'Matlock would be on a branch line', and he remarked that it would be a common thing to hear the porters call at Rowsley 'change here for the branch line to Matlock'. How true all this is we don't know. There is, we believe, something in it, but it behoves Matlock to look alive after its own interests. This would be best conserved by backing the new North Staffordshire and Mid-Derbyshire railway. Meetings ought to be held to take some steps to prevent such a calamity as that which may in all probability take place, in the event of the Whatstandwell line being still considered unsafe, of which there is such doubt.

Wirksworth station, probably taken around 1890. In the distance to the right (above the goods shed) is the station master's house from which a path led down to the station. The two Wirksworth Stone & Mineral wagons have dumb buffers, although the one furthest from the camera has sprung buffers at the far end. *Author's Collection*

Shottle station with station master Mr Herbert Barber in the foreground. The wooden lampposts and general cleanliness of the station could place this picture as early as 1880. The identity of other member of staff is not known. *Roger Holbrook*

Duffield station showing the Station signal box beyond Woodiwiss Bridge. The date can be fairly accurately pinpointed to around October 1897 when the new up goods line was opened through the station (behind the wall on the right). There is a connection visible just beyond the signal box, which would be where the up goods line from Milford Tunnel (opened June 1897) joined the station lines until it was extended. The equivalent down slow through the station, of September 1901, has not yet been opened, and the signal on the left of the bracket is the main to goods dating from May 1897. The light coloured (blue) oval plate on the signal box signified that the block instruments and telephone equipment were all in working order. The other side was black and, if hung horizontally, indicated that there was a defect with the block instruments. If there was a defect with the telephone equipment, however, the black side was hung vertically.   *V.R. Anderson Collection*

Judging by the position of the barrows by the wall on the left, it is reasonable to assume that this photograph was taken at the same time as that above. It is known that this one was taken by the Derby firm of Richard Keene. Points to note are the waiting room on the right, which appears identical to the one opposite. In later years part of the frontage was removed to create a bicycle shed. On the left-hand (up) platform is an additional, older, waiting room very similar to the one on the branch platform. This is probably the one dating from 1871, and mentioned in the text.   *R. Keene, Collection R.G. Cash*

A view of Wirksworth taken in the early years of the 20th century with much activity in the yard. The most prominent carriage, visible in the centre of the photograph, appears to be a 48 ft lavatory third with clerestory and square light windows to diagram D486, dating from between 1898 and 1900. On each side of it are arc-roofed vehicles. As the clerestory was of a type normally found on main line trains at that time, this was perhaps a special (possibly connected with the Well Dressings) hence all the activity in the yard. *Chris Mordey Collection*

78	DERBY and WIRKSWORTH.									
	WEEKDAYS.									SUNDAYS.
DERBY ....dep.	7 35	12 20	4 30	6 5	5 5	7 40	....	....		4 10
Derby (Nottingham Road)	7 38	12 23	4 34	6 9	7 43	..	..			..
Duffield	7 45	12 32	4 40	6 17	7 54	..	..			4 30
Hazelwood	7 54	12 37	4 52	6 23	8 1	..				4 36
Shottle	8 3	12 41	4 57	6 27	8 6	..				4 34
Idridgehay	8 8	12 46	5 2	6 32	8 12	..				4 40
WIRKSWORTH arr.	8 18	12 53	5 12	6 40	8 20	....	....			4 50

WIRKSWORTH dep	WEEKDAYS.								SUNDAYS.
WIRKSWORTH dep	....	8 30	1 10	5 42	8 35	....	....		5 15
Idridgehay	..	8 39	1 17	5 49	8 43	..	..		5 24
Shottle	..	8 45	1 22	5 53	8 47	..			5 31
Hazelwood	..	8 51	1 27	5 57	8 52	..			5 37
Duffield	..	9 0	1 32	6 2	8 57	..			5 46
Derby (Nottingham Road)	..	9 11	1 40	6 15	9 6	..			..
DERBY .. ..arr.	..	9 16	1 44	6 20	9 12	....	....		5 55

The timetable for July to September 1903.

Midland Railway railmotor No. 2233, which inaugurated the motor train service on the branch while on a visit to Derby in 1906. *Midland Railway Official Photograph in the Collection of the late George Dow*

It seems highly unlikely that the Midland would seriously consider extending the Wirksworth line to Rowsley because of a landslip on its existing main line. However, it may have thought that by resurrecting its earlier proposal, it would scupper the new line.

The December 1901 timetable shows a strange combination of four trains each way except on Saturdays when there were three from Derby to Wirksworth and four in the opposite direction. More curious still is the fact that the last trains of the day in each direction crossed at Duffield. On Saturdays, therefore, an extra engine seems to have materialised at Wirksworth and this can only be explained by either a light engine working or double-heading of one of the other trains, be it passenger or goods.

In the July to September timetable of 1903 there is a similar imbalance with five trains from Derby to Wirksworth and four from Wirksworth to Derby. This time, instead of trains materialising at Wirksworth, they seemed to be disappearing there! It would not have required much adjustment of the timing of the 5.42 from Wirksworth to return just after 6.00, and it has to be assumed that the engine came back on a freight working.

A major revision of services on the branch took place on 1st March, 1906 when a railmotor service was introduced to augment the normal passenger service. Trials were held on the Wirksworth branch from 6th February before the full service began. The railmotor also worked the Melbourne and Ripley branches covering about 100 miles throughout the day. Initially, there were two return trips to Wirksworth, three to Melbourne and one to Ripley, but in October 1906 the Melbourne trips were cut to two. The service was third class only and parcels and milk were not carried.

The railmotor consisted of a Hudswell, Clarke-built Midland & Great Northern Railway (M&GN) 4-4-0T coupled to a Midland Railway Pullman car of 1874. Four sets were converted by the Midland at the end of 1905 under order number 0/3053 and worked in the following pairs:

M&GNR Tank No.	Pullman Car No.
8	10
10	5
19	1
40	2

Pullman cars numbers 2 and 10 were later transposed and engine numbers were altered to correspond with the car numbers. Similar sets were put to work on the Higham Ferrers to Wellingborough and Hemel Hempstead to Harpenden services.

The locomotives, built originally for the Yarmouth & North Norfolk Railway, remained in their yellow livery when they first appeared on the MR although some Midland details were added and they were then repainted in crimson lake. The Pullman cars were fitted with side seats and a double wire cord running through the clerestory roof to the rear end where it was connected to the regulator handle. Other cords were provided for the whistle and the vacuum brake, and a gong and dial provided communication between driver and fireman.

An intriguing view showing railmotor No. 2233 or 2234 at Wirksworth alongside 0-6-0 No. 2261. Why both vehicles should be at the platform is not clear; the postcard was posted on 28th March, 1905, nearly a year before the motor train service began. No. 2233 was completed in June 1904 and 2234 a month later, but there is snow in the photograph, indicating that it was taken in the winter of 1904/5, so the photographer might have recorded one of the railmotors on a running-in trial after returning to Derby from Heysham for a modification not long after it had been delivered to Lancashire. *Collection R.G. Cash*

Midland & Great Northern Railway 4-4-0T No. 10 with a Midland Railway Pullman car stands at Wirksworth in 1906. The signal box is visible on the left. *Author's Collection*

MIDLAND 🦅 RAILWAY

RAIL MOTOR SERVICE

TO AND FROM DERBY.

Commencing March 1st, 1906,

THE FOLLOWING RAIL MOTOR SERVICES WILL BE IN OPERATION ON WEEKDAYS, IN ADDITION TO THE EXISTING ORDINARY SERVICE:—

DERBY & MELBOURNE.

		a.m.	p.m.	p.m. (Fridays excepted)				a.m.	p.m.	p.m. (Fridays excepted)
DERBY	dep.	7 40	12 5	4 55	MELBOURNE	dep.	8 12	12 38	5 23
Chellaston	,,	7 49	12 15	5 4	Chellaston	,,	8 21	12 47	5 32
MELBOURNE	arr.	7 56	12 22	5 11	DERBY	arr.	8 32	12 56	5 40

DERBY & WIRKSWORTH.

		a.m.	p.m.					a.m.	p.m.	
DERBY	dep.	8 45	1 55	...	WIRKSWORTH	dep.	9 45	2 50	...
Nottingham Road	,,	8 52	1 59	...	Idridgehay	,,	9 53	2 58	...
Duffield	arr.	9 1	2 8	...	Shottle	,,	9 58	3 3	...
Duffield	dep.	9 6	2 12	...	Hazelwood	,,	10 3	3 8	...
Hazelwood	,,	9 11	2 17	...	Duffield	arr.	10 7	3 12	...
Shottle	,,	9 16	2 22	...	Duffield	dep.	10 9	3 15	...
Idridgehay	,,	9 21	2 27	...	DERBY	arr.	10 18	3 25	...
WIRKSWORTH	arr.	9 29	2 35	...					

DERBY & RIPLEY.

		a.m.						a.m.		
DERBY	dep.	10 32	...	...	RIPLEY	dep.	11 25	...	...
Little Eaton	,,	10 41	...	...	Denby	,,	11 32	...	...
Coxbench	,,	10 47	...	...	Kilburn	,,	11 36	...	...
Kilburn	,,	10 53	...	...	Coxbench	,,	11 42	...	...
Denby	,,	10 58	...	...	Little Eaton	,,	11 48	...	...
RIPLEY	arr.	11 6	...	...	DERBY	arr.	11 57	...	...

THIRD CLASS ORDINARY FARES ONLY WILL BE CHARGED.

Tickets may be obtained at the Booking Offices in the usual way.

Derby, Feb. 1906.   JOHN MATHIESON, General Manager.

4,000-20-2-1906.   Bemrose & Sons Limited, Printers to the Company.

A delightful view of Idridgehay, most likely taken in the first decade of the 20th century.

Neville Dean Collection

Staff at Duffield station, probably taken before 1910, provided by Mr James Cooper of Duffield. Mr Cooper's grandfather, Charles Morley, is standing next to the platform edge; he was a porter at Duffield for 40 years. Standing next to him is the goods yard man, Arthur Flavell. Also standing (although it is unclear which) is Bill Wright, senior porter on the opposite shift to Mr Morley. Behind the group there appears to be a double bracket signal, different from that shown in the 1897 photograph on page 41, but also apparently not the bracket that crosses the running lines shown in the signal box diagram for February 1910 on page 188.

J.A. Cooper

Photographic evidence shows engine No. 10 with car No. 5 and (probably) engine No. 40 with car No. 10. In any event, these engines seem to have been the first to be converted.

Although it may have been intended to use these railmotors on the Wirksworth service from the start, contemporary press reports suggest that this was not the case and that two steam motor carriages were used for the first two weeks. These had been built for the Morecambe and Heysham line in 1904 to order number 0/2741. They were 60 ft long overall, weighed 36 tons and were numbered M1 and M2. They were also numbered in the carriage stock series as 2233 and 2234. Designed by David Bain, there was a passenger compartment with a vestibule at the rear end and a power unit at the front which was totally enclosed by the coach body. The vertical boiler had a working pressure of 160 psi and was mounted on a 0-4-0 chassis with Walschaert's valve gear.

Quite why they were brought to the Wirksworth branch is not clear. They had spent nearly two years on the Morecambe and Heysham line, and it is known that order number 2741A, dated 5th December, 1906, provided for the fitting of more powerful, horizontal boilers. It is not clear whether this alteration was ever carried out, but the existence of the order suggests that the Midland felt that the vehicles were underpowered for the job they were doing. Further details of these interesting railmotors are given in two articles by F.W. Shuttleworth in the October and November 1974 issues of *Model Railways*.

However, to return to the inauguration of the railmotor service, an eyewitness account of the events of 1st March, 1906 was given by writer Horace Merlin:

> The new railmotor service to Wirksworth had only just been started and on the first Saturday the afternoon car up the valley was well loaded. As it came along, towed by the 1.55 pm from Derby, the smoke issuing out of its diminutive chimney being a token of its efforts to prepare for the journey 'on its own' from Duffield to Wirksworth, it was evident . . . that very few empty seats remained . . .
>
> At Hazelwood, Shottle and Idridgehay every house and farm sent out an observation picket . . . Had the car been a flying machine it could scarcely have created more sensation.

By the time his report appeared, the 4-4-0T and Pullman car had replaced the motor-carriages.

The service lasted until 1911 and did not prove as successful as those on the Great Western Railway, for example. After a brief return to the M&GN, the engines were sold to the Government in World War I.

Over the years, the branch has often been used for experimental and testing purposes due to its proximity to Derby. One such experiment was heralded in a minute in the Midland Railway Way and Works Committee Minute Book, dated 5th April 1907; it read:

> Provision of Western Syndicate Co.'s Automatic Fog Signalling Arrangement. At the request of the Traffic Committee, ordered that the plan and estimate (£106 Rev.) prepared by the Engineer, and now submitted for the provision of experimental purposes, of the Western Syndicate Co.'s Automatic Fog Signalling Arrangement in connection with the distant signals on the Wirksworth Branch be referred to the General Purposes Committee, the necessary apparatus being lent for the occasion.

The apparatus was similar to that employed on the Great Western Railway and, under an order dated 4th June, 1907, was to be fitted to locomotives Nos. 1428 and 1429. A notice to drivers dated 30th January, 1908 begins:

> A system of electrical automatic signalling has been installed on the Wirksworth branch. This will be brought into operation on and from Monday, February 3rd 1908, and as many of the booked trips over the branch as possible will be worked by tank engine No. 1428 and autocar No. 5, which are fitted with the special apparatus.

There is no mention of engine No. 1429 in this notice.

Engine No. 1428 (2628 before 1907) was an 0-4-4T built by Dübs & Co. in 1900. For the purposes of the experiment, it was fitted with apparatus below the front buffer beam which was activated by a ramp placed between the rails. Situated just in advance of a distant signal, the position of the ramp caused one of two things to happen on the locomotive. If the signal was 'on', the whistle in the cab instrument would sound and the word 'Danger' appeared in the face of the instrument. If the signal was 'off' an electric bell rang. In both cases, the automatic signal continued until stopped by the driver.

A test ramp was fitted outside No. 4 shed at Derby to see that the apparatus was functioning properly before each day's work. The apparatus was only fitted on the Wirksworth branch and the locomotive and autocar were not allowed to work between:

Derby and Nottingham (via London Road Junction and Chaddesden)
Derby and Worthington
Derby and Ripley (via Denby)

Possibly, the experimental train also worked the railmotor service referred to earlier so there may have been a revision of these services at this time. The existing railmotor would have worked the Ripley and Melbourne branches only.

It is not known how long the experiment lasted, but a Midland Railway notice in 1909, over a year after the trial began, stated that

> . . . the electric automatic fog signalling apparatus working in conjunction with the distant signals on the Wirksworth branch will be disconnected for alteration to the ramps. The work at Wirksworth and Gorsey Bank will be carried out on the Monday (3rd May) and Duffield on the Tuesday (4th May).

The Midland also tried other systems but nearly 50 years would pass before this kind of apparatus became universally applied to the railway network as a contribution to safe travel. The Great Western Railway, which had perfected this system, began trials at Henley in January 1906. The idea was developed by making the system apply the brakes when a signal was on so what had been an automatic warning system became a system of train control.

By the 1900s railway travel had become the most effective means of mass transportation. People were now accepting holidays by the sea and excursions to not so local beauty spots as commonplace. The 1908 edition of Baddeley's *Guide of the Peak District* gives details of day-return 'Walking Tours':

Forward - Nottingham to Wirksworth
Return   - Derby to Nottingham

The cost was 3s. 9d. first class and 2s. 3d. second class. For this, the keen rambler had 14 miles of walking to do in order to catch the return train.

A survey of Midland Railway goods sheds of around 1912 revealed that four people were employed at Wirksworth station at a minimum wage of 19s. 0d. per week. The population of the town was 3,807 and the staple industries were Lead Mining, Farming, Tape Mills, Lime and Limestone Quarrying.

The passenger timetable for April 1910 shows seven trains each day on weekdays. Two of these were railmotor services except on Mondays when the railmotor operated only one out of the seven services. The Sunday pattern was as before with one train each way in the late afternoon.

On 1st January, 1917, the Midland Railway reduced passenger train services over the whole of its system. This was a wartime measure which all other main line companies introduced. In 1921, the weekday passenger service consisted of six trains each way with the Sunday service as before. There were two goods services daily. The first in the morning left Derby (St Mary's) at 6.25 am with mineral empties. Having shunted at the branch stations, it arrived at Wirksworth at 7.15 am. At 10.00 am it brought a load of limestone back, arriving at Derby at 12.08 pm. The second train was a stopping freight from St Mary's at 12.35 pm, which reached Wirksworth at 2.30 pm. It returned at 6.05 pm as another mineral working, arriving at Derby at 7.07 pm.

Milk traffic developed greatly during this time. F.S. Williams in *Our Iron Roads* (Bemrose 1883) noted that Wirksworth farmers forwarded:

> . . . their milk to Derby by the earliest morning and afternoon trains and by the 6 o'clock. In the evening, the middle platform at Derby will sometimes be crowded with cans ready to leave for London by the mail. The morning passenger train from Derby, soon after 8 o'clock, generally takes 8 or 10 vans of milk, each containing more than 40 churns, each churn holding 15 or 16 gallons.

By the end of the century, three or four vans of milk were leaving Wirksworth daily so that up to 800,000 gallons were leaving the station annually. This amounted to about 10 per cent of the total annual production for the whole of Derbyshire. Right up until early London Midland & Scottish Railway (LMS) days, so big was the traffic in milk that a travelling porter accompanied the milk trains to speed up the loading at the branch stations.

As the production and export of milk increased, there was a corresponding drop in the carriage of cattle. The cost of carrying milk was ½d. per gallon locally and double that for long distances. Farmers soon found that, at these prices, it made more economic sense to sell and transport milk to distant cities than the livestock that produced it.

In 1872, the number of trucks of cattle sent away from Wirksworth was 175 and, as more farmers took to using the railway, this rose to 441 trucks in 1880. From then on the figures declined until, at the time of World War I, about 250 trucks were sent annually.

Although the line was building up a sizeable turnover in goods traffic, be it coal, limestone, cattle or milk, the heyday of passenger services was fast coming to an end. Learning from their wartime experience, the Government had plans to create four large railway undertakings, each covering a roughly defined geographical area. Old enemies such as the Midland and the LNWR were soon to find themselves uneasy bedfellows in the London Midland & Scottish Railway, where rivalry between Derby and Crewe would continue.

Before leaving this period, though, it is interesting to look at the rivals to the Midland for traffic from and to Wirksworth. The opening of the railway in 1867 had an immediate effect. Prior to this date, a W. Smith had operated as a carrier from Wirksworth to Derby, leaving at 8.00 am on Monday, Tuesday, Wednesday, Friday and Saturday. He appears to have disposed of this business at the time of the commencement of railway services to a William Weston who, in 1868, was carrying to Derby. His service, however, was much reduced and only ran on Tuesday and Friday. Unaffected by all this was a Saturday service to Ashbourne run by one Francis Stone.

The nearest bus service to Wirksworth in this period was between Matlock and Cromford and was begun in 1902. From 1923 the familiar story of increasing bus services and decreasing passenger railway receipts became apparent and this will be described in the next chapter.

0-4-4T No. 1428 at Hazelwood in about 1920. The experimental automatic signalling equipment is just visible below the front buffer beam. *Sir Gilbert Inglefield*

Chapter Five

Under the LMS: 1923 to 1947

On 1st January, 1923 the London Midland & Scottish Railway became the largest joint stock railway company in the British Empire. The Midland and London & North Western railways, whose rivalry had resulted in the building of the Wirksworth branch, now found themselves as the largest constituents in the new company.

Initially, there was little outward evidence of any change apart from the appearance of LMS 'totem' nameboards at the stations. Train services on the branch remained as they had been with six passenger and two freight trains each day (one passenger train on Sunday). The freight service included an early morning train of empty mineral wagons which returned mid-morning with a load of limestone.

Soon afterwards, there was a slight re-scheduling of the afternoon freight train to accommodate an extra passenger train leaving Derby at 2.16 pm on Tuesday, Friday and Saturday only. Arriving at Wirksworth at 2.55, it started its return journey at 3.05 to arrive at Derby at 3.39 pm.

The first passenger train of the day brought the empty milk vans to all the stations on the line. On Derby market days the second train of the day picked up the cattle vans and conveyed the farmers to Nottingham Road to meet their cattle at St Mary's Goods Depot.

The final passenger train of the day picked up the milk vans on its way back to Derby, where a train was assembled to form the 10.55 pm departure to the Express Dairy at Cricklewood. The basis of this train was that from the North Staffs line and, as well as the Wirksworth portion, others were added from Ripley and Ashby-de-la-Zouch. At various times, milk also found its way to dairies at Leyton, Kentish Town, South Tottenham, Walthamstow and Sheffield. The bogie milk vans had a slate by each compartment door on which the destination of the milk in each compartment could be chalked.

In 1932, a new dairy was opened at Rowsley to which some milk was sent. As we shall see, from this time onwards, less and less milk was sent away by train. Milk is still the mainstay of Wirksworth farmers and much of it goes to London via the Express Dairy at Rowsley but, of course, it is now handled by bulk road-tankers. Such was the significance of the dairy produce in the valley that, to many, the branch was known as the 'Milk and Honey' line.

Passenger returns were diminishing, so the LMS instituted a series of trials on 9th-11th September, 1931 to see what saving of fuel could be made by reducing the weight of its trains. Although these tests were carried out on the Melbourne rather than the Wirksworth branch, it is interesting to see that the push-pull trains on trial used M&GNR 4-4-0 No. 9A and LMS class '1P' 0-4-4T No. 1408: an interesting throwback to 1906.

The 1931 freight timetable shows two regular workings each way as before, but, if required, there were two extra trains, one on Tuesday and Friday only and another Monday and Saturday excepted. This timetable actually shows a possible total of four freight trains from Derby to Wirksworth and five from

DERBY AND WIRKSWORTH.

	WEEK DAYS.								SUNDAYS.	
					Tuesdays, Fridays & Saturdays only.					
Derby ....dep.	6 45	8 18	....	12 10	2 16	5 15	6 28	7 30	4 5	....
Derby (Nt'm Road)	6 49	8 21	..	12 14	2 20	5 19	6 32	7 34	..	..
Duffield	7 4	8 29	....	12 24	2 30	5 28	6 44	7B55	4 20	....
Hazelwood	7 13	8 35	..	12 30	2 36	5 34	6 50	8A 8	4 38	..
Shottle	7 21	8 39	....	12 35	2 41	5 38	6 55	8A23	4 52	....
Idridgehay.. ..	7 29	8 43	..	12 40	2 46	5 42	7 0	8 29	5 5	..
Wirksworth arr.	7 40	8 50	....	12 49	2 55	5 50	7 9	8 39	5 14	....

	WEEK DAYS.								SUNDAYS.	
				Tuesdays, Fridays, & Saturdays only.						
Wirksworth dep	7 55	8 56	1 0	3 5	5 55	7 20	8 50	5 30	....
Idridgehay.. ..	8 3	9 3	1 7	3 13	6 3	7 27	9 0	5 39	..
Shottle	8 7	9 6	1 11	3 17	6 7	7 31	9 8	5 48	....
Hazelwood.. ..	8 12	9 10	1 16	3 22	6 12	7 36	9 13	5 57	..
Duffield	8 18	9 14	1 22	3 27	6 17	7C48	9 20	6 8	....
Derby (Nt'm Road)	8 27	9 22	1 30	3 35	6 25	7 58	..	..	..
Derby.. .. arr.	8 31	9 26	1 34	3 39	6 30	8 2	9 33	6 20	....

A Arrives Hazelwood 8.0 and Shottle at 8.14 p.m. **B** Arrives at 7.44 p.m. **C** Arrives at 7.40 p.m.

Timetable for 26th September, 1927 (until further notice).

The LMS (Midland Division) Working Timetable of Passenger Trains, 3rd May to 4th July (inclusive) 1937.

WIRKSWORTH AND DUFFIELD.

Miles.	For continuation of trains from junction, see page			WEEKDAYS.														SUNS.	
				1	2	3	4	5	6	7	8	9	10	11	12	13	14	15	16
					PASSENGER to Derby.	PASSENGER to Derby.		PASSENGER to Derby.	PASSENGER to Derby.	PASSENGER to Derby.	PASSENGER to Derby.	PASSENGER		PASSENGER to Derby.	PASSENGER to Derby.	PASSENGER to Derby.		PASSENGER to Derby.	
									F SO	SX	SO			SX	SO	SO			
					a.m.	a.m.		p.m.	p.m.	p.m.	p.m.	p.m.		p.m.	p.m.	p.m.		p.m.	
0		WIRKSWORTH........	dep.	....	7 55	9 1	....	1 0	3 4	5 52	5 59	7 23	....	8 42	8 42	10 21	....	5 30	....
3¼		Idridgehay.........⊕	arr.	..	8 2	9 8	..	1 7	3 11	5 59	6 6	7 30	..	8 49	8 49	10 28	..	5 37	..
			dep.	....	8 3	9 9	....	1 8	3 13	6 1	6 8	7 31	....	8 50	8 50	10 29	....	5 40	....
5		Shottle..................	arr.	..	8 6	..	..	1 11	3 16	6 4	6 11	7 34	..	..	8 53	..	..	5 43	..
			dep.	....	8 7	9 14	....	1 12	3 17	6 5	6 12	7 35	....	....	8 54	....	....	5 45	....
6¼		Hazelwood.............	arr.	..	8 11	..	..	1 16	3 21	6 9	6 16	7 39	..	..	8 58	..	..	5 49	..
			dep.	....	8 13	9 18	....	1 17	3 22	6 10	6 17	7 40	....	....	8 59	....	....	5 53	....
8¼	248	DUFFIELD.........⊕	arr.	..	8 17	9 22	..	1 21	3 26	6 14	6 21	7 44	..	9 0	9 3	10 39	..	5 57	..
			dep.	....	8 19	9 24	....	1 24	3 29	6 16	6 26	....	....	9 2	9 9	10 41	....	6 0	....

Miles.	For continuation of trains from junction, see page			WEEKDAYS.														SUNS.	
				1	2	3	4	5	6	7	8	9	10	11	12	13	14	15	16
					PASSENGER 6.48 from Derby.	PASSENGER 8.18 from Derby.		PASSENGER 12.10 from Derby.	PASSENGER 2.13 from Derby.	PASSENGER 5.[illegible] from Derby.	PASSENGER 5.15 from Derby.	MIXED 6.38 from Derby.		PASSENGER	PASSENGER 9.35 from Derby.			PASSENGER 4.[illegible] from Derby.	
									F SO	SX	SO				SO				
					a.m.	a.m.		p.m.	p.m.	p.m.	p.m.	p.m.		p.m.	p.m.			p.m.	
0	261	DUFFIELD..........⊕	arr.	....	6 58	....	....	12 23	2 26	5 18	....	6 48	....	....	9 44	....	....	4 35	....
			dep.	..	7 6	8 29	..	12 24	2 27	5 21	5 28	6 49	..	7 53	9 45	..	..	4 40	..
2		Hazelwood.............	arr.	....	7 11	....	....	12 29	2 32	....	....	6 54	....	7 58	9 50	....	....	4 45	....
			dep.	..	7 15	8 35	..	12 30	2 33	5 27	5 34	6 55	..	8 2	9 51	..	..	4 49	..
3½		Shottle..................	arr.	....	7 19	....	....	12 34	2 37	....	....	6 59	....	8 6	9 55	....	....	4 53	....
			dep.	..	7 23	8 39	..	12 35	2 38	5 31	5 38	7 0	..	8 7	9 56	..	..	4 56	..
5		Idridgehay............⊕	arr.	....	7 27	....	....	12 39	2 42	....	....	7 4	....	8 11	10 0	....	....	5 0	....
			dep.	..	7 31	8 43	..	12 40	2 44	5 35	5 42	7 5	..	8 12	10 1	..	..	5 4	..
8¼		WIRKSWORTH..........	arr.	....	7 39	8 50	....	12 49	2 53	5 43	5 49	7 14	....	8 21	10 10	....	....	5 13	....

Wirksworth. When required, a cattle train left Wirksworth at 9.04 am on Tuesdays and Fridays only. It was powered by an extra engine which came to Wirksworth on the first passenger train of the day. On these occasions, therefore, this train was double-headed from Derby.

The 1934 passenger timetable shows seven passenger trains each way with an extra train on Saturdays. This was a late night train which left Derby at 9.35 pm and arrived at Wirksworth at 10.10 pm. The return journey left at 10.24 pm, stopped only at Idridgehay and Duffield and arrived in Derby at 10.40 pm. Two Sunday trains are shown but the early afternoon train is labelled 'suspended'. This is just as well as the two trains were timed to cross on the single line stretch between Hazelwood and Shottle at about 4.52 pm! It is fairly certain that this train never ran but why was it ever included in the timetable?

The Summer 1937 timetable shows a pattern of six passenger trains each way on weekdays, with an extra mid-afternoon train (Friday and Saturday only) and a late-night train (Saturday only). The Sunday service remained as before.

The Winter timetable was similar but the Sunday service was timed an hour earlier with the promise that, from 1st May, 1938, it would revert to its later time. This was not to be, however, as the Sunday service ceased, due to the decline in milk traffic, from 8th May, 1938. At this time, for example, only two churns were being dispatched from Hazelwood each Sunday. After the withdrawal of the milk train, these churns were taken for collection at Duffield.

This then was the first step in the running down of services on the branch. Faced with competition from other forms of transport in the financially stringent pre-war era, the branch had to fight for its survival as a passenger carrying line.

The last passenger timetable to be issued before the war showed no change in the pattern of services except that the Friday- and Saturday-only mid-afternoon train was now just Saturday only. The following year saw the withdrawal of all milk trains from the branch. Lorries were now handling all this traffic, much of which went to Rowsley.

It seems appropriate at this point to look at the development of bus services in the area. Around 1921, Charles Rhodes of Warner Street, Derby began a Derby-Wirksworth service via Duffield. In 1925, he was joined by Frank Holland, also of Warner Street, and after operating as Rhodes & Holland, their fleet-name became 'Rhodeland' in 1926. They had three green and grey buses which ran every 1¼ hours. The Derby terminus was Bold Lane (where they had their office), and in Wirksworth they had a garage which was taken over by Trent when that company bought 'Rhodeland' in 1933.

A bus station of sorts was opened in Canterbury Road, Wirksworth in the mid-1930s. E. Webster & Sons of Hognaston operated buses to the surrounding villages, and services to the north were provided by the North Western Road Car Co., amongst which was a half-hourly service to Matlock. This had previously been operated by Watts Brothers, who also provided a service to the Baseball Ground on Derby County match days. Their three buses were called *Adam Bede* (described as 'black and rather ramshackle'), *Dinah Morris* ('a trim 14-seater') and *Seth Bede* ('a much larger half-cab machine').

There was also a company based at Duffield known as the 'Red Star Service', which ran daily between Derby and Belper. They had three buses, one

A milk train with at least four bogie passenger milk vans waits to leave Wirksworth station on 27th June, 1933.   *H.C. Casserley*

Johnson '3F' class 0-6-0 No. 3368 passes over Breadsall crossing with a freight train on 25th June, 1941. A 1934 Austin 10 is parked up on the verge.   *H.C. Casserley*

remembered as being elderly, with a bonnet out in front and a red star on the side, the other two being more conventional, but strangely, with yellow stars on the side. 'Red Star' was another company that sold out to Trent in the mid-1930s, and it is said that the proprietor, Mr C.E. Salt, insisted that his former passengers should travel at the same rate that he had been charging; they were issued with identity cards to ensure this! It is interesting to note that Salt occupied Tamworth House, which had been owned by the contractor Isaac Woodiwiss. This route was also operated by Mr T.C. Cox until a fire destroyed his garage in 1928. Tickets for Cox's and Salt's services were interchangeable.

Allestree and Darley Abbey (on the route of the railway but not served by it) were also served by Mr Fred Nichols with an old World War I Buick ambulance, complete with a red cross on each side which was still visible despite being painted over. In 1925, the route was taken over by Kingfisher, who were taken over themselves by Trent in 1935. Kingfisher's buses were a motley collection, comprising a yellow charabanc with a black canvas roof, two more conventional vehicles - one yellow and one 'teak', and finally two blue buses with red kingfishers painted on their sides.

As recently as 1974 there was a proposal to provide a railway station to serve Allestree and Darley Abbey though nothing came of it.

The bus service from Wirksworth to Derby took over an hour and the railway station at Derby was not very well situated. As a result, there was a movement of population between the wars from towns like Wirksworth to the new Derby suburbs like Allestree, Darley Abbey and Spondon.

Throughout my original researches I heard tales of the Royal Train being stabled at Hazelwood for a night. It was difficult to gain any hard facts, but Roger Holbrook, who lived all his life near Shottle station, made enquiries on my behalf and came to the conclusion that Hazelwood played host to the train at some time in 1939. No further details were forthcoming, so we were left to ponder who might have been aboard. That is until shortly after the first edition of this book was published, when I was contacted by Mr Robert Lobley, who provided the most comprehensive evidence of an auspicious visit. Mr Lobley was brought up at Hazelwood, and lived throughout the war at the Station House. Not only does he remember the Royal Train, but also the Army camped out around the station, the fire brigade running hoses from the River Ecclesbourne, and the fresh flowers placed on the platform. The train drew in at night, and left the next morning, but its occupants do not appear to have been the King and Queen. Mr Lobley's brother reported greeting Winston Churchill, who was leaning out of the window in the morning, and his mother claimed to have seen the Emperor of Ethiopia, Haile Selassie, on the train. The Lobleys had to be escorted along the line by soldiers when they went to feed the chickens by the siding, but, despite the security surrounding the train, Mr Lobley recalls a land mine being dropped on Idridgehay in an attempt (it was believed) to bomb the train.

Mrs Gwen Watts, who lived with her father and grandfather at Hole House Farm, Ashleyhay remembers that two bombs were dropped on her grandfather's land about 120 yards from the railway line that night. The next day her father took her to view the damage, and they stood on the edge of the crater, her hand in his. Although she was very small, this made a deep impression on her, and even now the fear and bewilderment of the occasion remains very clearly in her mind. The Vicarage at Idridgehay, and another large

Two views of Johnson '1P' 0-4-4T No. 1408 at Breadsall crossing with the Wirksworth branch train on 25th June, 1941. The train is comprised of a luggage composite and a brake third. The lower view shows the 5.52 pm service ex-Wirksworth. *(Both) H.C. Casserley*

house across the road, were both destroyed in the attack. Only later did they learn that Winston Churchill had been staying on a train that night, and many believed that the two large houses had been bombed because the pilots thought Churchill could have been staying in one of them. Whether the Germans even knew that he was in the area is open to conjecture, but on a later occasion a lone German plane was seen flying along the line, giving rise to a rumour in the valley that another VIP visit was expected.

Mr Lobley also remembered the porter finding an incendiary bomb on his way to work, putting it in his bicycle saddle bag, and keeping it at the station until the bomb disposal team arrived. One night after the war, a drunken driver drove his car onto the track, whereupon it was smashed to pieces by a train despite attempts by Mr Lobley's parents to warn the engine driver with a torch. No injury to the car driver was reported.

Inevitably, World War II saw a great reduction in passenger services throughout the country. The branch timetable for August 1942 shows only two return passenger workings, one in the morning and one in the evening for commuters. In addition, there was an early afternoon service on Saturdays intended for shoppers and Derby County supporters. This situation had, in fact, been the case from the outbreak of the war. At the same time, Trent service No. 37 ran 17 times from Derby to Wirksworth and 18 in the opposite direction.

The Derby-Wirksworth single train fare was 3s. 7d., first class and 2s. 2d., third class. From Derby to Duffield the respective fares were 1s. 6d. and 11d. Thus the third class fare was approximately twice the 'Gov' single fare that had applied when the line opened.

During the war, just south of Idridgehay station, construction of a blast-proof control centre began. Such centres were built at various strategic points on the railway network, and it was felt that Derby was particularly vulnerable to hostile action owing to the proximity of Rolls-Royce. For some reason though, only the foundations were built together with the steel reinforcing rods for the walls. All the years of exposure to the elements hardly touched the structure, which stood in its unfinished and abandoned state until recent years when the owners of the station building cut through the rods and built a workshop and store on the foundations.

During wartime (and until 1947) all railways had been under the control of the Government. There was a severe fuel shortage at the end of the war and, undoubtedly, a lingering 'Is your journey really necessary?' attitude prevailed. In addition there had been an extremely hard winter and all these factors combined to draw attention away from the announcement that the branch would close to passengers on and from 16th June, 1947. In view of the circumstances, it is remarkable that the service had not been withdrawn earlier. Those to Ripley, Melbourne and Castle Donington, for example, had gone in 1930, and the strong rumour (probably not without foundation) was that the line owed its longevity to the fact that a number of senior LMS officials lived in the area served by it.

The closure of the branch to passengers was said to be a temporary measure owing to the shortage of coal. With this, no-one could argue but it is probable that not many people really expected the service ever to be restored. By this time, fare-paying passengers were down to two a day, but there were many railway workers who went to work at Derby with free passes.

Two photographs of 'Station Working' being filmed at Shottle around 1945. The first shows the right way of doing things with the station master positioned where he can collect tickets and generally oversee things, the other shows how it shouldn't be done (but usually was!). The locomotive is a Stanier '3P' class 2-6-2T No. 112.   *Leslie Spears*

As a last fling, someone in the Commercial Department of the LMS suggested undercutting Trent's workmen's fare by 3*d*. No-one took this seriously though, in view of the inconvenient position of the station for prospective passengers from, say, Derby Road.

It is quite likely that the first the public at large heard about the impending closure was an article in the *Derby Evening Telegraph* of 3rd June, 1947. In an evocative, if slightly sentimental, article entitled 'Farewell to Shorr'll', Howard Channon lamented that:

> . . . we may no longer travel by train from Duffield to Wirksworth along that peaceful, jog-trot line which had so lively a personality, where station names were called out in a rich, local brogue endowing them with the mystic unfamiliarity of a foreign land.
>
> 'Shorr'll', 'Ith'see' and 'Wazzer' - cries, indeed to stimulate; small, sleepy wayside stations with little gardens, churns on the platform and a cob dozing in its shafts in the station yard. Anachronisms, I daresay, in this stern new world where values are assessed solely in account books and ticket offices, but attractive anachronisms for all that.

This was followed up in another article, again by Howard Channon, describing his journey on the last train '. . . for the time being'. 'A last minute rush got me the last return ticket but one - No. 900 - to be issued for the route. The man who got 901 must have been a sprinter.'

The train was driven by driver Arthur Harrison and fireman Ken Perry, and Mr Harrison recalled that his first trip on the line had been 40 years earlier. He was sorry to see the end of passenger trains on the branch. 'The scenery is so nice and so are the people who use the line.'

At Idridgehay, the train was bidden 'goodbye' by Col W.R.H. Whiston (of whom more later) who revealed that he had held a season ticket 'almost continuously from 1888 to 1945'.

Thirty passengers were on the train together with a few LMS official letters and a consignment of cattle food. At Hazelwood, the porteress and ticket collector, Miss Dorothy Malin, boarded the train and at Idridgehay a woman joined the passengers for the simple reason that her mother had travelled on the very first train in 1867.

'So at 6.40 we pulled into Derby. I still had my return (for sale cheap)', wrote Howard Channon at the end of his article. One wonders how much that ticket would be prized now!

At the end of each week in the *Derby Evening Telegraph* a cartoon used to appear lampooning high spots in the week's local news. The first of Howard Channon's articles was duly immortalised by cartoonist 'Sam' with 'Mester Channon' depicted in a first class compartment with a cow in the next compartment. Also depicted were the 'little gardens, churns on the platform and a cob in its shafts . . .'

At the time of the closure there were just two services each weekday leaving Derby at 6.55 am and 5.17 pm and returning at 7.55 am and 6.07 pm. An additional service ran on Saturdays at 12.50 pm ex-Derby and 2.00 pm ex-Wirksworth. This minimum service is hardly likely to have generated much support. The freight service shows three daily return trips one of which ran only when required (Saturdays excepted).

Ivatt '2MT' class 2-6-2T No. 1205 leaves Hazelwood with a Wirksworth-bound train in 1947. The locomotive is virtally brand new, only the first 10 members of this class ever carried LMS numbers.   *R.M. Casserely Collection*

For the last week of the passenger service 4-4-0 No. 416 was provided, and is seen here on the day before closure about to leave with the 6.07 pm train to Derby.   *W.A. Camwell*

On a very wet day that was typical of the 'summer' weather that week, the last passenger train on the Wirksworth branch draws into Idridgehay station behind 4-4-0 No. 416, witnessed by a few hardy souls. The line was closed from Monday 16th June, and there were no Sunday services, so this was the 6.07 pm ex-Wirksworth on Saturday 14th June. It is known that Colonel Whiston was present to witness the event (perhaps that is him on the left) and a contemporary newspaper report says that Mr W. Appleby was on duty at Idridgehay. Presumably, it is he who is attending to one of the ground frame levers, possibly to change a signal. *Neville Dean Collection*

The passing of the branch passenger service was mourned in the *Railway Observer* (published by the Railway Correspondence & Travel Society). In this, the point was made that Derbyshire had lost its last country branch line for passengers and that no other English county had suffered so severely in this respect.

It is, perhaps, appropriate that the closing of the line coincided with the end of the LMS era, but before closing this chapter mention must be made of a series of trials conducted at the end of 1947 and early 1948. Two '4F' 0-6-0s (Nos. 4585 and 4552) were converted to oil-burners and tested on the branch. The main problem was tailoring the burner to suit the rather short firebox; by using the branch, any shortage of steam would cause no hold-ups on the main line. Both Mr A.C. Sharpe and Mr George Williams, who were involved in these trials, have given me details of their experiences. Mr Sharpe recalls that the branch made a good test route with loads varying from 35 to 60 empties. Sometimes loaded trains were worked and the Idridgehay to Wirksworth stretch proved to be the most demanding. On this section, ½ regulator would be used with 45 to 50 per cent cut-off.

It was usual to have a van at the head of the train (often known as a 'road wagon', 'tariff van' or 'transit van') for sundry parcels to be dropped off at, or picked up from, the stations *en route*. One day, when this was left off, the footplate was littered with boxes of live chickens bound for Shottle. Being winter, this was a warmer place to put them than the brake van.

So it was that the LMS approached the end of its days. Nationalisation was about to take place and this 'new order' together with the post-war boom may have made people feel that it was only a matter of time before passenger services were reintroduced. Within two years, the temporary closure was indeed scrapped but not in the way that some people were hoping.

0-4-4T No. 58077 waits at Wirksworth with the SLS/MLS train on 25th April, 1953.

H.C. Casserley

A fine view of Wirksworth yard on the occasion of the visit of the SLS/MLS High Peak Rail Tour on 25th April, 1953.   *F.W. Shuttleworth*

Chapter Six

1948 to the Present Day

Soon after the formation of British Railways (BR) the permanent withdrawal of passenger services was announced. This was to be effective from 1st January, 1949. The service was shown in the timetables throughout this period of limbo as being temporarily suspended. Not until the publication of the summer timetable in May 1949 was it removed. However, excursion and special passenger trains continued to run for several years, and details of all those that have been traced are given in this chapter.

It was not long before further economies were made on the branch. The first involved the closure of Hazelwood and Idridgehay stations to goods from 5th January, 1953. The last load to be handled at Idridgehay was a coal delivery for Mrs Dean of Brownhouse Farm, the wagon label from which was saved for posterity by Roger Holbrook of Cowers Lane.

One feature of the period after closure to passengers was a series of railtours which included the Wirksworth branch. The first was organised by the Stephenson Locomotive Society in conjunction with the Manchester Locomotive Society on 25th April, 1953. After visiting the Cromford & High Peak Railway, and taking lunch at the 'Red Lion', Wirksworth, the participants made their way along to Wirksworth station ready for departure at 1.31 pm. The train to Duffield was hauled by Johnson 0-4-4T No. 58077. At Idridgehay, the token was collected and on arrival at Duffield, the engine ran round its train on the main line as by now the branch loop had been removed. At 2.15 pm the train left for Wirksworth with about 150 passengers. Waiting for them at the terminus was the Wirksworth station master, John Hall, who had borrowed the engraved spade to show the party. The return to Buxton was made on the C&HPR. So successful was the trip that it had to be repeated on 27th June, 1953.

Another feature of this period was the continued use of the line for testing purposes. Rumour has it that LMS diesel No. 10000 ran on trial on the branch, but while this remains only a rumour, what is certain is that between 1953 and 1961, the entire output of diesel-multiple-units from Derby works was tested and run-in on the branch. In all, 840 power cars were involved together with 618 trailer cars of light alloy ('Derby lightweights') and steel ('Derby heavyweights'). Also known to have been tested and officially photographed on the branch were the Birmingham Railway Carriage & Wagon units for the Calder Valley route.

Mr Pat Larkham was involved in the 'lightweight' dmu trials as an inspector for the Chief Mechanical Engineer's Department. He recalls that each set was tested twice - once by British United Traction (BUT) and then again by BR as an acceptance run. The BR driver would take each unit from Derby carriage & wagon works to Duffield, where the BUT representative or Mr Larkham would take over, and proceed non-stop to the Gorsey Bank down home signal, where they would reverse and go flat-out back to just short of Duffield tunnel. The round trip was then repeated before working back to Derby carriage & wagon works. Driving the units was considered essential, as it was found that, like a

0-4-4T No. 58077 emerges from Duffield tunnel with the SLS/MLS train after arriving from
Wirksworth on 25th April, 1953.   *H.C. Casserley*

Another view of the SLS/MLS train as it approaches Duffield from Wirksworth on 25th April,
1953.   *H.C. Casserley*

After the SLS/MLS train arrived at Duffield, No. 58077 ran round on the main line.

David Ibbotson

The SLS/MLS High Peak Rail Tour at Duffield before its return to Wirksworth on 25th April, 1953.

H.C. Casserley

Johnson '2P' 0-4-4T No. 58077 departs Duffield for Wirksworth with the SLS/MLS High Peak Rail Tour on 25th April, 1953. The wooden corn store of Fletcher Bros can be seen beyond the locomotive.   *H.C. Casserley*

One of the many Derby-built 3-car dmus that were tested on the branch in the 1950s. This one is seen at Shottle.   *Author's Collection*

car, it was possible to 'feel' if something was not quite right. On the up trip, the engine governor had to be tested. This cut in at about 72mph, and the only stretch of line where it was possible to attain that speed was on the downward gradient between Gorsey Bank and Idridgehay. Although the speed limit on the line was raised from 35 mph to 55 mph for the duration of the trials, the sight of dmus hurtling along the single-track branch line at twice the hitherto normal speed limit can only be imagined!

A former member of the Research Dept at BR, Mr Henry Pearce, also recalls running test trains on the branch on 7th, 14th and 16th September, 1960; he was looking at dmu exhaust pipe temperatures at the time, and the test train made three or four round trips each day. On the first occasion he remembers being told to enter Wirksworth station with caution, the reason being that the breakdown train was in the yard to sort out a derailment of wagons on the incline up to the Middlepeak exchange sidings. The practice was for the BR engine to run-round its train of empty wagons on arrival at Wirksworth, and then propel them, taking a run at the bank in order to get the train as far up as possible for the quarry engine to pick it up. On this occasion, the driver of the '4F' class locomotive had been given the signal to charge the bank, but there was a raft of wagons already on the incline beyond the Cromford Road bridge, and the result was inevitable, as the moving wagons made contact with the stationary ones. To make matters worse, some of the wagons were off the line just beyond the bridge, and the breakdown crane could neither get under the bridge, nor do anything from the station side of the bridge. How the wagons were eventually removed is not known.

While the dmus were being tested on the branch, there was also a need for driver training, so at the Railway School of Transport on London Road, Derby a series of courses was held for managerial staff and supervisors. Lasting for four weeks, the course involved learning about the mechanical and electrical components of the dmus. Part of the training consisted of a day's experience on the Wirksworth line learning such techniques as gear changing, braking and isolation of power units and final drives. The classes usually comprised 30 trainees who were split into two groups. While one group was gaining experience on the dmus, the other would witness the testing of lubricating oil at the Hazelwood firm of Lubrizol. Each session lasted three hours, lunch would be taken at the 'Railway Inn', Shottle, and then the groups would interchange.

These trials aroused considerable interest in the locality as many residents felt that the railcars might just as well be running a passenger service. On 5th May, 1956 the Clerk to Wirksworth Urban Council, Mr H. Haworth, was reported in the *Derbyshire Times* as having received 787 signatures on a petition to persuade British Railways to restore a service. Of these, 187 had signed at Middleton. In the same newspaper, an article appeared on 7th July, 1956 which reported that representatives of BR had attended a special meeting of the Council. The meeting was told that the cost of a single diesel railcar was £15,000 and a two-coach unit was £26,000. Running costs were 4s. 6d. per mile excluding maintenance charges and a minimum of 100 passengers would have to be carried per journey to make the service pay.

Among the more illustrious visitors was one of the Midland Pullman sets, that was brought to the branch for publicity photographs to be taken when new, probably around April 1960. Although most of the photographs taken at the time featured close-ups of the train with little clue to its whereabouts, here the photographer stood back to give us the shot above looking towards Gorsey Bank level crossing.   *(Both) Author's collection*

A BR representative heard that the Trent bus service was inadequate and often overcrowded so he promised to make representations to the Trent Motor Traction Co. It is not difficult to see why, on the basis of these figures, almost every passenger rail service in the country was losing money. Some members of the Council were not convinced, however, and Councillor K. Gell noted that it was apparent from the start that there was not to be even a trial railcar service. He pointed out, with some irony, that the railway representatives did not encourage efforts to restore a passenger service because they were major shareholders in Trent Motor Traction. It would not be in their interests to have a competing rail service.

At about this time, the *Derbyshire Advertiser* carried a pictorial feature showing the railcars undergoing trials. Three photographs were published, one of which showed a two-car set with a Derby (Friargate) destination panel. It is not difficult to understand the local residents' frustration in being denied a passenger service when dmus were going up and down the branch earning not a single penny in revenue. Later, one of the Blue Pullman multiple units was tried out on the branch and also on the Churnet Valley line in Staffordshire. Some of the publicity shots issued when the units were first introduced were taken on the Wirksworth branch.

On Saturday 30th January, 1954, an excursion (reporting No. M725) was run from Wirksworth to Nottingham, departing at 4.30 pm and arriving at 5.57 pm. Calling at Idridgehay and Shottle, a portion was added at Duffield, this being the 4.18 pm from Great Longstone. The return journey, leaving Nottingham at 10.35 pm, divided at Derby, the Wirksworth portion arriving at its destination at 11.51 pm. Attaching and detaching at small locations like this was an interesting throwback to Midland Railway and early LMS days.

On Friday 25th June, M706 ran from Wirksworth to St Pancras, leaving at 7.20 am and arriving back at 11.20 pm; this attached a portion from Belper at Derby. Another railtour traversed the branch on 21st May, 1955. Organised by the Gloucestershire Railway Society, it was hauled by class '2P' 4-4-0 No. 40416 (reporting No. M990) and left Derby at 12.13 pm.

The Stephenson Locomotive Society paid another visit on 21st April, 1956. Their train was hauled by Standard class '2' 2-6-2T No. 84008, and the proceedings were reported in the *Derbyshire Advertiser* of 27th April. Three pictures were published, one showing Mr W.A. Camwell (Hon. Secretary of the Midland Area of the SLS) about to board the train at Wirksworth. Later that year, on Tuesday 7th August, another excursion ran, leaving Wirksworth at 10.57 am and arriving at Duffield at 11.15 am, where it connected with the Halifax to Mablethorpe train. With reporting number M959, it returned early the following morning, leaving Duffield at 1.15 am and arriving back at Wirksworth at 1.34 am; it called at Shottle in both directions. This excursion was repeated the following year with the same reporting number. The train left Wirksworth on 6th August at 9.22 am and arrived at Duffield at 9.43 am to connect with the Halifax to Mablethorpe train. Arrival back was slightly earlier than the previous year, leaving Duffield at 12.15 am the following morning, and reaching Wirksworth at 12.34 am. Again, Shottle was served in both directions.

'2P' class 4-4-0 No. 40416 on the Gloucestershire Railway Society Tour at Wirksworth on 21st May, 1955.   *Knighton Collection*

Empty stock from the Gloucestershire Railway Society Tour being worked by '2P' class 4-4-0 No. 40416 between Wirksworth and Chaddesden sidings seen near Gorsey Bank crossing on 21st May, 1955.   *S.C. Nash*

Also in 1957, on 18th May, a special train ran to Wirksworth from Pear Tree & Normanton station. Laid on for the St Giles Sunday School Outing, and complete with headboard, the train ran again the following year on 17th May with reporting number M825. The timing of this train was Pear Tree & Normanton dep. 2.00 pm, Wirksworth arr. 2.35 pm, Wirksworth dep. 6.30 pm, Pear Tree & Normanton arr. 6.58 pm. The timings for the 1957 train were presumably very similar. On 18th June, 1958, a visit was made by the Leeds University Union Railway Society (their first-ever special train), the 20 members of the party being conveyed by a three-coach Cravens dmu (M50758, M59313, M50791 with reporting number M635). They left Derby at 2.45 pm and arrived at Wirksworth at 3.15 pm, the train being scheduled to return at 4.35 pm, to arrive back at Derby at 5.05 pm. However, there was a delayed start at Wirksworth of some five minutes, followed by an immediate halt to wait for late passengers, which added another two minutes. A further delay of three minutes at Derby Junction resulted in a late arrival at Derby by some 10 minutes. Cruising speeds of 50 mph on the branch and 70 mph between Peckwash Mill and Derby St Mary's were noted.

The branch was paying its way with some very healthy freight figures of mainly limestone traffic with some general merchandise to and from the remaining stations, Shottle and Wirksworth. On the main line there was still a regular stopping service at Duffield but threats that this might cease appeared in an article in the *Derby Evening Telegraph* of 13th May, 1959. This was the first time that Duffield had been proposed for closure but it was not to be the last.

From 30th November of the same year, Shottle became an unstaffed public siding. Also in that year, the newly restored Midland Compound No. 1000 was officially photographed at Wirksworth.

Another passenger special worked from Wirksworth to Derby on 15th April, 1961. The 'North Staffs. and C&HP Rail Tour' organised by the Stephenson Locomotive Society was a round trip beginning and ending at Burton-on-Trent and taking in Ashbourne, Buxton, Middleton Top and Wirksworth.

A red-letter day in the history of the branch was on 7th September, 1961. Arrangements had been made for four preserved locomotives, then in store at Derby locomotive works, to be filmed for the BBC television series *Railway Roundabout*. The Wirksworth branch was chosen as the venue for the filming and arrangements were made to bring the locomotives down the line. The operation was supposed to be unpublicised and Mr Hall at Wirksworth had been told not to mention it to anyone. Unfortunately (or fortunately?) a local paper not only 'spilled the beans' but even gave timings of the run. As a result, there were crowds of people at Wirksworth, and also on all the overbridges along the line. Barriers had to be erected at Wirksworth where a local school suspended lessons so that the pupils could witness the proceedings. One Duffield enthusiast, who had heard about what was to take place made sure he was there to see this little piece of history being made. This was the young Stefan Buczacki, better known these days for his gardening expertise as a Professor of Horticulture and presenter of television and radio programmes.

The engines were sent tender-first from Derby with MR 4-4-0 Compound No. 1000 hauling the other three. These were (in order behind the Compound) MR 2-4-0 No. 158A, London, Tilbury & Southend Railway (LT&SR) 4-4-2T No. 80

BR Standard class '2' 2-6-2T No. 84008 at Wirksworth with the SLS tour on 21st April, 1956.

G. Yeomans

Working timetable for September 1956 to June 1957.

H 48 WEEKDAYS — DUFFIELD AND WIRKSWORTH

DOWN

			H	H	J	
			5.40 am from Chaddesden	8.20 am from Chaddesden		
			52	39	39	
Mileage M	C		am	am	SX Q PM	
0	0	DUFFIELD .. .. arr	..	9 10	..	..
		.... dep	6 18	9 14	1 40	.....
3	35	Shottle .. .. .. arr	..	9 26	.....	
		.... dep	......	9 42	....	
4	77	Idridgehay	6 36	......	....	
8	29	WIRKSWORTH .... arr	6 53	10 10	2 20	.....

UP

			J	G	J	J
			To Chaddesden	EBV	To Chaddesden	To Chaddesden
			52	39	39	39
Mileage M	C		am	SX Q PM	SO PM	SX PM
0	0	WIRKSWORTH .. dep	10 40	12 30	5 5	7 40
3	32	Idridgehay	10 52	12 40	5 18	7 58
4	74	Shottle .. .. .. arr	10 58	..	..	..
		.... dep	11 0			
8	29	DUFFIELD .. .. arr	11 18	12 58	..	8*20
		.... dep	11X23 GL		5X35 GL	8*40

St Giles Sunday School outing in the platform at Wirksworth on 18th May, 1957. Note the 'Iron Ore' hopper in the background - many such vehicles were used for the transportation of limestone.   *Knighton Collection*

The Stephenson Locomotive Society's 'North Staffs. and C&HP Rail Tour' at Wirksworth on 15th April, 1961.   *John Langford*

Johnson 'Spinner' No. 118 with LT&SR 4-4-2T *Thundersley* at Wirksworth for the filming of the
BBC television programme 'Railway Roundabout' on 7th September, 1961.   *Eric Green*

Thundersley and MR 4-2-2 Johnson 'Spinner' No. 118. At Wirksworth, they were initially marshalled by the platform but the sun was in the wrong place so they were moved over to the other side of the yard. On arrival back at Derby, one of the engines derailed.

The episode was well reported in the local press with descriptions of the scenes surrounding the event, including motorists being held up at level crossings and leaving their cars to get a better view. Several photographs were published with a whole page of pictures in the Picture Edition of the *Derby Evening Telegraph* for 8th September. So, for a brief period, the line was in the limelight locally and nationally.

The Working Timetable for September 1961 showed the following trips on the branch:

Target 31 EWD Class '4F'	Shunt 1.15 pm to 5.00 pm SX; 10.05 am to 1.00 pm SO
Target 42 SX Class '4F'	Shunt 8.56 am to 10.55 am
	On return stops to pick up parcels traffic as required at Shottle 11.13 am to 11.15 am
SX 'Q'	11.15 am Chaddesden to Wirksworth, arrive 12.10 pm
	3.25 pm Wirksworth to Chaddesden

A year later on 29th September, 1962 the Railway Correspondence & Travel Society organised their 'Derbyshire Branch Lines Tour' which started at Nottingham Victoria. After travelling over the ex-Great Northern Railway lines in the area, the Melbourne, Wirksworth and Ripley lines were traversed before the return was made to Nottingham Midland.

The next landmarks were the complete closure of Shottle on 2nd March, 1964 followed three days later by the publication of the notice of closure of Nottingham Road and Duffield stations. This event was due to happen on 15th June, 1964 if no objections were received, and these were just two of the many stations nominated for closure between Derby and Manchester. This was not the closure of the whole line as 'The express service between Manchester Central and Derby Midland calling at Chinley and Matlock will still be available'.

The Parish Council at Duffield had, only a month earlier, decided to object to the proposed discontinuation of stopping services from Derby and Nottingham to Sheffield. This latest announcement would have resulted in the complete withdrawal of passenger services from and to Duffield.

The Parish Council's objection was sent to the Transport Users' Consultative Committee (TUCC) (East Midland Area) in April and letters of protest were sent to George Brown MP, Derbyshire County Council and Belper District Council.

In May, Councillors Bemrose and Hawley were appointed to attend a meeting at Derby Central Hall arranged by the TUCC. Their protests were successful as, in January of the following year, the TUCC informed the Council that they were satisfied that the withdrawal of the service would inflict hardship on certain categories of passengers.

In May 1965 the TUCC reported that they had made representations to the Ministry regarding these hardships and had pointed out that there would be much congestion of roads in and around Derby as a result of closure. Thus, the proposals were turned down - at least for the time being.

The aftermath of an accident that befell a limestone train just north of Shottle in October 1968. Some of the limestone can still be seen by the side of the line to this day.

(Both) Roger Holbrook

An interesting diversion (literally) took place in September 1964 when traffic to and from the Cromford & High Peak Railway had to be handled at Wirksworth. The reason was the installation of electrical winding gear at Sheep Pasture Incline which, up until then, had been worked by a stationary steam engine. 'J94' class 0-6-0ST No. 68006 was sent round to work the traffic and was stationed at Wirksworth for the duration. I have heard that two 'J94s' worked at Wirksworth taking turns each week and that on Sundays they were sent back to Rowsley.

The traffic was sent from Middleton Quarry by road to Wirksworth where 25-ton hopper wagons were used to take the stone away. These wagons could not be used on Sheep Pasture Incline, and this emergency working proved to be economically superior to that which it had replaced. As a result, on 1st April, 1967, the new winding gear having been in use for only 2½ years, Sheep Pasture Incline was closed, and all traffic sent away via Wirksworth. Pictures of No. 68006 working on the branch appeared in the *Railway Magazine* of February 1965; the second locomotive used was probably No. 68012.

On 17th October, 1965, the Locomotive Club of Great Britain organised a 'Derbyshire Branch Lines Tour'. Carrying the reporting number 1T25, class '4F' 0-6-0 No. 44113 hauled its five-coach train of ex-LMS 57 ft stock out of Derby station at 1.35 pm. It headed for the Ripley and Wirksworth branches and then returned to Derby for water. At 4.28 pm, it left Derby for Worthington and, thence, Nottingham, where it arrived at 6.30 pm. This was the last steam-hauled passenger excursion over the Wirksworth branch and the last passenger train of any sort for nearly 20 years.

Nottingham Road station was closed to passengers on and from 6th March, 1967 and, in December of that year, the *Derby Evening Telegraph* reported that stations on the Derby to Matlock line would become unstaffed halts. This was to have effect from Monday 1st January, 1968 and local stopping trains would be second class only. The line became grant-aided from October 1969. As a result, Duffield and the other stations on the line escaped complete closure and, at the time of writing, remain as unstaffed halts. Meanwhile, testing continued on the branch, and on 25th July, 1967, class '20s' D8179 and D8317 were noted on slow-speed trials, D8179 also appearing on its own the following day.

Wirksworth officially lost its goods facilities on 1st April, 1968 (the last cattle had been dispatched in 1962) although some public sidings were retained and, of course, the limestone traffic continued to be handled, so much so that after the closure of the main line to Manchester in July 1968, the best rail from that line (some laid as recently as 1964) was relaid on the Wirksworth branch. The Working Timetable for October 1968 showed the following trips on the branch:

Target 31 SX	Shunt 15.17 to 17.54
Target 42 EWD	Shunt 08.04 to 10.41 SX; 06.30 to 09.07 SO
	(SO worked by loco off 02.45 Etruria to Chaddesden)
Target 45 SX	Shunt 12.05 to 14.12
Target 66 SX 350 hp Diesel	08.50 to 15.30 Wirksworth shunt

Another major derailment took place on 9th October, 1969, when a class '45' diesel hauling 27 loaded stone wagons out of Wirksworth yard came off the

An unidentified class '45' hauls its stone train through Duffield tunnel towards the A6 road
bridge on 15th April, 1972.   *Author*

rails just south of Wash Green bridge. The engine toppled onto its side, taking with it a brake tender and the first wagon in the train. The driver, George Chadwick, escaped injury, and by the evening the same day, a breakdown gang from Toton had rerailed the brake tender and wagon, and tracklayers from Ambergate had slewed adjacent tracks so that trains could get past the still stricken locomotive, which was not rerailed until a couple of days later.

In the mid-1970s, another derailment was recorded at the same location, this time involving a class '25' locomotive that overturned and required the attendance of the Toton-based Cowans Sheldon crane for its recovery. Regrettably, the state of the track at Wirksworth, particularly at the foot of the incline, meant that derailments were commonplace, and barely a month went by without an item of rolling stock leaving the rails. Sometimes a breakdown crane was required, but on at least one occasion, when a train derailed at the Hannages, a fork-lift truck was pressed into service, although presumably to lift wagons rather than a locomotive.

On 7th April 1971, the down branch sidings at Duffield, together with the associated ground frame, were taken out of use, and as recently at 29th May, 1977, a new facing connection to the branch was provided.

The 1974 Working Timetable of Conditional Services showed a maximum of four freight workings daily either to Whitemoor, Lloyd's Sidings (Corby) or Purfleet. In 1977, only one service was shown (again conditional) to Lloyd's Sidings, but by 1979/80, two conditional services to Whitemoor had been added. These services carried what was euphemistically known as 'sugar-stone' to the sugar refineries in the Ipswich area, where the stone was used to blanch the sugar. Because of the nature of sugar production, the demand for this stone was seasonal, and loads were usually sent between November and January in 21 ton iron-ore hoppers. The Working Timetable for October 1979 showed only one regular trip on the branch:

Target 42 SX 2 x class '25' Diesel   Shunt 07.00 to 10.55 SX; 13.20 to 16.50 TWFO

Throughout the 1980s there was a steady reduction in services, not least because of the closure of the steelworks at Corby, and the fact that the loading facilities at Wirksworth were far from ideal, with only six wagons at a time being able to be handled on the exchange sidings. With the number of stone trains down to about two a week, there was much speculation in May 1985 that Tarmac Roadstone Ltd was wishing to move its limestone by lorry in preference to rail. Local residents were very concerned about the prospect of more heavy lorries passing through the town.

Despite the gradual loss of traffic, however, improvements were still being made to the branch. At Idridgehay, an interesting experiment took place whereby solar energy was used to provide power for the level-crossing lights and equipment. This began early in 1982 with the mounting of solar panels on a gantry and the construction of several battery boxes that could (allegedly) store sufficient electricity for the system to work through 40 completely sunless days. The system was monitored remotely by the Railway Technical Centre at Derby, and the hope was that similar equipment could enable power signalling

Wirksworth yard, photographed on 15th December, 1977. This was the heyday of its life as a stone terminal with sidings full of loaded and empty hopper wagons, and a couple of class '20s' in attendance - locomotives that typified the motive power at this time.   *R.G. Cash*

On 15th December, 1977 an unidentified class '25' brings a train of loaded hoppers down from the exchange sidings and under Cemetery Lane bridge.   *R.G. Cash*

A lone class '20' No. 20072 hauls its train of quicklime (judging by the sheeted wagons) under Wash Green bridge towards Duffield on a snowy 10th April, 1978.   *R.G. Cash*

A double-headed stone train from Wirksworth hauled by class '20s' Nos. 20005 and 20178 at Gorsey Bank crossing on 20th October, 1978.   *A.R. Kaye*

Above: The Middlepeak exchange sidings looking towards the station from Cromford Road on 24th July, 1982. *Author*

Above right: After passing under Cromford Road, the line from the exchange sidings ran into a dead-end on the line of the extension to the Cromford & High Peak line. Trains were then propelled up the left-hand line into the loading area. (At this point, WyvernRail are building a platform called Ravenstor Halt, which will give access to the National Stone Centre.) *Author*

Right: This is the standard gauge feeder line looking in the direction of the tunnel under Middleton Road that led into Stoneycroft Quarry. The picture was taken on 24th July, 1982. *Author*

to be installed at remote country locations where there was no mains electricity. In reality, Idridgehay was never wholly solar powered as the track circuits and treadles continued to be fed from the mains. The current owners of the line, however, are determined to make the experiment work, and 20 years later have installed modern solar panels (a fraction the size of the originals) connected to Nickel Cadmium cells to supply the track circuit. Second-hand cells have been installed in the original battery boxes and connected to the existing solar panels, which were found to be still in working order, although in need of a good clean.

Ironically, in the same month that locals were speculating that Tarmac Roadstone Ltd was wishing to move its limestone by lorry, the Spring Bank Holiday saw the reopening of the line to passengers in connection with the Well Dressing festivities. This was a joint venture between British Rail, St Mary's Church (Cromford) Restoration Committee, the Branch Line Society, the Arkwright Society and Hertfordshire Railtours. The service operated on 25th, 26th and 27th May, 1985 with six trains each way on the Saturday and Monday and five each way on the Sunday. Running as the 'Wirksworth Phoenix', at least 5,000 passengers were carried by class '150' dmus over the three days, and the 10.39 train from Derby on 25th May reportedly had 200 standing passengers. Two of these 'Sprinter' units worked the service (sets Nos. 150 001 and 150 002), and special day return through tickets were available from 62 stations as far apart as Edinburgh and Plymouth. Prior to the first trains running, it was necessary for a clearance test to take place, and this as done on 13th May, when the 16.51 Birmingham to Derby scheduled service was extended to Wirksworth for the purpose.

Unit No. 150 001 was in use on the Saturday, but after some faults had been discovered, No. 150 002 took over for the rest of the weekend. However, the service proved so popular that an extra train had to be provided to supplement the final Wirksworth to Derby train on the Monday. As a result, both units were in action at the same time. The fares were £2.50 return, £1.50 single and £1 child/OAP single or return.

This first series of excursions set the scene for more of the same. On 1st September, 1985, a special from Plymouth worked down the branch, and the weekend of 14th and 15th September saw a repeat of the 'Wirksworth Phoenix' services. The Arkwright Society and Cromford Church Restoration Committee were again the prime movers and banded together under the name Venture Rail. The occasion was the Wirksworth Festival, and there were six trains a day for the same fares as before. This time, the service was provided by class '151' dmu No. 151 002.

Venture Rail repeated the runs again for the 1986 Well Dressing festival. Dmu No. 151 002 was used on the six trains each day, and an extra train was required again on the Monday. The fares remained much as before, but an additional feature was a series of coach excursions from Wirksworth to the Cromford & High Peak line, sponsored by Derbyshire County Council. At last it seemed that BR was becoming aware of the potential for such trips as these, for on the Monday, special trains were also run from Derby to Sinfin Central on the former Melbourne branch.

The 'Wirksworth Phoenix' rose from the ashes one more time with six return trips on Saturday 23rd and Monday 25th May, 1987, but the trains made a loss,

The 'Wirksworth Phoenix' (13.51 ex-Derby) on arrival at Wirksworth on 26th May, 1985.   *Author*

Having left Wirksworth at 18.15, the 'Wirksworth Phoenix' formed by 150 002 waits at Duffield for its last journey of the day to Derby on 26th May, 1985.
                                                         Author

Charter control   2nd
The Wirksworth Phoenix
Sunday, 26th May, 1985
Derby or Duffield
to
Wirksworth and back
Valid for one return journey only
For conditions see over (M)   1444

0510

The 14.37 ex-Wirksworth 'Phoenix' at Shottle on 27th May, 1985. The oil storage tanks here are prominent in this picture. *Author*

No. 151 002 has just arrived at Wirksworth with the 08.50 ex-Derby 'Wirksworth Phoenix' on 14th September, 1985. *Cyril Sprenger*

Brakes are being pinned down on wagons prior to leaving the exchange sidings at Wirksworth. The train is the 6E28 to Purfleet on 27th November, 1985 with No. 45104 *The Royal Warwickshire Fusiliers* in charge.   *Peter Gater*

No. 45007 at the exchange sidings with train 8P07, the 13.16 Wirksworth to Derby St Mary's limestone train, on 15th January, 1986. The train will then go forward to King's Lynn via Whitemoor Yard, March.   *C.J. Tuffs*

and there were no more. On 22nd April 1989, the 'Denby Dawdler' railtour visited the line, also becoming the first passenger train for over 20 years to reach Denby on the Ripley branch (from which the tour took its name). In a manner reminiscent of the 1906 railmotor service, three runs were made over the Ripley and Wirksworth branches starting from Derby at 08.40, and ending there at 19.15. The train was 'topped and tailed' by class '20s' Nos. 20114 and 20127, the former leading from Derby, the latter from Wirksworth. On the first run, an attempt was made to storm the incline, but one of the locomotives stalled half-way up. The second and third trips were more successful in this endeavour, both trains making it all the way to the loop at the top.

The last sugar-stone working and, as it turned out, the last-ever revenue-earning service over the line under BR, was hauled by BR class '47' No. 47373 on 4th December, 1989. The following years were to see several attempts to reinstate the line as a freight, and even a passenger route, as residents and local councillors watched huge tonnages of stone and carloads of commuters pounding along the roads in the area. In anticipation of an upturn in traffic, some continuous-welded rail had been laid in the 1980s, but on 20th July, 1990, the Freight Network Manager at Birmingham advised that 'the line is not expected to carry any Railfreight traffic for at least three years'. Some track was made available for use elsewhere in the Nottingham area and would 'not be replaced for the time being – therefore the line will cease to be operational, i.e. mothballed'. Sure enough, in February 1991 came news that some trackwork near Idridgehay had been removed for use elsewhere. In the same month, it was suggested that Hawley Colours of Duffield might buy the stretch of line between their factory and Duffield Junction, and turn it into a road so that their lorries could bypass the village, but nothing more was heard of the idea.

The last trainload of limestone departs from Wirksworth on 4th December, 1989 hauled by class '47' No. 47373. ꟻ ueson   *Neil Ferguson-Lee*

A prospect of new stone traffic occurred early in 1992, when BR bid to transport limestone by rail from Wirksworth to a 'pollution-free' power station at Radcliffe-on-Soar. The scheme was reckoned to save up to 120 lorries a week leaving Wirksworth, but although Derbyshire County Council were reported to be considering buying the line itself in order to ease the impact on its roads, the contract for supplying the stone went to the quarries at Peak Forest. The final nail in the line's coffin was an announcement by Tarmac at the beginning of November 1992 that Middlepeak Quarry was to be mothballed, no doubt as a result of the failure of the scheme to supply stone to Radcliffe-on-Soar.

Shortly afterwards, a determined bunch of local businessmen and BR managers formed WyvernRail Ltd, with the express purpose of returning a passenger service to the line. Accordingly, they applied for a Light Railway Order, but at this point, things became complicated with the privatisation of Britain's rail network, the end of BR, and the arrival on the scene of Railtrack. Having started negotiations with BR, WyvernRail found itself back at 'square one' with Railtrack, but carried on undaunted. As part of the privatisation activity, the yard at Wirksworth was designated a Strategic Freight Site to safeguard it from non-rail development.

This change in political ideology surrounding rail transport, while regretted by many, did at least provide an atmosphere in which initiatives such as WyvernRail could prosper, and the Light Railway Order was duly granted by the then Transport Secretary, Sir George Younger, coming into force on 16th October, 1996. Somewhat optimistically, the company announced that a seven-day-a-week passenger service would be running within two years, the intention being to use dmus, with the option of a steam service at weekends and during holidays. For this reason WyvernRail does not see its proposal as 'just another preservation scheme', but as a serious rail option for the local community that will encourage commuter traffic off the roads, and serve the various tourist attractions that have sprung up in the Wirksworth area.

Regrettably, things haven't moved quite as swiftly as WyvernRail had hoped, but the project is still very much alive, and was boosted at a public meeting on 2nd October, 1997 by the launch of the Derby & Wirksworth Railway Association. Since renamed the Ecclesbourne Valley Railway Association, its aim is to apply for charitable status, and provide a volunteer labour force to restore the line. There is a wealth of support in the area, and the efforts of all concerned were rewarded on 8th November, 2000, when Railtrack granted the Association access to the branch in order that they could begin clearing the line of the vegetation that had accumulated over the intervening 11 years. This monumental effort is now virtually complete, and the line has emerged once more from the canopy of trees that had almost obliterated it.

WyvernRail has secured a 15-year lease-purchase of the whole branch from Duffield Junction to the quarries at Middlepeak, excluding that part of the yard which forms the Strategic Freight Site, for which it has a separate lease renewable every three years. The hope is that, boosted by a share issue on 19th April, 2002, WyvernRail will start a limited service in the second half of 2004. The company is not content just to return passenger trains to the branch, however. Mindful of the line's history as a location for experimentation and innovation and its proximity to Derby (still an important railway centre), a new company, MyTestTrack.com, was formed in August 2003 to offer testing services and a training environment for the various privatised railway companies, at a location away from the main railway system.

In the meantime, the line has remained in the ownership of Railtrack (and now Network Rail) and early in 2001 was officially classed as being under an 'extended Engineer's possession', a copy of the relevant notice being attached over the representation of the branch on the panel at Derby. In January 2003, Network Rail contractors began to erect an 8 ft high steel palisade fence along the boundary between the main line and the branch. This was but one aspect of a major track renewal scheme on the old North Midland line, culminating on the morning of 8th February, 2003, with the removal of the trailing crossover between the up and down main lines, together with the facing connection from the down main to the Wirksworth branch. As a result, both running lines at Duffield were 'plain-lined', and the line 'Duffield Junction to Wirksworth Station GF' was severed from the network and officially put out of use.

Throughout the many years of disuse, the two colour light signals controlling movements on the branch at Duffield remained stubbornly, if understandably, showing red. Bizarrely, despite the line being officially out of use, and physically disconnected from the rest of the railway network, signal DY547 was still shining brightly in 2004, as if to underline the fact that access to the main line was not possible. By now, however, someone had replaced the red glass (long since smashed) with a piece of concrete slab in order to reduce the annoyance to nearby residents of a bright white light burning day and night.

As if in defiance of the events taking place at the junction, at around 6 pm on 7th June, 2003, the first steam-hauled train to run over the entire length of the branch through the Ecclesbourne Valley for nearly 38 years, ran from Wirksworth to Duffield and back behind 0-4-0ST *Whitehead*. This was followed on 7th July, 2004 with a visit by the Her Majesty's Railway Inspectorate, who had no hesitation in pronouncing the section between Wirksworth and Gorsey Bank fit for public operation - a wonderful tribute to those who worked so hard to breathe life back into the line. As this book is published, timetabled passenger services will begin over this short stretch of line just over 57 years since the last passenger train ran under the LMS. This will represent a remarkable transformation in the fortunes of the line, and a huge step towards its eventual reopening throughout.

When I wrote the final words in the first edition, I little thought that it would be BR and not the Wirksworth branch that would disappear in the intervening years, but it was a close-run thing! For observers of the railway 'scene', privatisation and its ramifications have provided much of interest nationally, and the advent of a serious proposal to restore services to the branch is a portent of more interesting times ahead for this interesting town and its surrounding area. If you would like to know more about WyvernRail and the Ecclesbourne Valley Railway Association, you can visit their website at www.e-v-r.com.

Looking at the branch now, it is not hard to picture it in its heyday with passengers, milk churns and parcels waiting on a platform for the next train. It is this picture which epitomises the life of a branch line railway in a way which facts, figures and dates can never do. The rest of this book, therefore will concentrate on the incidents and happenings in the line's life, the recollections of those who knew it and the place of the branch in the lives of the local inhabitants.

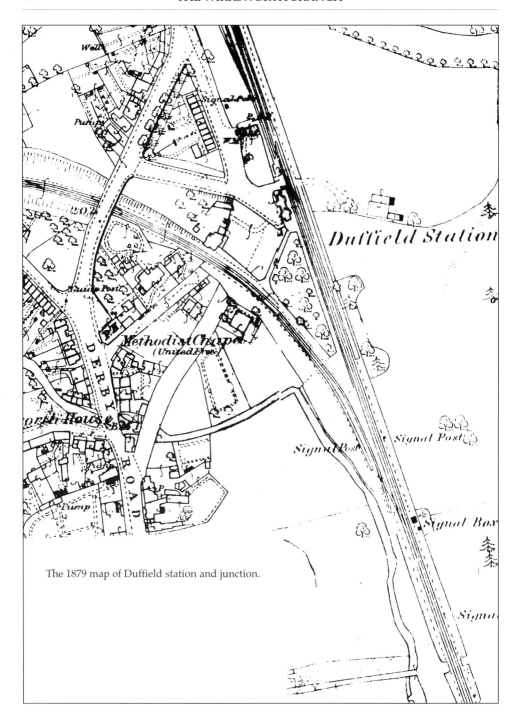

The 1879 map of Duffield station and junction.

Chapter Seven

Derby to Duffield

Since most branch line trains ran from Derby it seems only right and proper to begin a description of the route from Derby Midland station. Had we been travelling by the 5.17 pm departure in 1942 we would have departed from the north end of platform 4. In the same year we would have had to cross to platform 6 for the Saturday 12.45 pm departure. In earlier years, the situation would have been complicated by the presence of Ripley branch trains.

Wirksworth-bound trains would travel towards Duffield on the down fast with a first stop at Nottingham Road station some ¾ mile distant. In the last century, just north of Derby Midland was Derwent Bridge Ticket Platform where up trains would be stopped solely for the purpose of checking tickets. It must be remembered that, in those days, there were no corridor-trains and that this was the only way in which tickets could be checked. The last trains to use the platform did so on Monday 19th September, 1892 from which date tickets were checked at Duffield (except for the 2.25 am mail train from Leeds on Sundays which had tickets checked at Belper).

Nottingham Road station only ever had passenger facilities as its close proximity to St Mary's goods yard made goods facilities unnecessary. It was opened on 1st September, 1856, some 16 years after the opening of the North Midland Railway and on the same day as the opening of the Ripley branch. Most Wirksworth branch trains stopped at the station but it never opened on Sundays.

Little Eaton Junction lies some 3¼ miles from Derby just north of the erstwhile Breadsall Crossing where the line crossed Ford Lane. A magnet for train-spotters, this site was always referred to by them as 'Ford Lane' and never by its official title. At the junction the Ripley branch left the main line and a little further on, at Peckwash Mill, Wirksworth trains were switched to the down slow line. Workings in the reverse direction were routed on to the up fast immediately at Duffield and continued on this line into Derby. This was because the up slow was not signalled for passenger working. To be accurate, the down slow line was designated 'goods' from Derby to Peckwash, 'slow' from Peckwash to Duffield and 'goods' again from there to Milford tunnel where the four tracks became two.

A siding was opened to Tempest's Peckwash Paper Mill on 15th December, 1877, and crossed the River Derwent on a wooden pile bridge. The line was worked by a small steam locomotive that hauled coal and rags into the factory, and drew out wagon-loads of paper for dispatch. The siding was taken out of use in 1917, but the earthworks for the bridge can still be seen. The junction between the siding and the main line was controlled by Peckwash Mill signal box, opened originally at the time the siding was opened, but replaced with a new box with 22 levers (5 spare) on 14th March, 1897. In 1901 in connection with new slow lines being laid to Duffield, the box was reframed with 32 levers of which 5 were spare; it remained open until 24th January, 1965.

Chapel Street, Duffield in January 1904, with the Methodist Chapel on the right and Duffield station in the distance. The down platform home signal gantry, installed when the down goods line was added in 1897, is also visible.   *Knighton Collection*

Duffield looking south with all four running lines in use, thought to have been taken before the Station box was taken out of use (*see Chapter Eleven*). Interestingly, there is a line running from the up goods, which (according to a plan that is not suitable for publication) crossed the up and down main lines to join the down goods line.   *Author's Collection*

Five and a quarter miles out of Derby is Duffield station, junction for the Wirksworth branch, and opened on 6th April, 1841 as the first station out of Derby on the NMR. The 855-yds-long Milford tunnel between here and Belper was completed in October 1839 and Chevin Hill, through which it passes, is still surmounted by George Stephenson's sighting tower. This is a tall gritstone building, 47 ft high by 21 ft square which was built as a look-out and instruction point from which the progress of the tunnelling from each end could be monitored. Since 1939 it has been roofless as a result of a fire.

The portion of line through Duffield as far as Milford (including the tunnel) was built by David McIntosh of Bloomsbury Square, Middlesex. The main road (now the A6) was taken over the railway in order to avoid a level crossing, part of the hillside east of Duffield Castle having to be cut away.

The railway was opened as far as Masborough on 11th May, 1840, and to Leeds (Hunslet) on 1st July of the same year. A celebration feast was given to all the navvies who had worked on the line, and this was held at Duffield.

Much of the stone used in the construction of the line is thought to have come from Duffield Bank Manor Quarry which closed in 1897 but presumably this was not the only source. A lot of stone was needed, particularly for the stone-lined cutting through Belper. Bricks came from a brickworks in the grounds of what is now a house called 'The Glen' on Hazelwood Road. The bricks were stamped 'I.J.' and 'Duffield', the 'J' standing for Jennens, the proprietor of the brickworks.

As previously mentioned, the station building was erected at the time of the opening of the branch. The former station master's house had an office with a weighing machine, but when it was vacated it was converted to two houses for pointsmen.

In addition to those who moved to Duffield from Derby as a result of the opening of the line, several of the sub-contractors who built it chose to live in the village. The early service was about five trains each way per day.

A census of 7th June, 1841 showed that amongst the population of Duffield there was a 'Railway Agent' (station master), two platelayers, one contractor for public works and four civil engineers. There were also 27 quarrymen and 13 stonemasons who doubtless had much to do with the building of the North Midland Railway.

Ten years later the census showed a station master, two railway labourers and a railway carpenter who possibly worked at Derby. Overall, the population had decreased by 150 as a result of the movement away from Duffield of the navvies.

White's 1857 Directory names the station master as Samuel Jennens (though Kelly's 1855 gives 'Jennins') who was possibly related to the aforementioned brickmaker. Harrison, Harrod & Co.'s Directory of 1860 lists John Jenner as the station master. The similarity of the names suggests that some of these entries may be inaccurate, and the same person is being referred to.

In August 1865, the MR received an application from a Mr Eddowes who wished to purchase about ¼ acre of land near the 'Crab Yard' for the erection of a gasworks. His application was turned down, however.

The line through Duffield was originally double-track with platforms serving each line, that on the up line having a waiting room. The 1879-83 series of Ordnance Survey maps still shows a double track, but by then, the Wirksworth platform had been added. A store had been built alongside the main building

A view of Duffield looking north with all four running lines apparently in use and the Station box still in operation. This suggests a date some time before 1910.   *Author's Collection*

Duffield station looking north in about 1950. Notice the footbridge supports and wooden handrails.   *Lens of Sutton*

Duffield station looking south in June 1969. The up goods line has been removed, and colour light signal DY547 has been installed on the branch, but is not yet in use. *V.R. Anderson*

The Wirksworth branch platform, Duffield in about 1950. *Lens of Sutton*

The main building at Duffield looking from the station approach in June 1969.   *V.R. Anderson*

The platform side of the main building, also in June 1969.   *V.R. Anderson*

and this is now the only remaining feature of the original station. On the branch platform was the waiting room and to the north of the station on the down side were two sidings. For most of the life of the station this site was covered by a large timber yard, but it has now been built over.

In 1895 and 1897, plans were submitted showing extra land that the Midland Railway wished to buy on either side of the line between the station and Milford tunnel. Both show the continuing existence of a double track, and are an indication of the desire of the company to provide additional lines at this point, even though the tunnel would continue to be a bottleneck. The down goods line between Duffield and Milford tunnel was brought into use on 16th May, 1897, and the up goods line between these points a little later on 14th June. These predated the new lines to the south, the up goods line from Duffield station signal box to Peckwash Mill being brought into use on 4th October, 1897, followed by the down slow line between these points on 8th September, 1901. The new up goods line necessitated the rebuilding of the up platform, which according to the 1898-1899 Ordnance Survey map had two buildings on it, one of these being the waiting room that survived until the station became an unstaffed halt. This map also shows that the waiting room that later became a bicycle shed had been added on the down platform and two footbridges had been built, one linking the platforms and another at the north end of the station.

This latter footbridge was constructed in 1897 together with a level crossing to provide access to Eyes Meadow to the east of the station. The owner of this land was the contractor, Isaac Woodiwiss, who was given exclusive use of the bridge and crossing when he sold part of his land to the MR for its track widening scheme. Officially known as the Woodiwiss bridge (No. 19B) the right to use it and the crossing passed to successive owners of the land and, in 1974, the parish council took it over. In late 1982, however, a new road was built from the church to Eyes Meadow on the trackbed of the old up slow line. The level crossing was removed, and the bridge demolished.

The station footbridge was built slightly earlier in 1892 and is numbered 19A. The present brick piers were built in the mid-1950s and replaced wooden (or concrete) piles, those on the down side having themselves been replaced in 1929.

Another footbridge was built over the Wirksworth line to provide access to the branch platform from Chapel Street. The nameboard on this platform read:

DUFFIELD
Change for MANCHESTER
LIVERPOOL and the NORTH

How interesting that in contrast with the sentiments expressed at the meeting of would-be promoters at the Moot Hall on 8th June, 1859, no mention was made of any points to the south, but of course, passengers would have been expected to stay on the train and change at Derby.

Plans for new down sidings were included in the 1895 submission and can be seen at the Derbyshire Record Office (No. 238) together with the 1897 plans (No. 246).

According to the 1904 edition of the *Railway Clearing House Handbook of Stations* the goods yard was equipped with a 5 ton crane. This feature was still present in the 1956 edition.

Duffield waiting room and footbridge in 1969. The brick piers to the bridge were added at some time in the early 1950s, and provided additional storage below the steps on each platform.

David Ibbotson

In a similar style, the bicycle shed stood on the down platform at Duffield, and had originally been completely enclosed like its twin on the island platform. It was demolished along with the rest of the main buildings shortly after this photograph was taken in June 1969.

V.R. Anderson

At the turn of the century, almost everything came and went by train and many of the local men were employed at the locomotive and carriage and wagon works at Derby. Work started at 6.00 am and a train left Duffield at 5.20 am to accommodate them. Many would walk quite a distance to catch this train and one is known to have come from near the 'Tiger Inn', Turnditch, over three miles distant.

The 1914 map shows everything as before, but the fourth running line had been added. This layout remained virtually unaltered until the late 1960s when the wholesale destruction of the station occurred in connection with the beginning of the grant-aided Derby-Matlock service.

Quite naturally, the station was one of the focal points of the village and figures in many tales of village life. Part of the daily routine was the delivery of milk to the station for dispatch to the dairies. At about 7.00 am and 6.00 pm, the farmers brought their churns on horse-drawn carts to the 'Milk Yard'. The milk was taken away to Sheffield and Manchester in the morning and to Derby (for Cricklewood or Kentish Town) in the evening. Tom Naylor of Meadows Farm used a horse called 'Prince' to haul his cart, and evidently the horse very much enjoyed his visits to Duffield station. After galloping down to the loading dock and backing up, he would often start away on hearing the tailboard being raised, unfortunately before the driver had taken his seat. Inward goods included coal for the local merchant, S.F. Upton, colour for Hawley's dye works, and grain waste from the breweries for use as animal feed.

Another time of great activity in the 19th century was during Wakes Week when all Duffield exiles would try to return. This was hardly surprising when on each night of the week at least one public house would offer free beer, cold beef and mashed potatoes. In the club room of the 'White Hart', dancing took place nightly and throughout the week there was a fair.

For much of this period, the station master was Frederick Perry, his reign covering the last quarter of the 19th century and the first 10 years or so of the 20th century. He was succeeded by William Cope who, after a short stay, was followed by Joseph G. Goss at the time of the Grouping, and, from 1954 to 1960, the station master was Mr Hill. Other staff at the station, according to a book published by the National Union of Railwaymen in 1930 included C. Morley and W. Wright (leading porters), C.H. Yeomans (signal lampman), C. Warrington, J. Tebbutt and H.J. Rose (all signalman class 2C, Duffield Junction).

The relative importance of Duffield in the 1930s and 1940s can be judged by the fact that W.H. Smith ran a bookstall on the station. The manager from 1933 to 1938 was Harry Brown who had had experience at both Derby Midland and Friar Gate before coming to Duffield.

It has already been mentioned that the old school room in King Street was owned by the railway and rented to the Parish Council as a Parish room. The Council paid £7 per annum rent and rates and, in November 1948, enquiries were made regarding the outright purchase of the room; this request was turned down. Then, in 1958, it was realised that repairs were urgently needed which BR estimated would cost £200. They were prepared to do the work but only if the rent went up to £65 per year plus rates. Not being prepared to pay this, the Council again offered to buy the property. BR again refused but offered to lower the rent to £50 and, later, to £32. However, in November 1959, the Council were told that the premises were unsafe and advised to vacate the room.

The Wirksworth branch platform at Duffield, thought to have been taken in January 1904, and evidently after Duffield Junction signal box was extended, giving weight to the belief that the extension was not added as late as 1910. Also shown is the footbridge that allowed passengers to gain access to the station directly from Chapel Street. Notice also the waiting room on the branch platform to a design that was repeated on the island platform on the main line.

Knighton Collection

The Woodiwiss bridge at Duffield pictured shortly before demolition in May 1982.

Derby Evening Telegraph

Soon afterwards, the Parish Council were involved in another wrangle with British Railways. A wooden footbridge had, for many years, provided an easy route from the village centre to the branch platform (and hence the station) via Chapel Street. This street had been the main road until the present road was built to accommodate the Wirksworth branch and, by using it, visitors to the station avoided a long walk round to the main entrance.

Towards the end of June 1961, a notice was displayed at the station entrance. Written in chalk on a sheet of cardboard, it read:

> Special Notice. Will passengers please note that, in the near future, the bridge over the Wirksworth line will be closed to the public and the right of way from Chapel Street to the station will be dispensed with. A further notice will be issued of the actual date of closure of the bridge. It is expected to be closed on or about 1st July, 1961.

A protest was lodged against the closure on the grounds that this was a public right of way. There was no doubt that, having been in uninterrupted use for more than 20 years, this would have been the case were it not for the fact that the bridge had been built solely for the convenience of rail passengers. It was thought doubtful whether it could be proved that its use was not merely for railway business so BR carried out their closure threat.

On 10th October, 1961, the Parish Council received a letter from BR which informed them that the bridge would be closed from the 12th October and removed shortly afterwards. A Mr F. Butt commented that if the railway did not want people to get to their platform that was all there was to it.

This was the first act in the destruction of Duffield station, but by no means the last. Further rationalisation took place in 1969 when the station was reduced to an unmanned halt. I was at school in Duffield at the time and paid regular visits to the station. At every visit, something seemed to have disappeared, and my diary of the time reveals that the signal box met its demise on 8th October, 1969 and the up waiting room on 15th October, together with the bicycle shed on the down platform. The main building, branch waiting room and up slow running lines all went at about the same time. The down slow was the next to be removed so that all trains now pass either side of the island platform, for which reason the station footbridge has been retained. A 'bus shelter' is the only building on the platform and gives scant comfort to users of the Derby-Matlock service. It must be at the time of this demolition that the characteristic BR totems were removed, and although the fate of all of them is not known, at least one was saved, selling at a railwayana auction in 2003 for £1,050.

Before leaving the main line for a trip up the branch, it should be pointed out that test work has been carried out here as well as on the branch. The 'Fell' locomotive made test runs from 1955 onwards, as did the prototype APT-E in 1972. In the same year, a mile-long stretch of line between Little Eaton and Duffield became the first piece of Inter-City route to be laid with continuous reinforced concrete paved track. Intended for use in locations where maintenance was a problem, the design was thought to have a possible use in the Channel Tunnel and for allowing higher speeds in less-difficult locations. The track gained a judges' mention in the Concrete Society's 1973 award scheme, but in recent years it has ceased to be used because subsidence has cracked the concrete.

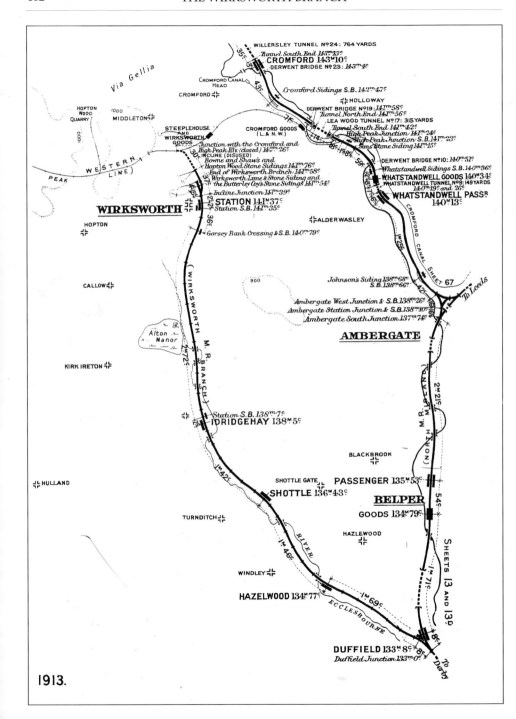

1913.

Chapter Eight

Along the Branch

Hazelwood

On leaving the branch platform at Duffield, trains faced a continuous, but not difficult, uphill route all the way to Wirksworth. The steepest gradient is 1 in 100, but apart from a few level sections, all the gradients are adverse in this direction.

The first notable feature is the 52 yds-long Duffield tunnel (one of the shortest in the country and numbered 2 by the Midland Railway, bridge number 1 being the one taking the A6 over the line); only the presence of a crossroads above the line meant that a tunnel rather than a bridge had to be built. In common with all the engineering works on the line, it was built to take double track, and this feature was utilised by extending the branch siding at Duffield through the tunnel to terminate at buffer stops just outside the northern portal. From here the line was single all the way to Wirksworth except for passing loops. The keystone of the tunnel's southern arch has the initials 'J B' carved on it, which might be those of the 'Master Mason' or the gaffer of the masons who, during the course of the work, would it apply his 'mark' somewhere on the stones. Interestingly, the initial 'B', preceded by another which has been worn away with time, can also be seen on the southern side of one of the Cemetery Lane bridge arches at Wirksworth, and it is possible that this was made by the same mason.

The branch runs in a cutting for nearly ½ mile after leaving the junction but then comes out into the broad expanse of the Ecclesbourne Valley as it approaches Hazelwood station, 1 mile 77 chains from the junction and 7¼ miles from Derby. The station is situated next to the bridge which carries Nether Lane from Hazelwood village south to the Wirksworth road. Nearby, on this road, is an inn called 'The Puss in Boots' and it was suggested before the opening of the line that this might be a suitable name for the station.

There was a single platform with a loading dock and a passing loop beyond from which sprang a siding back towards the main building. Two small ground frames controlled the points for the loop, one at each end. The main station building, now a private residence, was built in the same style as the other three on the branch and is really a smaller version of that at Duffield. Two gabled ends are joined by a narrower section from which springs a canopy with an interesting fretted ironwork lintel. This was a common style at that time, as similar station buildings were built at locations as far apart as Bitton, near Bristol (now preserved) and on the Settle & Carlisle line.

There was sufficient capacity in the yard for 38 normal-sized wagons, but I have found no evidence of the existence of a yard crane. Similarly, there was never a signal box at Hazelwood, although a list of 'signal posts' returned to the Board of Trade in November 1880 shows some centralised control from before August 1877. This was provided by a ground frame on the platform south of the station building.

The northern portal of Duffield Tunnel in 1953. The A6 road bridge can be seen in the distance.
David Ibbotson

Mr Herbert Swift with Cadet Mr (later Sir) V.M. Barrington-Ward. Probably taken just before World War I.
Mrs Land

The first station master at Hazelwood was Anthony Swift, but it is not exactly clear whether he took up his duties on the opening of the line in 1867 or in the following year. He came from Armley in Yorkshire and it is known that he arrived at Hazelwood before the station house was finished, which I think supports the earlier date of arrival. On his death on 12th April, 1890, he was succeeded by his son, Herbert Swift, who held the post for exactly 39 years, retiring on 12th April, 1929, by which time he was also responsible for Shottle station. While there have been other recorded cases where a son succeeded his father as station master, it is doubtful whether any family régime has ever lasted as long as this.

The Swifts also became coal merchants and rented some land adjacent to the station as their depot. In 1926, Herbert moved out of the station house into a house called 'Sunset'. This was followed later by the building of a second house called 'Sunnette' for his assistant Mr W.H. Allsop.

Allsop eventually took over the business but when the station closed in January 1953, he moved the business to Shottle. In March 1964, this station lost its goods facilities, so the business (which had been sold) was again moved, this time to Belper. Swift owned two 12 ton private owner wagons, thought to have been painted red-oxide with:

SWIFT HAZELWOOD

written in white paint on each side, although Mr Allsop's son remembers:

H. SWIFT
HAZELWOOD

appearing on the top left-hand corner of the wagon. There could, of course, have been different lettering styles at different periods.

After the milk traffic had declined on the railway, Swift and Allsop started a milk-haulage business. Milk was collected from the local farms and taken to Brightside Dairy, Sheffield. *Kelly's Directory* of 1928 refers to Swift as 'Coal Merchant and Income Tax Collector'.

During the first half of this century, the Swift family was synonymous with the Wirksworth branch. I was able to talk to Mrs Land of Sycamore Farm, Hazelwood, who knew the line for most of her long life. Her father was Andrew Swift, who was, for a time, the station master and goods agent at Wirksworth; he was brother to Herbert, and therefore son of Anthony. It was from Mrs Land that I first heard about the visit of the Royal train, the story being confirmed by Bill Allsop who also confirms a date at the beginning of the war. He remembers Herbert Swift well, and the Clyno car which he owned for many years.

Swift's replacement was Gemalial William Marple who combined his railway duties with those of a local preacher. It is thought that shortly afterwards there was a reorganisation whereby Hazelwood was run together with Duffield under its station master, and Shottle and Idridgehay were 'twinned' under Mr Marple, who had held this position for a few years before Swift's retirement at Hazelwood. It is probable that Marple was only a 'caretaker' station master at Hazelwood for a brief period until the reorganisation took effect. As such he

Mr Herbert Swift at Hazelwood *c*.1913.   *Sir Gilbert Inglefield*

was in charge of all three intermediate stations. At this time, there were two porters at Hazelwood, W. Greenhalf and H. Wagstaffe.

After his retirement, Herbert Swift wrote a history of the village entitled *Hazelwood in the Forest of Duffield* and this was published in 1931. He was a remarkable man and evidently held in high esteem by his employers, for at some time after 1910 he was entrusted with no fewer than four 'cadets' (equivalent to present-day 'management trainees'). These were Messrs V.M. Barrington-Ward, J. Maxwell Stewart, Meredith Lewis and Bernard Smith. While at Hazelwood, they lived with the Scotney family of Firs Farm. Alas, World War I intervened and all but Barrington-Ward perished on active service. The three are remembered on memorial tablets in the church and the Memorial Hall. Barrington-Ward, however, progressed very well in his chosen career. After wide experience on the Midland Railway and later the North Eastern Railway, he joined the LNER at the Grouping. In 1927, on the retirement of W.M. Clow as Southern Area Superintendent, it was decided that his area should be divided into two parts. Barrington-Ward was given the post of Superintendent, Western Section, which consisted of the former Great Northern and Great Central lines. The Eastern Section (ex-Great Eastern Railway) became the responsibility of Col H.H. Maudlin and on his promotion, in 1939, the Eastern and Western Sections were combined under the overall supervision of Barrington-Ward.

In 1942, he became Assistant General Manager (Operating) and, in September 1945, became Divisional General Manager, Southern Area. From 1938, he had also been Chairman of the Operating Committee of the Railway Executive which had been brought into being by the Ministry of Transport to prepare for the eventuality of war.

At Nationalisation, Barrington-Ward became a member of the new Railway Executive under the British Transport Commission with responsibility for 'Operating and Marine'. He finished a distinguished career as Sir Michael Barrington-Ward.

One of the first telegraph offices in the district was opened at the station in October 1879 and, thanks to the efforts of the Revd W.H.M.G. Aitken of Holmeside, became available for public use. So anxious was Aitken to send the first telegram that he handed it in the previous night to ensure transmission at the first opportunity the next day.

The first farmer to use the railway to take away his milk was Thomas Travis of Postern Lodge Farm, who sent his first consignment to Manchester around 1880. Other farmers prophesied ruin, but the practice quickly spread and soon milk was established as one of the principal exports of the valley. By 1931, from the Wirksworth branch, there were up to 11 full vans of milk being dispatched each night, equivalent to 440 cans of milk or 7,000 gallons. Morning milk was to be at the station by 6.00 am and friendly rivalry between farmers resulted in competition to be first with their consignment.

On 20th February, 1935, a derailment occurred at Hazelwood which resulted in the death of the driver. The 8.40 pm Wirksworth to Derby passenger train left the rails some 900 yards south of Hazelwood station, and as well as the fatality, the fireman was badly injured and the guard slightly injured. Significantly perhaps, there were no passengers on the train.

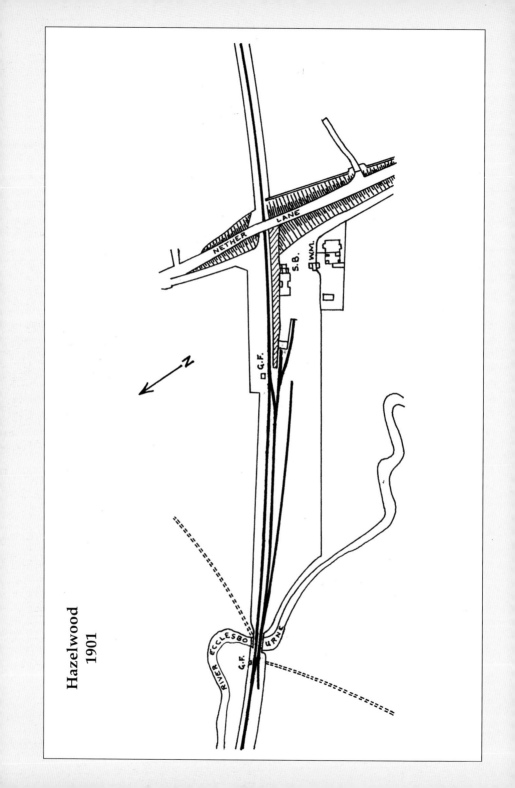

Hazelwood
1901

N

NETHER LANE

S.B.

WM.

G.F.

RIVER ECCLESBOURNE

G.F.

The train consisted of three bogie coaches and a 6-wheeled brake van marshalled between the second and third coaches. It was hauled by class '417' 0-6-0 No. 4402 built in 1927. As a result of the derailment, the engine and tender fell onto their left side and were considerably damaged. The coaches remained upright but all were completely derailed and the first coach was leaning to the left. A rail had been caught by the rear axle of the tender and forced into the leading coach for a distance of 12 feet 6 inches, its end appearing under the seat of the third compartment.

In his report on the accident, Colonel A.C. Trench noted that the Wirksworth branch was classified as a third class line and that the rails in the vicinity were 21 feet in length. These rails had been laid as far back as 1885 and the line re-sleepered in 1910. It is quite clear from his comments that the track maintenance left much to be desired and this factor was singled out as a prime cause of the derailment. The gauge varied considerably at some points and fish-plate bolts (in some cases all four) were found to be loose. In addition to all this was the presence of a 'clay hole' north of Hazelwood which would give a varying degree of support to the track depending on how wet or dry the weather had been.

A further contributory factor was the speed of the train which, although said to be not greater than 40 mph, would have been very difficult to judge in the dark. It is interesting to note that although this class of locomotive had been used for many years on goods trains, its appearance on passenger trains was only a feature of the previous two years.

Fireman Bill Robinson was able to describe the events leading up to the accident, culminating in a sudden lurch to the right before the engine toppled over to the left. He fell into the escaping steam and, as a result, was badly scalded. Of the driver, Gould, with whom he had worked for about 11 months, nothing could be seen so he crawled back to the brake van for assistance. (It is to be noted that on a previous trip on the branch that day he had noticed nothing out of the ordinary but the difference was that on that working the train was booked to stop at Hazelwood.)

On that particular run each day the guard was always accompanied by a porter from Derby who would help with the milk churns. So it was that guard Owen and porter Clark found themselves in the trailing end of the second coach, a bogie third brake. After the crash, Owen and then Robinson were able to run and walk the 1½ miles to Duffield signal box, leaving Clark to look after the train. It was Clark who found the body of the unfortunate Gould.

In summing up, Trench remarked on the standard of maintenance of the track, the speed of the train (which could have been as high as 50 mph) and the presence of old and badly worn 21 ft rails. These rails in themselves would, it was stated, have made maintenance very difficult.

Whatever the ultimate cause of the accident, it is perhaps ironic that the track was due for renewal the following year and that casualties could have been much worse had passengers been on board.

After Mr Allsop had moved his coal business and the goods facilities had been removed, the station was used as a depot by Messrs Buxton and Dawson. All items associated with the yard were removed, the last to go being the weighbridge. The station building remained, however, and, in 1963, an indoor

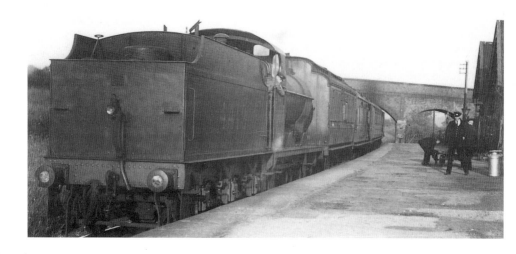

MILK TRAIN DERAILED

A press cutting relating to the accident between Hazelwood and Duffield on 20th February, 1935 that resulted in the death of the driver.

Class '4F' No. 4419 with the branch train on 27th June, 1933. Unusually, the engine is running tender-first, suggesting that the Wirksworth turntable was out of order.   *H.C. Casserley*

riding school was built on the station site by Mrs Judith Yeomans, later to be taken over by Mr and Mrs King. The site has since been redeveloped as a timber merchant's depot following the closure of the timber yard next to Duffield station in the 1990s.

When Mr Marple was succeeded at Shottle and Idridgehay he was replaced for a short time by Mr Webb but he seems to have been in charge of Shottle and Hazelwood, not Idridgehay. Evidently he did not stay long, and on his departure, Hazelwood went back into partnership with Duffield and Shottle with Idridgehay. From 1941 until closure in 1953, Hazelwood was unusual in having a lady porter called Mrs Malin.

Before leaving Hazelwood, it seems only fitting to include some reminiscences of Sir Gilbert Inglefield who spent his early years at 'Flower Lilies', Windley. From his bedroom window he could see the smoke and steam from the engines as they started from Hazelwood. He sometimes accompanied the milk-float from the estate farm on its two mile journey to the station and watched the churns being loaded into the wagons that had been left in the siding. At other times he would accompany his Grandfather in his elderly, chain-driven Daimler when he took the train to Derby.

Sir Gilbert remembered Herbert Swift well and described him '. . . as a tall, dignified person, always most courteous to my Grandfather and with whom I had many pleasant encounters'. As boys will, the young Sir Gilbert asked Mr Swift if he thought it would be possible for him to have a footplate ride. The regular driver, who was finishing his career on the local line, agreed and soon the two became firm friends. While at home one holiday, Sir Gilbert saved up and offered him 'a pecuniary reward' if he would teach him how to drive the engine; '. . . this beautiful little tank engine painted immaculately in the colours of the Midland Railway, hauling four or five coaches. He agreed'. Evidently Sir Gilbert already had some experience of driving motor cars but this was nothing compared to the 'entrancing experience' of driving a steam engine. 'One had to keep an eye on the steam pressure gauge and on the water gauge too, to be economical in stoking up so that the safety-valve did not blow off steam, and this one learnt by judging the noise the exhaust made out of the funnel.' Driving the engine became a fairly regular activity, but judging the application of the vacuum brake could be difficult; on one occasion he nearly overshot the platform at Wirksworth. His regular engine was the 0-4-4T No. 1429 but he was not allowed to drive the 0-6-0 engine which hauled the goods train. What a fascinating childhood!

As an aside, Mrs Gwen Watts, of Hole House Farm, Ashleyhay remembers the Inglefield brothers' love of the railway, and also remembers being taken with her brother, Peter, to 'Flower Lilies' when the house and contents were being sold. The large conservatory was filled with a wonderful railway layout some of which her father bought and took home in two large wooden tea-chests for her brother.

On leaving Hazelwood there is an initial gradient of 1 in 246 for about ½ mile which steepens to 1 in 164 for nearly a mile on the approach to Shottle. The only feature of interest apart from the odd road bridge or culvert is the occupation viaduct mentioned in Chapter Two - and what a feature of interest!

Very much run down, Hazelwood station is seen here on 3rd June, 1967.   *G. Yeomans*

Hazelwood station on 20th September, 1969 showing the indoor riding school built on the site of the goods yard.   *D.F. Tee*

As we have seen, there is only scant mention of the viaduct in the Construction Committee's minutes so one can only assume that the Midland Railway was intensely embarrassed at having to build such an enormous structure simply to provide access from one part of a farm to another. In setting this precedent, other land-owners could easily have argued for the same treatment.

The popular story, locally, is that the farmer, Thomas Travis, insisted on a bridge in preference to a level crossing. This is the same man who was later to be the first to take advantage of the railway for the transportation of his milk - not without reason, then, was he known as 'Canny Travis'. Having agreed to his request, the company found that, because of the marshy ground on either side of the line, 19 arches had to be built in all. This exercise cost about £10,000 and no sooner had the work been finished than Travis announced his intention to use 16 of the arches for storage and shelter for his cattle. The Midland was not amused and promptly dug a ditch and put up a fence around the structure to deny him access. For this reason, the bridge became known as 'Travis's Folly'. Officially, it was called 'Hazelwood Viaduct' or sometimes 'Hazelwood Bridge'.

Though much of this story is basically true, in reality, the situation was slightly different. Although Travis farmed the land on either side of the line, he was only a tenant of the Duke of Devonshire and it was his agents who insisted on the bridge. Two farms were involved, Postern Farm and Postern Lodge Farm, and the need for access was because Travis ran both farms as one. However, shortly after the bridge was built, the two farms were separated and run as separate units. As a result, the bridge fell into disuse and remained so for the rest of its life. Nowadays the farms are run together and are still part of the Duke of Devonshire's estate.

The bridge was 400 yards long and, because of its almost total disuse, the roadway became overgrown with grass, so much so that William Watt, a neighbouring farmer, had occasionally obtained a crop of hay off it! Understandably, this kind of treatment took a heavy toll on the structure and it became increasingly expensive to repair. This, together with the fact that it was so rarely used, prompted the LMS to do away with it. The job was offered to the military as a training exercise and the time was set at 7.30 am on Sunday 24th September, 1933. The military grabbed at the chance of experimenting with such a structure in order to find how to obtain the maximum effect with the minimum of explosive. A report of the results was to be sent to the School of Military Engineering at Chatham.

Preparations began the preceding week with LMS workers removing the coping stones. Permission had also been obtained from the Duke of Devonshire to put a level crossing in place of the bridge. At either side of it, the ballast was built up over the track to avoid damage from fallen masonry, and it is interesting to note that farm implements had to be removed from on top of the bridge where they had been stored.

Entrusted with the job were a detachment of 24 Royal Engineers from Catterick and units from the Northumberland Territorials. More than 2,000 spectators and 1,000 troops gathered in the surrounding fields to watch the proceedings and roads in the area were blocked by cars. In order to avoid injuries, a cordon of troops prevented unauthorised persons from venturing

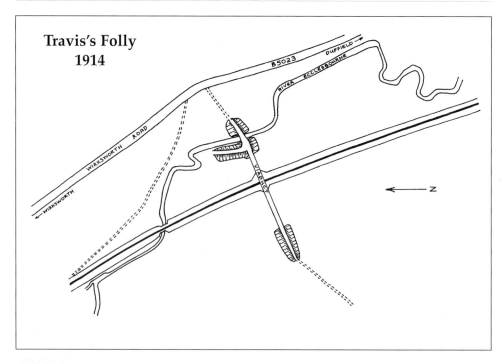

Travis's Folly
1914

A close-up of the central arches of 'Travis's Folly'.   *Roger Holbrook*

Travis's Folly, a bridge at Hazelwood, Derbyshire, so called because a farmer of that name, some 80 years ago, insisted upon the Midland Railway Co. building it to enable his cattle to cross their branch line passing through his land, was blown up yesterday by a detachment of Royal Engineers [*from a local newspaper*].

The remains of 'Travis's Folly' after demolition.   *Author's Collection*

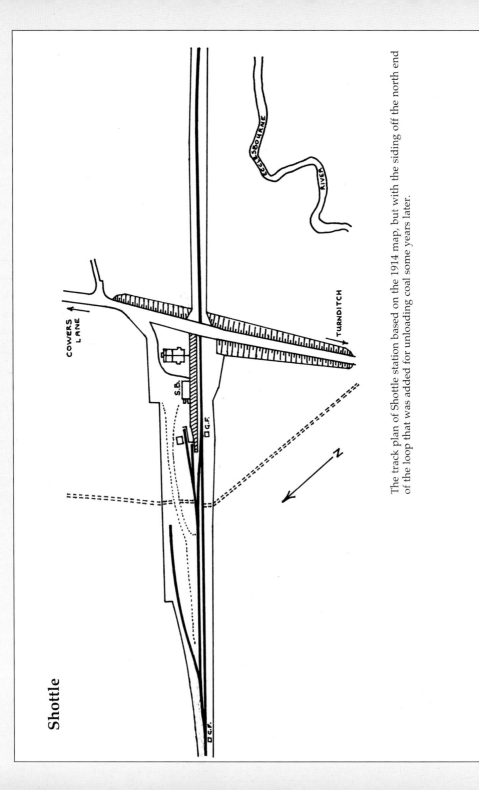

Shottle

COWERS LANE

S.B.

G.F.

G.F.

TURNDITCH

SOD LANE

RIVER

N

The track plan of Shottle station based on the 1914 map, but with the siding off the north end of the loop that was added for unloading coal some years later.

any nearer than 300 yards from the bridge. In drizzling rain, the crowd waited for the action to commence.

The 'Regulars' were the first to attempt the demolition and concentrated on five of the arches. Explosives were laid in holes made by pneumatic drills and these were ready for firing by 9.00 am. A warning bugle was the signal for the crowds to draw back and a second bugle signalled the detonation. The bridge rocked slightly but stood its ground.

The three central arches were the next to be tackled and these were entrusted to the Northumberland Territorials. At 10.00 am they were flung into the air to the accompaniment of loud cheering. The remaining arches were similarly dispatched, three at a time, including the five which had withstood the initial onslaught. Guncotton and gelignite were used and no two arches or piers were destroyed in the same way. Variations were made in the type of explosives used and the timing and spacing of the charges.

At around midday, the crowd started to disperse - possibly slightly bored and probably rather cold. New arrivals maintained the number of observers, however. LMS workers were able to clear the track for the passage of the evening milk train and the last charges were laid at 8.00 pm. Three pillars remained and were demolished the next day.

So ended the curious story of Travis's Folly although there are remnants of the bridge left. If you travel along the Wirksworth Road between Duffield and Cowers Lane and look to your left just after crossing the railway, you will see two arches which remain to take the footpath over the River Ecclesbourne. Much overgrown now, there is little to suggest what momentous events took place at this spot.

Shottle

Shottle is, as mentioned previously, some distance from the village. It is actually at the small settlement of Cowers Lane and was known as such until the opening of the line. The road from Cowers Lane to Turnditch crosses the railway at the station and even this latter village is nearer than Shottle itself.

In appearance, it was virtually a mirror image of Hazelwood with a similar arrangement of sidings and a loop, but on the other side of the line. There was no signal box, but from the list of 'signal posts' provided to the Board of Trade in November 1880, a centralised ground frame was in existence from before August 1877. In the 20th century, if not before, there were two such ground frames or 'stages' controlling the points to the loop at each end. The station was 8¼ miles from Derby and 3 miles 43 chains from Duffield Junction. The yard capacity was 40 wagons.

The station master when the 1871 census was carried out was John Towler, originally from Settle in Yorkshire. Whether he was in place at the time of the line's opening is not known, but it seems likely. Also listed in that census was a platelayer by the name of John Moreton, who presumably was employed on this line. The 1881 census lists another platelayer by the name of George Heathcote, and also reflects the arrival in 1875 of station master Herbert Barber, who remained in this position until about 1920. He was the great-grandfather of

A postcard of Shottle station published by George Marsden & Son in 1908. The wooden lamp-posts have been replaced by cast-iron ones.   *Author's Collection*

Shottle station in its days as the only intermediate goods yard on 2nd August, 1954.
H.C. Casserley

Roger Holbrook, who spent all his life living near the station, and who helped me greatly with the history of this part of the line. Ten years later, and the census shows that Barber's 15-year-old son, also called Herbert, was working as a porter at the station, and James Holbrook (almost certainly related to Roger Holbrook) was employed as a clerk.

Sir Gilbert Inglefield did not remember Mr Barber but had heard about him from his elder brother, Sir John Crompton Inglefield. Mr Barber evidently held Sir John in high regard and on one occasion, presented him with a pair of pistols, telling him in his slow Derbyshire drawl, 'Never point 'em at anyone'.

A porter recalled by Sir Gilbert was H. (Bert) Wagstaffe, who has already been mentioned as porter at Hazelwood (possibly later). Mr Wagstaffe enjoyed cricket and played for Turnditch village cricket XI. The Inglefield brothers also used to play in these matches, and Sir Gilbert remembered one or two occasions when Wagstaffe was at the crease but had to stop the game to be on duty for the arrival of a train. 'I can see him now on the platform dressed in his cricketing clothes but wearing his uniform coat over his white flannel trousers. He was a great man.'

After the departure of Barber, Shottle was put together with Hazelwood under Herbert Swift and, on his retirement, with Idridgehay under Mr Marple. It was again twinned with Hazelwood when Mr Webb briefly took charge in the 1930s, and then back with Idridgehay at the end of that decade under Mr Harrison. He was succeeded by Mr Cooke in the early 1940s who looked after the two stations until 1947 when Mr Soar took over. By the time he left in 1955, Shottle was the only remaining intermediate station and, by then, John Hall was in charge at Wirksworth. He then took charge of Shottle until its closure.

During the 1930s and the early war years, Edgar Rogers was the porter at the station and lived in the station house. He remembers the traffic well and, as might be expected, most of the inward goods were for the farms in the area. Brewers' grains came from Newark and Burton-on-Trent, and beet pulp came from Colwick. Other provisions included lime and fertilizer which farmers would travel miles to collect. On Fridays, the farmers with their families and employees would all travel into Derby and, in the winter months, wait in the station master's office as there was not enough coal to heat the waiting rooms. In 1941 Mr Rogers was moved to Chaddesden Sidings and out of his house at Shottle - a move which he considers to have been very lucky as shortly afterwards the roof of his old house was damaged by a land-mine.

Mr Rogers remembers one particular red-letter day for Shottle. I have already mentioned the fact that the line's proximity to Derby made it a natural test-track for innovations and rolling stock. This also resulted in the use of the branch for the making of an LMS educational film. Shottle station was chosen for scenes in the film 'Station Working' which, as its name suggests, was used to show staff how trains should be dealt with. Earlier scenes had been shot at Leicester and Mill Hill. In an article entitled 'Shottle "Shot"' the *Derbyshire Advertiser* described the filming:

> The train filmed had an engine, three passenger coaches and a guard's van. When the filming was completed, the party had lunch at the Cross Keys Inn, Turnditch.
>
> Mr A.W. Cave responded to a vote of thanks that was accorded to all taking part by representatives of the LMS Publicity Department.

O. Whiston was porter at Shottle after the departure of Mr Rogers until 1959. After moving to Belper goods yard for a while he returned to the branch, this time to Wirksworth.

At about this time, Will and Charlie Booth had a cattle feed business, and stored feed-stuffs at the station. Will Booth's daughter, Mrs Gwen Watts, spent as much time as she could with her father, and he always took her with him whenever he could. She particularly recalls the sugar beet pulp trucks coming into Wirksworth, and sitting for hours as they were unloaded into the lorry. The smell of the beet pulp is still a memory, as is the need to unload the trucks as quickly as possible in order to avoid demurrage charges being levied for the wagons' undue retention.

Between 1953 and 1964 Shottle was the only remaining intermediate station on the line, so W.H. Allsop moved Swift's coal business from Hazelwood. He died while the firm was at Shottle, but the business was carried on for a while by his widow. Two other coal merchants had their coal delivered to Shottle at this time, but carted it to their premises at Ashbourne. One of these firms closed down in 1955 and, as a result, the weighbridge was removed.

This facility had been kept for the convenience of the coal merchants but only brought the railway some 10½d. a month. Since it cost over £70 a year to maintain, its retention was hardly viable. When it became necessary to replace it, a figure of £4,000 was quoted. While there were three merchants, they were prepared to 'club together' to meet the cost, each one paying according to the amount of use. After the closure of one of the businesses, however, this plan was abandoned.

The station is now owned by Peak Oils and used as a fuel-oil distribution depot with oil-tanks standing on the site of the sidings. The main building remains, but has been much altered internally for use as storage and office space. The Ladies waiting room has been modified by the addition of a window adjacent to the former Gents toilet, which is now a store, and is slightly shorter than when built. Externally, the building has been maintained in its original style, and until recently, all the doors still had their nameplates attached. At the rear of the yard a new building has been erected in connection with the business. This began life as the first depot for the National Tramway Museum at Crich, and was moved to Shottle many years ago. The station houses remain and both are inhabited.

Before leaving Shottle, it is appropriate to mention two accidents remembered by Mr Holbrook. The first occurred one Saturday evening in 1946, and involved a train that had been standing at Idridgehay. While the engine was shunting in the yard, the train started to run away. With a favourable gradient all the way down to the junction it soon gathered momentum. Mr Holbrook remembers it roaring through Shottle, still accelerating as it careered down the line to be stopped rather untidily, at the stop-blocks at Duffield.

A similar incident happened in 1967 when a train ran away from Wirksworth. With the benefit of the extra stretch from there to Idridgehay it was fairly flying by the time it reached Shottle. Mr Holbrook estimates that at this point it was travelling at around 60 mph and I have no reason to doubt his judgement. This time it did not reach Duffield as a stone train was travelling towards the

A limestone train passes Shottle behind an unidentified class '4F' on 14th June 1957.

G. Yeomans

junction and the runaways caught up with it at the road bridge between Shottle and Hazelwood. The results can be imagined.

Bearing in mind the continuous downward gradient for the whole length of the line, it is amazing that no-one was killed in these incidents. Had the 1967 runaway not met with another train but continued to Duffield gaining speed all the way, it is doubtful whether it would have stayed on the branch siding but would have, more likely, jumped across the main lines at the junction. What would the consequences have been if it had met a passenger train there?

Idridgehay

The last and most important (some say the prettiest) intermediate station on the branch was Idridgehay, 5 miles 5 chains from Duffield and 10¼ miles from Derby. Its yard had room for 22 wagons. Although it is not certain who the original station master was, it is likely that it was Benjamin Tomlinson, who held the post at the time of the 1871 census. Also mentioned at this time is the coal agent in the village, John Greatorex. Ten years later, Tomlinson was still in charge and Greatorex was still supplying coal, but the staff now boasted a porter, Joseph Wright and a platelayer, who was presumably employed on the line, called William Oakley.

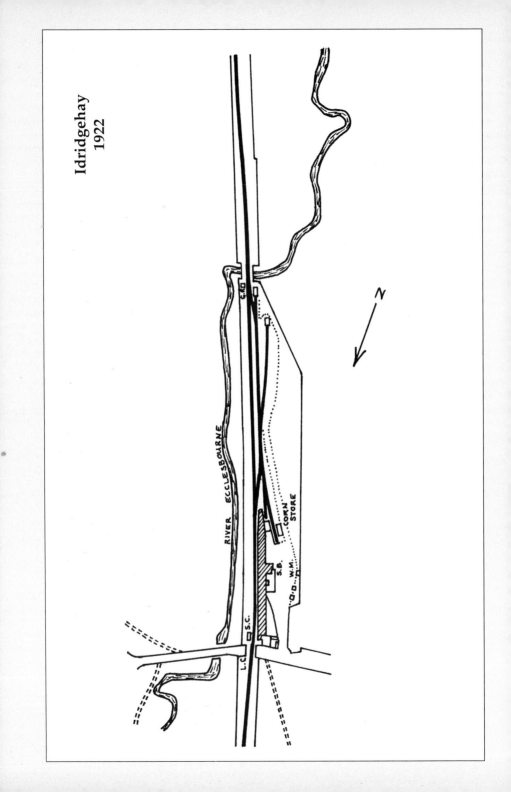

Idridgehay
1922

N

RIVER ECCLESBOURNE

G.K.

CORN STORE

S.B.

W.M.

W.D.

L.C.

S.C.

The Station, Idridgehay.

Idridgehay station with a good collection of churns on the platform. The exact date is unknown, but is probably around the turn of the century.   *Lens of Sutton*

One of the earliest mentions of the station arose as a result of an accident which occurred on 14th January, 1884 involving the 7.45 am Derby to Wirksworth passenger train. Its engine was 2-4-0 No. 81 and behind the tender were a brake van, composite, bogie third and bogie composite carriages and a rear brake van.

Approaching Idridgehay, the train became derailed at the facing points to the loop, the engine coming to rest some 51 yards up the siding, the front brake van on its side across the main line and the composite on its wheels across the main line. The third class carriage and the leading bogie of the second composite were derailed but the carriages were in line. The rear brake van was unaffected. There were no injuries but the guard in the leading van was shaken.

Most puzzling was the fact that the points had been properly locked but some time later a miscreant had unlocked them and wedged them partly open. It was never discovered who was responsible but much of the inspecting officer's report was taken up with criticisms about the circumstances which allowed such a thing to happen. The points were locked in the position for main line running by means of a pin and padlock, an indicator showing which way the points were set. The points and signals were not interlocked and the facing points, being worked from a lever alongside, lacked the proper safety appliances of facing point bolts and locking bars.

It was recommended that the only way to prevent such accidents would be the concentration of the points and signals in a 'proper signal cabin' and the provision of the aforementioned safety appliances at the facing points. In fairness to the Midland Railway, it was pointed out that whoever was responsible had obtained possession of a key and must have had some knowledge of railway working. It is worth noting that from the list of 'signal posts' returned to the Board of Trade in 1880, a centralised ground frame had been in existence from before August 1877. No blame was attached to any employee of the MR, but the driver and fireman were criticised for not having noticed that the point indicator was not showing properly for the main line and, it was felt that they should have seen this in good enough time to stop the train. Some years later, on 8th September, 1890, the signal box at Idridgehay was brought into use.

Perhaps the most interesting aspect of the report is the amount of detail given about the employees of the company. The driver and fireman were, respectively, Joseph Roberts Bakewell and John Naylor, the former having been a driver for 26 of his 33 years with the company, the latter a fireman for five of his nine years' service. William West was the guard riding in the rear van and, in evidence, he pointed out that the train was running 104 minutes late as a result of another derailment of wagons at Duffield. It must be said that there was never any suggestion that the driver had been trying to make up time, and none had been made up between Duffield and Idridgehay. The proper arrival time should have been 8.17 am but the accident happened at 10.01 am.

Also mentioned is the station master of the time Benjamin Tomlinson and his son of the same name who was the station porter. The Superintendent of Police on the MR was Henry Carr and although he mentions that one or two Idridgehay inhabitants were under suspicion, no further details are given.

The next station master that I have been able to trace was Alfred George Beeton, who is mentioned as being in this position from about 1885 until at least 1908, according to *Kelly's Directory*. His position is confirmed by the 1891 census, which also lists signalman Charles F. Jacklin and porter George Thistleton. Other railway employees listed in the village, who presumably (but not necessarily) worked at Idridgehay station were clerks George Hurt and Joseph Taylor and junior clerk Alfred Beeton, the 15-year old son of the station master. There was also a railway labourer in the village by the name of John Duroe, and the coal agent was given as William Dean.

A Midland Railway notice records that on 27th May, 1907, the stage at the Duffield end of Idridgehay goods yard was replaced. This is the ground frame working points 'X' on the signalling diagram shown on page 190, and was implicated in the 1884 accident.

After Beeton left, it is known that Mr Peat was in charge for what appears to have been a brief reign until about 1910 when Mr Marple took over. We have met Mr Marple before, of course, in connection with Hazelwood and Shottle but he had started in the office at Wirksworth before his promotion to station master. Idridgehay was his first station but he took over Shottle and, briefly, Hazelwood after the retirement of Herbert Swift. As we shall see, he was also in charge of Wirksworth and thus had the distinction of having been, at some time, station master of all the stations on the branch. In addition to all this, he was responsible for Ireton Wood Methodist Chapel.

One family who had a long connection with the line was the Whiston family. Colonel William Reginald Harvey Whiston was Clerk to Derby Magistrates, and travelled into Derby every day from his house, 'The Cottage', at the top of Station Lane. Remembered as a confirmed bachelor, he had in fact married the Vicar's daughter in May 1905, but she tragically died just three weeks later, and Col Whiston never remarried. He had held a season ticket almost continuously from before the turn of the century to 1945, and the train would always be held for him at the station. In his use of the line, however, he was predated by his father, also Clerk to the Magistrates, who regularly drove to the station in a dog-cart, accompanied by his wife and groom (a Mr Aikman) from his house, 'Holmeside', on Hillcliffe Lane.

Apparently, one frosty morning his horse slipped and fell, and the passengers of the dog-cart were all ejected. The horse, however, blissfully unaware of the chaos in his wake, did what any horse in his position would have done and continued down to the station. His appearance, 'sans passengers' naturally caused some consternation, and confusion reigned until the groom arrived to explain the situation. Although unharmed, Whiston decided to forego his trip to Derby, which was just as well as, by then, the train had been sent on its way.

At the closure of the line, Colonel Whiston's remarks encapsulated the affection of the local population for their railway. 'I feel very grieved that it is being taken off. It is like losing an old, old friend.'

I was provided with much information about Idridgehay by Reginald Brown whose family was involved with the branch for many years. His recollections cover a period of around 20 years from about 1910. Between 1908 and 1934 (when the signal box closed) his father, John Thomas (Jack) Brown was the Idridgehay signalman, and his elder brother, Edward (Ted) was also employed as a porter. Before coming to Idridgehay, his father had been a lampman at Duffield where Mr Brown's maternal grandfather, Edward George, was a signalman at the Junction box. As well as his brother, there was another porter at Idridgehay by the name of T.J. (Jack) Walker, and a porter-signalman, F.J. Thorne.

The Browns lived in the village, the station master living in the station house. Mr Brown well remembers the system of station grading which was in operation at that time, whereby Idridgehay was classed as 'silver braid' (the braid being worn on the station master's hat). Wirksworth was 'gold braid' and so too was Mr Swift, though this was probably due to his own status and the fact that two stations were under his aegis rather than any reflection on the standing of Hazelwood and Shottle stations *per se*. At larger stations such as Derby, the braid system did not operate but the station master was decked out in silk hat and tailed coat.

While his father was employed at Idridgehay he looked after the station garden, consistently appearing in the list of winners of the 'Best Kept Garden' competition. This was organised for stations in the Derby area and Cromford, Sawley and Borrowash are remembered as also being in contention for honours.

A particular memory is the handling of the milk at the station. The normal weekday pattern was for milk vans to be left in the dock for farmers to put milk in at their leisure. Things were a little more hectic on Sunday, however, when there were no vans in the dock and all milk had to be loaded on the train when it arrived. Accounts had to be paid at the end of the month and if this

A member of staff at Idridgehay poses with a chalked notice advertising trains to London for the Silver Jubilee of King George V and Queen Mary in 1935.   *Knighton Collection*

The station house, level crossing and ground frame at Idridgehay on 14th June, 1957.
G. Yeomans

happened to fall on a Sunday a very hectic day could be expected. When the train arrived, empty churns had to be unloaded, full churns loaded, accounts settled and, in addition, the books balanced so that the cash itself could be taken away by the same train. This activity was repeated at each station on such days.

There was a wooden corn-store in the station yard owned by Fletchers of Duffield. Indeed, their main depot was next to Duffield station with another large depot next to Wirksworth station. In charge of the Idridgehay store was Daniel Petts; he was not in attendance every day, but when he was needed there, travelled from Wirksworth. In about 1946, Fletchers were bought out by Spaltons of Derby.

There was also a coal merchant in the yard at Idridgehay named Smithers. At some time in the 1930s, however, he closed down. Shortly afterwards, the weighbridge was done away with but the office remained for a while afterwards. When it was demolished it disappeared 'overnight'.

Apart from the milk vans being left in the dock other wagons were, of necessity, left in the yard. Two milk vans were brought on the early morning passenger train and left in the loop; the mid-morning goods train stopped at Idridgehay and its engine was used to shunt them into the dock. Any other goods wagons were cleared from the sidings by trains running from Wirksworth to Derby. At Shottle and Hazelwood, it was Wirksworth-bound trains which picked up the loose wagons. Mr Brown remembers the milk going either to Kentish Town, London or to Attercliffe, Sheffield.

At about the same time that Idridgehay lost its signal box, there were some personnel changes on the line. Mr Marple became responsible for Wirksworth station only and was succeeded at Shottle and Idridgehay by Mr Harrison. He stayed until the early 1940s when Mr Cooke took charge of the two stations. From 1947 until closure, Bert Soar was appointed station master of both.

In 1950, Mrs Pike became the porter-signalwoman at the station, later becoming crossing keeper until the gateless crossing was installed. Only four years before the gates were removed, they had to be repaired as a result of a collision. At this time, apart from the signalling equipment, the booking office had been stripped of all its fittings, and similarly, the fireplaces and woodwork had been removed from the other rooms, although strangely, the brass handles on all the doors, including those to the derelict rooms, were brightly burnished!

The main building was bought for conversion to a private dwelling and, through the kindness of the new owners, I was able to see the conversion taking place. The most interesting feature is that the single-storey building has been turned into a two-storey house by the insertion of a floor at a level just below the height of the side walls. Skylights have been placed in the roof to light the upper floor but despite this, the character of the building has been completely preserved. Neither water nor electricity was present in the building and had to be installed as part of the conversion.

Idridgehay station looking towards Duffield on 20th September, 1969.   *D.F. Tee*

This grounded coach body stood for many years on the east side of the line near Idridgehay station, the main building of which can be seen behind the trees on the left; 3rd May, 1982. While the author was being interviewed for local radio when the first edition of this book appeared, a Mr Peter Bussell phoned in to say that when he and his wife first got married, they had made it their home.   *Author*

Wirksworth

From Idridgehay the gradient becomes increasingly severe as the line approaches the head of the valley and its ultimate destination. There is a subtle change of character from here onwards; the lush, green, wide vale of Hazelwood and Shottle gives way to a harder, more confined landscape. Thoughts of milk and honey are replaced by visions of lead and stone, and the climate seems to become just a little colder - a feeling heightened by the snow-like covering of limestone dust that was ever present, even in the height of summer, until the quarries ceased production.

Two miles from Idridgehay is Alton Manor, designed for its owner, James Milnes (who vexed the Midland so much with his demand for a private siding), by Sir George Gilbert Scott, the architect of St Pancras. Before reaching Wirksworth, we first pass the level crossing at Gorsey Bank, 7 miles 79 chains from Duffield Junction and, but for the length of a cricket pitch, 141 miles from St Pancras; a milepost 22 yards up the line tells us so. The signal box was opened here on 8th September, 1890 and was 15 ft long by 10 ft wide.

The earliest crossing keeper I have been able to trace was Charles Casterton, who is first mentioned in the 1871 census, making it likely that he was in place when the line opened. He was still in charge at the time of World War I, by which time he must have been a considerable age as he was already 72 by 1911. Someone who remembered Wirksworth well from the period of the Great War was my great-uncle, Albert Goodwin, who was a boy when Mr Casterton was at Gorsey Bank. Casterton was an old soldier and had a peg-leg. When he retired, he came to live in a cottage opposite the Goodwins in Coldwell Street. Noticing my uncle's interest in reading, he lent him a volume of *Robinson Crusoe*, which was rather like a family bible in size. When Mr Casterton died, his son visited my uncle to give him two mementoes - not the book which he would have valued greatly, but a drainpipe which the old man had used as a stand for his walking stick and umbrella, and his wooden leg, which was certainly not expected, nor desired. My uncle 'buried it deep in the garden. Has it ever come to light again?'

The next crossing-keeper was Mr H.J. Bailey who, with his family, moved into the house alongside the crossing. He was a keen gardener and is well-remembered by another local inhabitant, Mrs Kathleen Winson. Her father, William Franklin, was a porter at Wirksworth for many years, but on the retirement of Mr Bailey was offered the crossing-keeper's job. Unfortunately, the house was not given with the job as the Baileys were entitled to stay there until Mr Bailey died, or whenever it was convenient for them to move. For this reason, Mr Franklin turned down the job, though he did serve there temporarily at one time. At about the same time, another crossing-keeper is recorded, Mr H. Brailsford, but he could have worked as a relief keeper.

I do not know whether Mr Casterton or Mr Bailey was responsible, but my great-uncle clearly remembered several occasions when trains were held up at the crossing because the keeper had fallen asleep. Nor were the gates here safe from attack by errant trains. The LMS Works Committee Minute Book No. 1 records that on 4th December, 1923, at about 7.25 pm, the 6.28 pm passenger train from Derby passed a signal at danger and collided with the two 14 ft gates, smashing them and also 'one gate lamp and stand'.

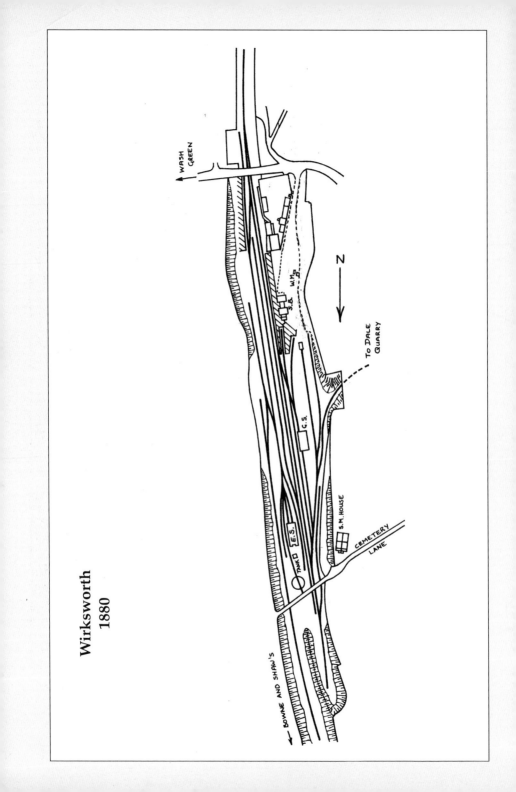

Wirksworth
1880

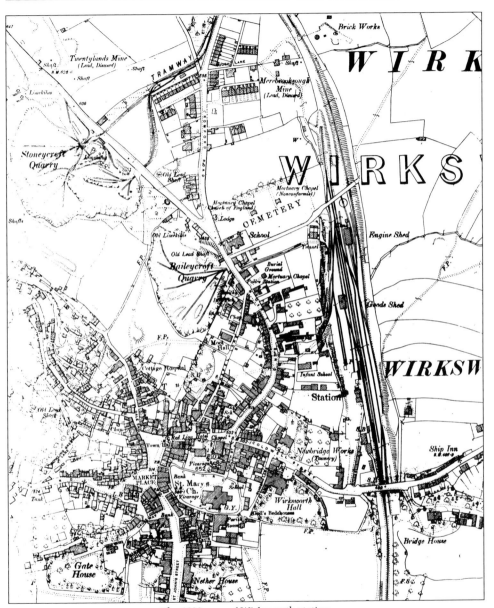

The 1899 map of Wirksworth station.

A fine array of wagons is shown in this postcard of Wirksworth station taken in 1938.
Tony Holmes/Wirksworth Heritage Centre

Wirksworth station seen through the Wash Green road bridge around the turn of the century.
Author's Collection

After World War II, the crossing was looked after by Mrs May Smith or 'Little May Smith - LMS' as she was affectionately known because of her size (less than five feet tall). Her husband, Jack, was employed on the High Peak line, and when the family were given the opportunity to take over the crossing keeper's house, a condition was that Mrs Smith should take the job of crossing keeper. Initially, the traffic was easy to cope with, but as the stone traffic increased (and particularly during the 'sugarstone' season) Mrs Smith, aided by her husband, was working the box from 7.30 in the morning until 9.00 at night. When the box closed, Mrs Smith was 62 and had been in charge for over 30 years.

Gorsey Bank saw some development when a loop was put in just south of the crossing. This was brought into use on 9th November, 1970, and enabled a stone train to be left for collection after the signal box closed for the night. It was operated by its own ground frame rather than from the box, and was taken out of use on 24th December, 1977.

In 1978, the gates were taken away and formal closure of the crossing took place on 3rd June, 1979. The gates and box were acquired by the Peak Railway Society, and the box transported to Buxton in August 1985 where, complete with Buxton station nameboard, it was restored to its former glory. However, its stay was short-lived, as Peak Rail (as it is now called) decided to concentrate its efforts at the Matlock end of its line, and the box was again moved, this time to Church Lane Crossing, Darley Dale where, in a slightly extended form, it controls the level crossing. The lever frame from the box did not travel around Derbyshire with the rest of the box - it now resides as an exhibit at Derby Industrial Museum in the Old Silk Mill, which is also home to the Midland Railway Study Centre.

After the broad expanse of the Ecclesbourne Valley, the line is increasingly squeezed by the surrounding hills and almost creeps into Wirksworth unnoticed. After threading its way through the Hannages, however, it emerges under the Wash Green road bridge into a vast yard whose size reflects the importance of the terminus for stone traffic. 8 miles 37 chains from Duffield junction and 13¾ miles from Derby, the station is built on an incline of 1 in 192.

The station building was in a similar twin-gabled style to the others on the line, though larger in conception. Also on the single platform was the signal box, opened on 8th September, 1890, and to the north end of the platform was the goods shed. Across the yard stood the engine shed, water tank and turntable, and beyond this a single line rose into the exchange sidings for Middlepeak Quarry; the line is still there, but the exchange sidings have long gone. A crane stood in the station yard, and was rated at 6 tons, although this was later replaced by a 10 ton crane according to an LMS rating plan. Below it all, from before the time the station was built to this day, ran several watercourses, including Lees Sough, which drains Northcliffe vein and runs into the site just north of Cemetery Lane bridge. For the station to be built, these were diverted through a 5 ft diameter culvert from a point north of the bridge and along the back of the platform to surface a quarter of a mile or so south of Wash Green bridge. Various inspection points are dotted around the yard, and it was not unknown for staff to have secret hideaways underground!

Prior to the building of the signal box it is evident from the list of 'signal posts' returned to the Board of Trade in 1880, that some centralisation of signalling by ground frame was in existence from before August 1877. The

An interesting photograph of Wirksworth taken around 1930. The station nameboard is the original Midland Railway one, as are the notice boards, although they have been updated with LMS lettering. At the end of the platform is the stop signal, which was abolished with the signal box in July 1934. *Knighton Collection*

An overall view of Wirksworth, taken from the Wash Green road bridge on 12th February, 1949. *D.F. Tee*

engine shed was little used and appears to have housed no engine since the turn of the century. It was of typical MR design with a pitched roof very similar in style to that at Hitchin. In later years it was used as a wagon repair shop. Recently, the turntable pit was excavated and was found to have a blue brick base and dressed stone walls, the top few feet of which had been smashed. It was backfilled and its reinstatement might be considered, but it is on the line of two sidings which are in regular use. Similarly, the engine shed foundations have also been located and one of the inspection pits has been rebuilt and put back into use.

An early mention of the railway appeared in 1891 in a book entitled *Picture of the Peak*, by 'Strephon' (the *nom-de-plume* of Edward Bradbury). 'Special trains bring thousands of excursionists of the Wirksworth "Tap" Dressings each Whit-Wednesday.' A pattern was thus set for a regular series of excursion trains which used the branch over the years, Well Dressing time being a high-point in the year.

The earliest known station master, possibly the first, was Samuel Hodgkinson. He was succeeded by Luke Fox, who reigned from about 1875 to about 1890, when Thomas William Cox took over. It is thought that he was succeeded by Andrew Swift (brother of Herbert) in about 1920 and approximately 10 years later by Mr Marple.

As is often the case when a large commercial interest comes to a small tight-knit community, there is an expectation of support, usually financial, for any new project of benefit to that community. In 1896, therefore, an approach was made by the Wirksworth National Schools Building Fund to the Midland Railway inviting a donation for the building of what is now the Church of England Infants' School. As a large ratepayer, it was felt that the Midland was obligated in some way and as a result it subscribed £116 towards the cost of the project out of a total requirement of £1,448.

I have been able to obtain many names of personnel who worked at Wirksworth in the inter-war years from Reginald Brown, Albert Goodwin and Mrs Kathleen Winson. What follows is an amalgam of their recollections.

From c.1920 to the beginning of World War II, the porters were William Franklin (Mrs Winson's father) and Alfred Boden; one of the goods shunters was Mr A.W. Roughton.

Signalmen remembered include Albert Doxey who was a porter-signalman from August 1912, rising to relief signalman by September 1924. While in this post, he studied and eventually became a station master elsewhere. Mr Doxey was a keen gardener who won prizes for Wirksworth as Mr Brown had done at Idridgehay. The prize was 10 shillings, which was awarded to the station master! Other signalmen were Messrs Jack Allsop, Sam Bowler (who also farmed at Wash Green) and Ernest Pidcock, whose brother Billy was employed as a ganger between Idridgehay and Wirksworth. In time, Billy was replaced by Bill Boden, another member of the gang being Sam Bunting.

Several booking office clerks are mentioned, including Andrew Swift's daughter. Others were Messrs Moore, Pettit, Alan Causer (who lodged with the Goodwins for a time) and Billy Haywood.

There was a carrier (complete with LMS horse and cart) called Mr Hill and in the yard, two coal merchants by the names of Mr Isaac Bunting and Mr Hawley.

An overall view of Wirksworth yard on 10th October, 1951, with No. 43763 shunting in the distance. On the right is the loading dock from which the narrow gauge line ran to Baileycroft Quarry, and, beyond this, the track can be seen curving away to the Dale Quarry tunnel.

F.W. Shuttleworth

Class '3F' 0-6-0 No. 43763 and brake van No. M1603 in the yard at Wirksworth on 10th October, 1951.   *F.W. Shuttleworth*

The engine shed at Wirksworth in about 1967. *R.J. Essery Collection*

Stanier '8F' class 2-8-0 No. 48003 in the yard on 1st September, 1965. A dmu can be seen at the platform, no doubt under test from Derby works. *H.N. James*

Right: Wirksworth was provided with a substantial water tower, despite the assertion at the opening of the line that it was possible to run from Derby to Wirksworth and back 'without water'. *R.J. Essery Collection*

Below: Wirksworth goods shed in about 1967. *R.J. Essery Collection*

Mrs Winson remembers much about Wirksworth at this time. Her father had been a porter at Derby before World War I and, on moving to Wirksworth, was employed at the rate of £1 19s. 1d. per week. He supplemented his wage by being a member of Wirksworth Fire Brigade, for which he was paid a yearly retainer of £3 plus 2 shillings per hour while on duty. From the railway he was entitled to a new uniform every six months and a new overcoat every five years or so. There were two shifts, 8.00 am to 4.00 pm and 1.00 pm to 9.00 pm, though on Saturday, this would be extended to cope with the 10.30 pm train. The porters took it in turns, weekly, to work as either a porter or as a kind of general assistant, unloading goods. Among the goods which had to be regularly dealt with was cement from Earle's which was distributed by the station master who received a commission on each bag sold. Fish and newspapers were distributed by the Franklin children and Mrs Winson remembers receiving 2d. for taking the papers to the newsagent. This would have been on weekdays; Sunday papers were delivered to Cromford station.

As at Idridgehay, there was a very busy time when the milk train arrived. This was particularly so on Sunday when this was the only train. Naturally there were fewer people on duty on this day so the porter had to collect and issue tickets, couple up the train, help load the milk and any other luggage and inform the Gorsey Bank signalman when the train was due to leave.

Albert Goodwin, has similar recollections of the train services at this time and particularly remembers the 'motor-train' which, unlike other passenger trains, was propelled back to Derby by virtue of the control arrangements mentioned in Chapter Four. Normally-worked trains had their engine turned on the turntable before their return journey.

A handful of men from the town fought in the Boer War and when hostilities ceased they returned one-by-one. It was always arranged that they should arrive by the last train in order to be given a hero's welcome by the Town Band and local dignitaries. Each would be placed in an open carriage and paraded through the town followed by a torchlit procession of the local population. It was because of the desire to make this as effective as possible that the returning warrior was prevented from arriving by an earlier train. If he happened to arrive too early at Derby he had to 'kick his heels' before boarding the Wirksworth train. Unfortunately, this sometimes proved disastrous as the day-long opening hours placed severe temptation in the way of the war- (and travel-) weary soldier. As a result the hero was often in too sorry a state to take part in any procession.

The Well Dressings have been mentioned and throughout this period interest in them continued to such an extent that on Whit-Wednesday special trains arrived from Leicester, Nottingham, Chesterfield and Sheffield. Exiled townspeople always tried to return on this day and would be given a similar welcome to the war veterans with the town band meeting each train.

An interesting incident relating to these specials is believed to have occurred in the late 1920s. Prior to the arrival of one of the special trains one year, the normal branch train derailed at Wirksworth and prevented the special from reaching the station. The passengers were helped down from the carriages, and were escorted across a field to reach their destination. The owner of the field is said to have charged them one old halfpenny each to cross his land, and so profitable was the exercise that the village began seriously to consider ways in which the line could be blocked again the following year! The local constable learned of their plans, and threatened gaol if anything happened to the train. He is even said to have spent the whole day sitting in a chair by the railway to make sure that nothing untoward took place!

Another regular excursion, this time from Wirksworth was held on a Monday in September. For about 3s. 6d. travellers could catch a train at 6.00 am to Belle Vue, Manchester which returned in the early hours of Tuesday morning.

A similar annual event was the Mill Trip. Employees of Wheatcroft's Mills (Haarlem and Speedwell) used to have a few pennies deducted from their pay each week to pay for their yearly foray to the coast. A vote was taken to decide which resort would be visited and Blackpool was usually the one chosen. On the eve of the outing the workers were given tickets to the value of their contributions and, since many received more than they needed, the 'extras' were sold off at a handsome profit to finance the day's activities.

On Saturdays when Derby County played at home, a special train was run for which the return fare was one shilling. This train was always packed as many people took advantage of the cheap fare to go shopping or to visit the theatre.

Again, milk is remembered as a large contributor to the line's takings and the 'Sunday rush' resulted in a long line of milk floats stretching back through the station yard. The other major export, stone, would require two long mineral trains leaving the station each day.

A curious incident is said to have occurred some time after World War II, when a van full of newly-minted cash from the Royal Mint was found abandoned in the yard at Wirksworth. Why it should have been there in the first place is anyone's guess, but presumably it was misrouted. Nor is it known how long it was there before its contents were discovered, although it is hard to believe that a vehicle could remain unnoticed for any length of time, particularly one that had arrived unexpectedly.

In 1946 Mr Marple was succeeded by Mr John G. Hall who was destined to be the last station master on the line. From 1955 he was also responsible for the only other station open at that time, Shottle. Although not a Wirksworth man he took a great interest in local history and affairs and can truly be said to have adopted Wirksworth as his home town. On his retirement he bought the station house for what he described as 'a knock-down price' and continued to live there until his death, which regrettably occurred during the preparation of the First Edition of this book. I am pleased to say that I was able to meet him shortly before he died and, although not in the best of health, he reminisced enthusiastically about the railway, its people and Wirksworth in general.

He did not recall ever seeing the engine shed being used for its intended purpose. Occasionally, wagons were kept in it and, for a time, two men went into business making concrete blocks, using the shed as their factory. They were unsuccessful, however, and went out of business within a matter of weeks.

The sale of Earle's cement continued during Mr Hall's time and an enamel advertisement on the goods shed bore witness to this. The arrangement whereby the station master acted as agent for Earle's dated back to Midland Railway days and at certain stations a stock of the firm's cement was always kept. For his services, Mr Hall was allowed to keep 2½ per cent of the sale price but he was much relieved when Buxton's took over the agency as '. . . it was a nuisance to me!'

The bridge at the far end of the station which carries Cemetery Lane had been declared unsafe before World War II so materials were delivered to strengthen the structure. Nothing was ever done, however, and over the years these materials gradually disappeared. The bridge could not have been too unsafe as it was not until about 1980 that remedial work was finally carried out.

The late 1960s saw the rationalisation of the station area into a dedicated stone terminal, a large 'dust dock' being built where lorries could discharge limestone dust into waiting wagons. The embankment for this was formed by using the rubble from the demolished station buildings, probably at the end of 1966 or early 1967 to coincide with the closure of the Cromford & High Peak Railway. This line's demise was no doubt hastened by the successful routeing of stone traffic away from it 'temporarily' in 1964 (as mentioned in Chapter Six) and the changes were largely to the benefit of the Middleton Limestone Mine, whose output had hitherto been taken away over the southern section of the High Peak line. The quarry owners (Derbyshire Stone, who had by then taken over Hopton Wood Stone Firms) would have preferred to retain their direct connection, but they also wanted to use larger wagons than were permitted on Sheep Pasture Incline, and as this requirement had not been addressed by the 1964 modernisation of the incline, closure became inevitable. Dan Jones had been the driver at Cromford Goods, and when the traffic transferred to the Wirksworth line, he became the shunt engine driver at Wirksworth.

As an interesting postscript, in July 2003, volunteers working to restore the yard at Wirksworth received a visit from a gentleman who asked whether they wanted the door to the station master's office - an item that had evidently been in his possession since the building was demolished. His offer was accepted and the door is now stored awaiting the building of a suitable structure to hang it on.

Two particular incidents recalled by Mr Hall were a train running away from Wirksworth taking the Gorsey Bank gates with it (fortunately it was stopped before reaching Idridgehay) and the events which occurred in a bad winter in the 1940s. The weather was so bad that a passenger train became stranded at Wirksworth. A second engine was sent from Derby with the idea of meeting the train as it battled its way along the branch. At a point near Idridgehay the progress of both the train and the light engine was halted by a solid wall of drifting snow which separated them by a matter of 15 feet or so. As fast as the snow was cleared it was blown back but, eventually, the two engines were coupled up and proceeded back to Wirksworth. As they approached the terminus, the whole train shuddered to a halt. Ice had formed between the motion and the bottom of the boiler barrel on one of the engines and this had to be chipped away by the fireman lying on his back. In addition the packed snow had actually lifted the engine some four inches off the rails. Wirksworth was finally reached at about 3.00 am when it was decided to give up.

The coal merchants at this time were Isaac Bunting (again) and F. Slater. Mr Hall recalled that both of these traders had a couple of small coal wagons each but he did not remember them lasting very long. The 1945 *Colliery Year Book and Coal Trades Directory*, however, only shows a J. Slater working from Wirksworth.

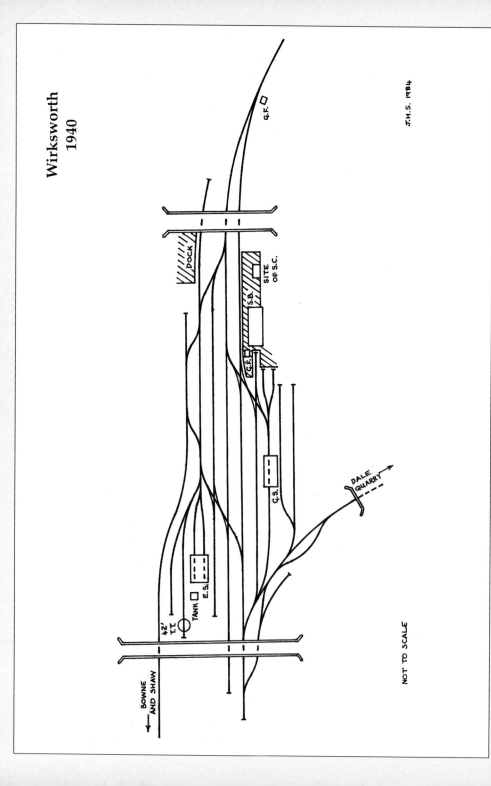

Wirksworth
1940

BOWNE
AND SHAW

42'
T.T.

TANK

E.S.

DOCK

S.B.

G.F.

SITE
OF S.C.

G.S.

G.F.

DALE
QUARRY

NOT TO SCALE

J.H.S. 1984

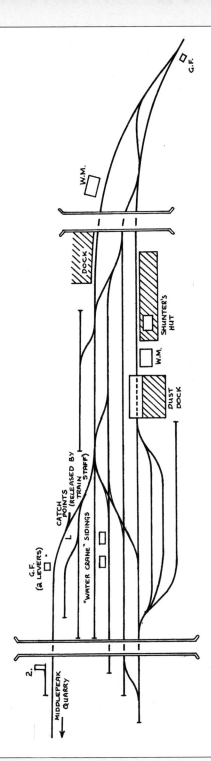

Wirksworth
1982

J.H.S. 1984

NOT TO SCALE

G.F.

W.M.

DOCK

SHUNTER'S
HUT

W.M.

DUST
DOCK

CATCH
POINTS
(RELEASED BY
TRAIN
STAFF)

"WATER CRANE" SIDINGS

G.F.
(2. LEVERS)

2.

MIDDLEPEAK
QUARRY

Much activity at Wirksworth on 7th September, 1982 when, in addition to a class '20' shunting at the 'dust dock', an engineer's train was also present.   *Cyril Sprenger*

Two other names are remembered from this period. Jack Washbourne was in charge of the goods shed and the booking office clerk was Mr Fry.

After the withdrawal of passenger and goods services, and the subsequent removal of facilities, the yard was completely refurbished as a limestone terminal. There were two main loading areas: the dust dock and a loading dock by the Wash Green bridge. Both of these were served by lorry from the quarries, the remainder being handled at the exchange sidings 'up the incline'. It is not known exactly when these were laid in, but it must have been after 1922, and the gradient must have been eased considerably to allow wagons to be left there. Loaded wagons were brought in by the quarry company's own locomotive and marshalled into a train to be collected by the British Rail locomotive, empty wagons being similarly deposited here to be hauled back into the quarry complex, as required. A separate shunting locomotive was provided by BR up until the 1980s, after which train engines were called upon to do their own shunting. The shunting engines (a single class '25' or two class '20s') were never stabled at Wirksworth, but came up on the first train, and stayed all day shunting in the yard while other trains came and went. At the dust dock and just south of Wash Green bridge, there were weighbridges (in earlier years, there had been a weighbridge on the far side of the yard near to where the incline line diverged from the sidings). Apart from a few offices and huts, there were no other buildings.

Further improvements were made in 1972, largely to provide easier handling at Wash Green. This part of the yard was also separated from the line to the incline for safety reasons. A new ground frame for the incline was brought into use on 29th September, 1973.

The history of the quarries and their associated traffic is so enmeshed with that of the branch that to ignore it here would be to tell only half a story. A later chapter will deal with this traffic, and details of the quarries will be included.

Chapter Nine

Beyond Wirksworth

It will be remembered that the original intention of the Midland Railway was to proceed from Wirksworth to Rowsley if the LNWR succeeded in gaining absolute control of the Matlock line. The Act which authorised the construction of the branch was passed in July 1863 and included the construction of a link from Wirksworth to the Cromford & High Peak Railway near the foot of Middleton Incline.

The Midland thought that if it did lose the Matlock route, it would still have a connection with the C&HPR via Wirksworth. I cannot see the logic of this because, even with the Matlock line in LNWR hands, the Midland would have taken all the traffic at either Rowsley or Ambergate anyway. However, had the Wirksworth branch extension become operative, the section of the High Peak line to the east of the junction would have become practically redundant, thus giving the LNWR even less reason to acquire sole rights to the Matlock line. If this was the thinking behind the MR decision to go ahead with the extension, it goes to show the extraordinary lengths which one company would go to in order to thwart another. In this case the Midland was prepared to build a branch to Wirksworth, an extension to the C&HPR and draw up plans for an independent line to Rowsley. By this can be measured the strategic importance of that 'little line' from Ambergate to Rowsley.

By February 1870 the Midland was sure that it was to have the Matlock line to itself, and abandoned the planned Wirksworth to Rowsley line as a result. In May of the same year it was ordered that 'Mr Crossley be requested to obtain tenders for the construction of the works required for making the junction with the Cromford and High Peak Railway'.

Perhaps it was taking a 'belt and braces' attitude, but why did the MR proceed with the building of the extension knowing that the Ambergate to Rowsley line would soon be its own? Whatever the reasons for wanting the link in the first place, it would seem that the reason for actually building it was either to avoid the financial penalties that were written into the Act (which were to apply if the whole line was not completed within five years, but nearly seven years had passed before Crossley was ordered to obtain the tenders) or to divert mineral traffic onto the Wirksworth branch. The branch was hardly busy, so putting slow mineral traffic on it from the C&HPR would ease the pressure on a main line that was unlikely to be quadrupled north of Duffield. An alternative reason is that the Midland might have been casting a covetous eye on the C&HPR. If they had managed to take it over, the incline to Wirksworth would have resulted in the abandonment of the stretch from Middlepeak Wharf down to High Peak Junction, indeed the LNWR might have considered such an abandonment anyway if traffic were to have been siphoned off to Wirksworth.

An equally intriguing question arises over the submission of the tenders. Only one was received, from Messrs I. & G. Tomlinson, for £5,814 2s. 6d. compared to Crossley's own estimate of £5,828 16s. 8d. Naturally, it was resolved to accept this, the only tender, which just happened to be within £15 of the Engineer's costing.

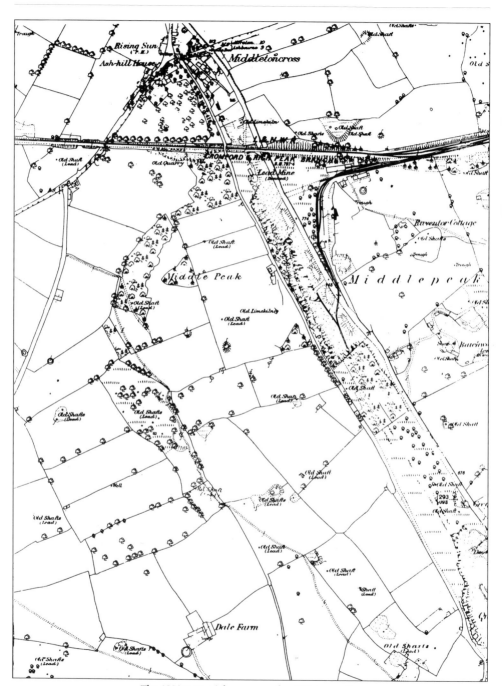

The 1880 map of the area north of Wirksworth.

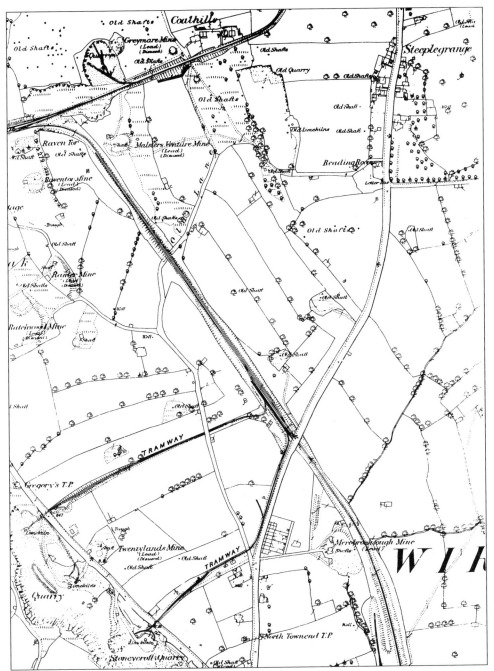

The 1880 map of the area north of Wirksworth.

This Lilywhite postcard of Bole Hill taken in the 1920s shows wagons in the loading area at Middlepeak with Old Lane in the foreground and Cromford Road behind. Rock House, home of the Shaws, is in the right foreground.

Tony Holmes/Wirksworth Heritage Centre

Reports of the building of the line were submitted to the Duffield and Wirksworth Construction Committee until 2nd May, 1871, when the last official mention of the line's progress is made. Five thousand yards of earthworks and 300 yards of masonry were done and all bridges were complete. Nowhere is there any record of completion, connection to the C&HPR or of opening to traffic. Just one year had elapsed from the date when tenders were invited and only two months were to pass before the Midland took sole possession of the Matlock line. Nearly six months later, on 22nd October, the *High Peak News* reported that:

> . . . the new branch to connect the High Peak Railway with the Midland line at Wirksworth is rapidly progressing, large bodies of men being employed for this purpose by the spirited contractor Messrs Tomlinson of Derby.

It is not known, with any certainty, when work ended on the line, but it cannot have been long after this report was written.

It is dangerous to speculate about some of the decisions made at this time but I think it can safely be said that all concerned quietly 'forgot' about the extension. It has been said that an engine house was built to haul the wagons up to the junction. I have found no evidence of this whatsoever nor, indeed, have I found any reference to plans or estimates for such a building. It has also been suggested that the extension was never opened because it did not obtain Board of Trade sanction. Again, I have found no evidence that Board of Trade sanction was ever requested and why should it have been for a junction between two goods lines? Surely, it is beyond the bounds of credibility to imagine that thought was ever given to running a passenger service from Wirksworth to Whaley Bridge!

The plan of the extension shows the following:

5	chains at 1 in 220
20 ½	chains at 1 in 30
15 ½	chains at 1 in 15
14 ½	chains at 1 in 6
6	chains on the level

As built, however, the incline left Wirksworth at 1 in 33, steepening slightly to 1 in 30, and then completing its climb at 1in 5, with Old Lane being crossed about half-way up this steepest part. The junction with the C&HPR was built on the level 9 miles 28 chains from Duffield and 142 miles 26 chains from St Pancras. It should be stressed, however, that no official railway plans or records have been found to confirm that the junction was actually ever laid.

A look at the Ordnance Survey maps over the years shows the life of this little line quite clearly. The 1880 edition shows the full extent of the incline as built, but the junction is shown as being laid into Middlepeak Siding alongside the High Peak line, so a zigzag shunt would have been necessary to gain access to the main C&HPR running lines. Oddly, only the eastern line of the two is actually shown connected; the western line stops short of the junction, and in this form it is difficult to see how the incline could ever have been worked,

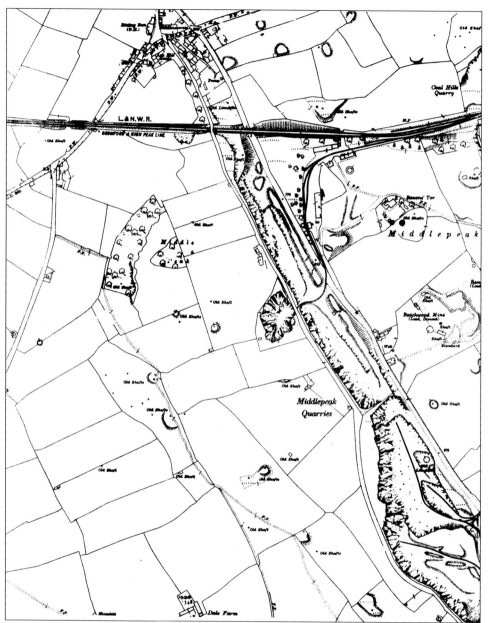

The 1922 map of the area north of Wirksworth.

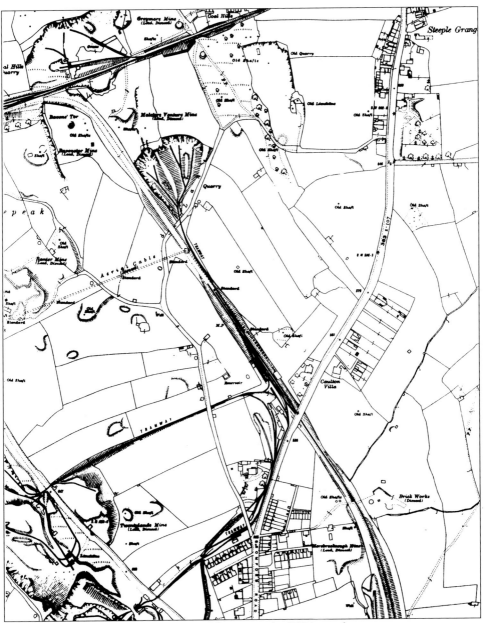

The 1922 map of the area north of Wirksworth.

A view down the incline in 1932. The bridge in the distance carries Cromford Road, and the large building in front of it is a stone crusher. The narrow gauge track running down the left-hand side of the incline is from Colehill Quarry, and there appears to be another set of rails running through the field on the left. This is not shown on any map, but seems to run from Colehill Quarry behind the stone crusher and possibly to a loading chute out of sight in this shot. (Remnants of such a chute can be located at the time of writing.) It is not known why there would have been two mineral lines running from Colehill Quarry to the loading area.   *LGRP*

Fifty years later, Colehill Quarry had made large inroads into the incline. The modern conveyor from Middlepeak Quarry to the loading hopper can be seen in the middle distance, and the trees to the left of the hopper obscure the site of the bridge over Old Lane. The track leading out of the quarry at bottom left marks the start of the narrow gauge line that can be seen on the 1932 photograph.   *Author*

Two photographs that show the top of the incline. The C&HPR is behind the wall, and the trackbed of the incline can be seen curving away to the left. What is particularly interesting about these pictures is that the first was taken in 1932, and the second, 50 years later. So little had changed even to the extent that the indentations made by the sleepers were still visible when the 1982 picture was taken.   *LGRP and Author*

whether by simple balancing of loaded wagons coming down with empties going up, or with the aid of winding gear. Two narrow-gauge tramways from what later became Middlepeak Quarry ran onto a loading dock parallel to the lower part of the incline just north of Cromford Road.

The 1899 edition shows little change save that the quarries and their associated tramways had developed in the intervening years. The 1922 edition, however, shows that the rails from Old Lane to the junction had been removed, and it is believed that this was done in 1914. The two former tramways were still in evidence but a further tramway now ran down the route of the incline from Colehill Quarry. This consisted of flat-bottom rail laid to a gauge of 3 feet, and was rope-worked, the anchor block for the winch mechanism still being *in situ* near the Old Lane bridge to this day. There was also a weighbridge at this point, which had narrow gauge track on the table, and this was used in later years for weighing lorries (although it has to be said that there is no evidence that the weighbridge was contemporary with the narrow gauge line). Recently, while excavating the site south of Old Lane in order to build a new halt to serve the National Stone Centre, WyvernRail volunteers uncovered a section of double track, that had become buried many years ago. This was bullhead rail, inside keyed on MR chairs, and was probably brought in 'used' from another location. Sections of 'lighter' standard gauge track have also been unearthed further up the incline.

Colehill Quarry has now obliterated the upper half of the incline, although the bridge over Old Lane is still there. The tramways from Middlepeak Quarry were converted into roads, and an overhead conveyor was built to connect the quarry to the railway. All is now disused, of course, but the tramways can still be traced, and the huge conveyor and loading hoppers continue to dominate the site.

If the original line to Wirksworth seemed to have been both costly and unnecessary, the extension can only be said to have been a profligate waste of money. Including the cost of land, approximately £7,500 was spent on an enterprise which cannot have earned its promoters one single (old) penny. The only distinction that the junction with the High Peak line ever gained (if it was ever laid) was to mark the boundary between the Derby and Manchester Divisions of British Railways, London Midland Region.

Chapter Ten

Stone Traffic

A whole book could be written about the history of quarrying in the Wirksworth area but, although I propose to do no such thing here, some background details might not come amiss.

A total of five quarries had some form of rail link to Wirksworth station. The picture is complicated by the fact that some quarries had rail links to the Cromford & High Peak Railway as well, and others which were linked to this line would also use the Wirksworth branch via a road link. Add to that the numerous amalgamations and takeovers among the various companies and the physical amalgamations of quarries as they expanded into each other, and quite a confused picture emerges. The quarries are dealt in order working around the railhead in a clockwise direction, starting with Dale Quarry.

Dale Quarry

Known locally as 'Big Hole', Dale Quarry was linked by a tunnel under the town to the station yard. It dates back to March 1862 when an area of land in The Dale was purchased by Arthur Harward who further extended his property in 1876. In about 1874 he started quarrying and formed the Wirksworth Dale Stone and Lime Company. Initially, horses and carts carried the stone to the station but his trade developed so rapidly that he looked at ways by which the stone could be delivered to the railway more easily. His first idea was to build a tramway through the town. The proposed route was surveyed by an engineer from Manchester by the name of Wilkinson, but local residents objected to stone-laden trucks passing by their doors on a steep gradient. Despite a public meeting where Harward's scheme gained the approval of the ratepayers, he decided to abandon the project in favour of a tunnel under the town.

The work was carried on around the clock with men working in eight-hour shifts. Shafts were sunk at various places, tunnelling began from both ends and in less than 18 months the project was completed. Several accidents occurred but only one was serious and resulted in the death of a workman.

The opening on 17th November, 1877 was carried out with great ceremony. All those who had been engaged in its construction, together with quarry workers and friends of Harward, were invited to join a special train through the tunnel. They gathered at the station at 2 pm and filled the six wagons that had been provided. A large crowd also assembled, and were entertained by the Band of the 10th Derbyshire Rifle Volunteers. The company's own locomotive hauled the train but it was stopped about 25 yards from the tunnel end because of flooding. Nevertheless most of the party walked through to the quarry with candles provided by Harward. At one point they inspected a shaft which had been sunk some 108 ft from the floor of the quarry above.

After their return to the station the members of the party proceeded to the Town Hall where about 240 guests sat down to a meal of roast beef, plum pudding and ale. Speeches then followed, first by Harward's brother, the Revd Cuthbert Harward, and then by the quarry Manager, Mr Hodgkinson. After toasts to the Army, Navy and Volunteers it was Harward's turn to speak.

He revealed that although his original scheme to build a tramway had met with popular favour, a number of property owners had threatened him with legal proceedings. Although he could have appealed to the Board of Trade he was anxious to ruffle as few feathers as possible (and save considerably on legal fees, no doubt). As a result he looked into the possibility of building the tunnel and had received much encouragement from the Engineer, Wilkinson and his Manager, Hodgkinson. An unexpected bonus had been the discovery of a bed of 'beautiful cream rock, free from dirt, of precisely the same quality as the famous Hopton Wood stone'. No wonder he was pleased with his efforts.

At the same time as constructing the tunnel, he had built lime-kilns which were producing some 30 tons of lime per day. Stone was being dispatched at the rate of 1,000 to 1,200 tons per week and he confidently expected to increase production dramatically in the future. He seems to have been quite an philanthropist and made it known that he wished to offer employment in the quarries to those who had worked so hard on the tunnel. He also put forward an idea to build lime-kilns at the station end of the tunnel which would produce lime for instant loading onto the trains. This would increase lime production threefold.

Before the festivities ended Wilkinson said a few words about the quality of the stone produced at the Dale and foresaw an enormous trade growing up in the district. He even went so far as to suggest that Wirksworth might become a second Birmingham. At 8 pm the party adjourned to the Market Place for a firework display by Messrs G.F. Brock & Co.

A Deed of Grant to Arthur Harward by Philip Hubbersty gave the right to 'make and forever maintain a tunnel from the Station'. The plan accompanying the deed shows the route of the 491 yds-long tunnel and that the total area of land involved was 286 square yards. The cost of the right to build the tunnel was one shilling per square yard; a total of £14 6s. 0d. Sadly, the cost of the tunnel was Harward's downfall for he was forced into liquidation in December 1879. The quarry was sold to John Gilbert Crompton of Derby, the parcels of conveyance describing the tunnel as:

> . . . leading from the Station of the Midland Railway Company . . . to the Stone Quarry of the Wirksworth Dale Stone and Lime Company . . . such tunnel to be 17 feet in height and 15 feet in width . . .

It appears that Crompton was only a lessee, the owner of the quarry being George Miller of Holcombe, Somerset for in March 1884 Miller leased the 'Lands, Houses, Limestone Quarry and Tunnel' to George Colledge, and in the 1887 edition of Kelly's Directory he is named as 'Proprietor'.

In 1895, 22 men were employed at the quarry, and at some time after this, the quarry was leased by the Butterley Company who then bought it outright in

July 1900 (hence the reference to the Butterley Company's Stone Siding on the 1913 MR distance diagram shown on page 102). On buying the quarry, the company bought a Peckett 0-4-0ST (Works No. 822 of 1900) but the quarry was closed down in the early 1920s, and the locomotive was moved to Bull Bridge. The area quarried by 1920 was some 2.6 acres, the 1922 Ordnance Survey map showing the quarry as 'disused'.

In February 1925, the quarry was sold to the London-based Wirksworth Quarries Ltd, and after a couple of company takeovers, came into the hands of Tarmac Ltd. However, for most of its life between 1925 and closure in 1968, it was run by Wirksworth Quarries Ltd, and it was this company's wagons that were most commonly seen on the branch (*see page 132 and 158*). Many of them were purchased by BR in the 1950s, becoming LMR Nos. M360466-M360578 (purchased 1950), M360663-M360690 (purchased 1954), M360693-M360711 (purchased 1950), M360772-M360808 (purchased 1954), M360818-M360819 (year of purchase not known). All were 12 ton 7-plank wagons, and were included in LMR diagram D2157 (BR type code 141).

Mr Hall remembers the company's wagons being used for the transportation of tarmac (presumably in addition to the carriage of stone) but when bitumen-based compounds replaced tar the traffic was transferred to road as it had to be used within 24 hours of mixing.

On 12th November, 1927 Wirksworth Quarries ordered a Hudswell, Clarke 0-4-0ST (Works No. 1611). It had outside cylinders (11 in. x 16 in.), 2 ft 9½ in. diameter driving wheels, weighed 13 tons 10 cwt and left the works on 25th January, 1928 at a cost of £1,300. Lamps were fitted at the front and rear of the locomotive for use in the tunnel. It is not known when it left Wirksworth, but by 1960 it had found its way to Gyproc Ltd, Hawton Gypsum Mines and was scrapped in 1963.

Traffic through the tunnel was controlled by a three-aspect colour light signal (red, amber, green) which was operated from a hut in the yard opposite the tunnel mouth.

Mr A.C. Sharpe, while testing oil-burning '4F' engines on the branch in 1947/48, recalls seeing 'little Simplex diesels' working through the tunnel. The ballast was built up to enable lorries to run through as well, and the tunnel was well lit with light bulbs every few yards.

In 1965, the quarry was providing stone for concrete aggregates as well as the manufacture of tarmacadam. Some stone went to the sugarbeet factories, and 55 men were employed in producing 390,000 tons per year. By this time, the tunnel was still in use but not by trains, lorries having taken over the transportation of the stone to the station yard. The tunnel is now blocked at the quarry end, there being several thousand tons of spoil blocking the way, but sufficient space has been left for the tunnel to continue to act as the quarry's drain, which it does by virtue of a large ditch at one side.

After it closed, the quarry was almost joined by Middlepeak Quarry. The tunnel became waterlogged and impassable, even on foot, and at the station end it became so overgrown that it was almost impossible to locate. Clearance in recent years has made the entrance visible again, but it has been wisely fenced across to prevent access.

Hudswell, Clarke No. 1611 of 1928, which worked for many years at Dale Quarry. The lamps on the smokebox and bunker were needed when working through the tunnel. The date of this picture is not known, but the locomotive appears to have been attempting some quarrying of its own judging by the shape of the cab. *Real Photographs*

Although the quality of this 1933 photograph is poor, it does show an interesting pair of Wirksworth Quarries wagons, the lettering on the fourth plank down reading 'Tarmacadam & Asphalte Manufacturers'. The unidentified class '4F' is running around tender-first indicating that the turntable was out of commission. *A.C. Sharpe*

In the 1980s, a new use for 'Big Hole' was proposed; known as the Wirksworth Astropit Project, the quarry would have been roofed over with glass and stocked with an assortment of tropical plants and animals. Supporters of the project were in negotiation with British Rail, Tarmac Roadstone Ltd and the County Council to run excursion trains from Derby to Wirksworth and then through the tunnel. A fascinating project, there were many at the time who scoffed at the idea, but perhaps they were forced to modify their earlier views when the Eden Project opened in 2001 in a disused china clay quarry near St Austell in Cornwall. (There is no evidence that the two projects were linked in any way.)

Baileycroft Quarry

This quarry, also known as North End Quarry, is first mentioned in an agreement dated 14th March, 1871 between John Smith of Bole Hill and George Colledge (Cromford) and John Williams Keene (Oldbury, nr Birmingham). In this, Smith agreed to let to Colledge and Keene '. . . all that stone quarry situated in and underneath such portion or portions of a field of land in Wirksworth called or known by the name of Baileycroft'. George Colledge would later be concerned with Dale Quarry.

The rent payable to John Smith was to be £35 per annum and the maximum amount of limestone to be sold annually was 8,400 tons. If more than this was produced in any one year, an extra rent of one penny per ton was to be paid.

On 28th March, 1877, Colledge and Keene entered into an agreement with John Waterfield of Wirksworth whereby, for a consideration of £10, Waterfield granted them the right to make and maintain a tramway in a tunnel from the quarry to the railway:

> . . . under, upon or through the southwardly side of a certain plot of garden ground and croft or piece of land situated at the north end of Wirksworth, adjoining the Wirksworth lockup, the Baptist Cemetery and land of George Frost.

The tramway was not to exceed 15 ft in width. John and Nathaniel Waterfield were lime-burners and dealers at North End as early as 1835, though Nathaniel had dropped out of the picture by 1860.

Colledge and Keene were now trading under the name of 'The Wirksworth Stone & Mineral Company' and were to pay an annual rent of £30 for the tunnel. In fact, there were two short tunnels connected by a cutting. These appear on the Ordnance Survey map of 1880 but no lines are shown as being laid. At this time, 1.9 acres were quarried and Colledge was known as 'Managing Partner'.

It must have been soon afterwards that the narrow gauge lines (unfortunately the gauge is not known) were laid, and a siding put in the station yard to receive the stone (shown on the 1913 MR distance diagram on page 102 as Wirksworth Lime & Stone Siding, although by then out of use). The tunnel was quite near the surface, and residents of Cemetery Lane have, on occasion, struck the top of the tunnel whilst digging their gardens. The tramway came out from a brick arch beneath the garden of the station master's house, and ran onto a loading bank where the stone was tipped into standard gauge wagons (see overleaf).

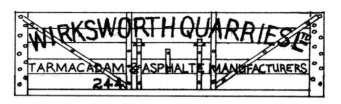

Body: Black
Lettering: Plain white

Livery: Possibly grey
Lettering: White, shaded black

Dumb-buffered at one end.

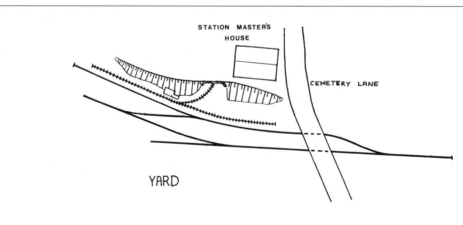

**Exchange Sidings
Baileycroft Quarry
Tramway**

The purpose of the small building shown is not known.

In 1887 Colledge is named as proprietor but by about 1906 the quarry had been closed, 3½ acres having been quarried to a depth of over 100 feet. The 1922 Ordnance Survey map shows that the Urban District Council was using the site at this time as a refuse tip. The life of this quarry was, therefore, quite short compared with others in the area. Private owner wagons belonging to the company were in operation over the branch but, obviously for only a relatively brief period at the turn of the century *(see opposite)*. The 1904 edition of the *Railway Clearing House Handbook of Stations* shows that the company's siding at Wirksworth was in existence at that time. It also reveals that the same company owned Brittains or Manystones Quarry which was near Longcliffe on the Cromford & High Peak Railway.

In the 1930s, in an effort to improve the flow of traffic through the town, it was decided to build a new road at the site of the quarry. The quarry face between the footbridge and the Red Lion Hotel was removed and the quarry filled in with dust from Dale Quarry. At that time, this dust was a waste product, but nowadays is used as a constituent of 'wet mix' road making material. Harrison Drive was the result and made a great difference to the traffic situation, all traffic previously having had to go along North End. A garage, fire station and telephone exchange have been built in the quarry.

Middlepeak Quarry (Bowne & Shaw's)

Travel between Wirksworth and Middleton and you will find that all the land to the left of the road is now quarried away. This series of quarries is collectively known as Middlepeak, but originally there were two groups of quarries: Stoneycroft at the bottom of Middleton Road, and Middlepeak towards Middleton. It is the quarry to the south that concerns us here, for it was owned by Bowne & Shaw's, and produced enormous amounts of stone.

The quarry was started shortly after 1830 by John Shaw of Steeplehouse, a smallholder and victualler at the 'Green Man', who began burning lime on the west side of Middleton Road. Having been left a fair-sized plot of land by his father-in-law, and realising that the stone made farming almost impossible, he started quarrying. The produce was carted to Cromford by road and loaded onto barges on the Cromford Canal; the returning boats brought coke for the kilns. By 1857, Shaw had moved to Bole Hill and was listed in the directories of the time as a limeburner only.

After opposing the new railway from Duffield, Shaw joined forces with Mr Bowne and they began trading as Bowne & Shaw. Quick to realise that perhaps the new railway was not such a bad thing after all, the firm reached an agreement on 21st July, 1876 with the MR to provide a railway connection. *Kelly's Directory* 1881 lists Bowne & Shaw (Lime and Limestone works) and John Shaw (farmer and stone merchant).

Shaw bought out Bowne in 1905 but the firm carried on trading under the same name. In 1910, on the death of John Shaw, his sons took over and continued trading as Bowne & Shaw.

A very early picture of Stoneycroft Quarry with Midland Railway and London & North Western Railway wagons in evidence.   *Collection R.G. Cash*

Primitive wagons are evident in this early picture of Stoneycroft Quarry.   *Collection R.G. Cash*

An owner's plate on a derelict wagon photographed in the Middlepeak loading area on 26th December, 1969.   *R.G. Cash*

A view into Stoneycroft Quarry taken in around 1935. A Stanton hopper wagon can clearly be seen.   *Author's Collection*

A postcard view of Bole Hill in around 1930, showing the more northern of the narrow gauge tramways running in from the bottom left-hand corner. The absence of overgrowth compared with the current scene is quite spectacular. *Tony Holmes/Wirksworth Heritage Centre*

Two trains of wagons have just passed on the loop that is visible behind the nearer train on the more northern of the two narrow gauge tramways linking Middlepeak Quarry with the loading area. The loop points were evidently worked automatically by the wagons themselves, which were remembered as being wooden although those in the picture appear to be heavily riveted, suggesting metal bodies. The photograph was taken from Old Lane where the line passed under a bridge. *Collection R.G. Cash*

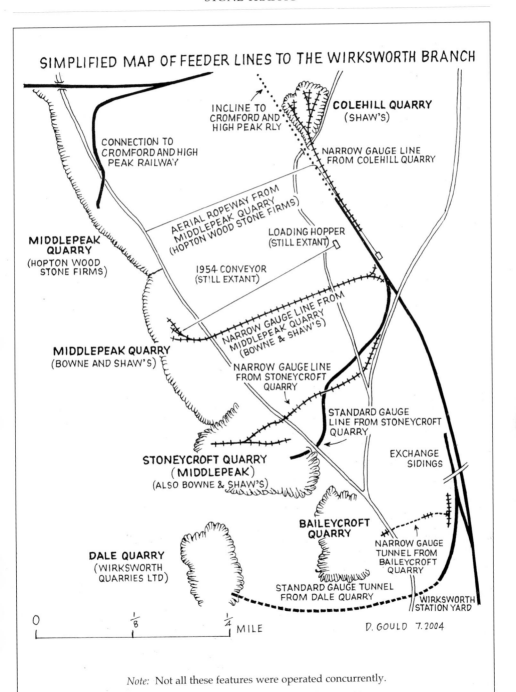

SIMPLIFIED MAP OF FEEDER LINES TO THE WIRKSWORTH BRANCH

INCLINE TO CROMFORD AND HIGH PEAK RLY

COLEHILL QUARRY (SHAW'S)

CONNECTION TO CROMFORD AND HIGH PEAK RAILWAY

NARROW GAUGE LINE FROM COLEHILL QUARRY

AERIAL ROPEWAY FROM MIDDLEPEAK QUARRY (HOPTON WOOD STONE FIRMS)

LOADING HOPPER (STILL EXTANT)

MIDDLEPEAK QUARRY (HOPTON WOOD STONE FIRMS)

1954 CONVEYOR (STILL EXTANT)

NARROW GAUGE LINE FROM MIDDLEPEAK QUARRY (BOWNE & SHAW'S)

MIDDLEPEAK QUARRY (BOWNE AND SHAW'S)

NARROW GAUGE LINE FROM STONEYCROFT QUARRY

STANDARD GAUGE LINE FROM STONEYCROFT QUARRY

STONEYCROFT QUARRY (MIDDLEPEAK) (ALSO BOWNE & SHAW'S)

EXCHANGE SIDINGS

BAILEYCROFT QUARRY

NARROW GAUGE TUNNEL FROM BAILEYCROFT QUARRY

DALE QUARRY (WIRKSWORTH QUARRIES LTD)

STANDARD GAUGE TUNNEL FROM DALE QUARRY

WIRKSWORTH STATION YARD

0   1/8   1/4   MILE

D. GOULD 7.2004

Note: Not all these features were operated concurrently.

A poor quality, but interesting view of wagons on the more northern of the two narrow gauge tramways linking Middlepeak Quarry with the loading area. The line appears to be double track throughout indicating that the photograph was taken in later years. Judging by the elevation of the photographer, the picture must have been taken from the bridge on Old Lane.

Tony Holmes/Wirksworth Heritage Centre

For many years a major customer was the Stanton Iron Company, so it was no great surprise when, in 1921, that company bought a 50 per cent share in Bowne & Shaw's, later taking over completely. Stanton was taken over by Stewart & Lloyds, but when steel was nationalised, a new company was formed called Stewart & Lloyds (Minerals) Ltd. However, the quarry was always referred to locally and by the railway as Bowne & Shaw's. On 1st January, 1966 another transfer of ownership took place, this time to Derbyshire Stone Ltd who more recently sold out to Tarmac Ltd.

The quarry operated on two levels, the lower level (Stoneycroft) was worked by standard gauge steam locomotives, and later diesel. The upper level was horse-worked, and altogether, three railway lines connected the quarry with the Midland Railway at various times. A standard gauge line (the southernmost and most recent of the three) crossed under the Middleton road; the two lines further north were 3 ft gauge, and crossed the road on the level, one (like the standard gauge line) came from the old Stoneycroft quarry, and the northernmost led from the original Middlepeak Quarry. They were worked by self-acting inclines down to the exchange sidings, where one, possibly two, internal combustion locomotives moved the wagons around. A small engine shed, a miniature of the standard gauge shed, stood to the north of the tipping dock and was demolished around Christmas 1980. The northernmost narrow-gauge line was (around the 1920s) single track with a passing loop, the points for which were set by the wagons themselves as they approached, but, by the 1950s, this had been altered to double track throughout. At this time, the lower narrow gauge line (by now superseded by the standard gauge line further to the south) was out of use. Both narrow gauge lines were later converted into roadways for internal lorry traffic.

By the 1960s, the overhead conveyor and hopper were already in use, and the demise of the remaining narrow-gauge line was hastened as a result. Stone that had been crushed and graded in the quarry was carried by the conveyor, which, with its associated paraphernalia, is still very much in evidence. Iron-ore tipplers, standard 16 ton mineral wagons and hoppers could all be seen, the tipplers being the most common. These were loaded in Stoneycroft Quarry, and ran through the narrow tunnel under Middleton Road. However, the larger hopper wagons were loaded under the conveyor at Cromford Road, and it is likely that these never ventured through the Middleton Road tunnel.

In 1965, 34½ acres of land were quarried and 104 men were employed. Half of these men worked on the lime-kilns, one of which was coal-fired, the other oil-fired. Two-fifths of the output was dispatched by rail and the rest by road. An interesting insight into conditions of work in the quarry is given by the the remarks of a pensioner in the 1980s who had been a mining engineer at Middlepeak: '4½d. per ton shifted out of the quarry, and you bought your own explosives and detonators'.

Mr Albert Goodwin recalls that the 'senior Shaws' lived at Rock House which soon became surrounded by the tramways and paraphernalia attached to the quarries. As a result, they had a house built further up the Cromford Road and let Rock House to one of the foremen.

Above left: The old Stoneycroft Quarry was linked to the Middlepeak loading area by narrow gauge and standard gauge lines. This photograph shows the route of the southernmost narrow gauge line converted for internal lorry traffic by the time it was taken on 24th July, 1982. This line originally crossed both the standard gauge feeder line (which superseded it) and Old Lane on its way to the loading area.   *Author*

Above right: The third of the rail links to cross Middleton Road, this is the course of the narrow gauge line that linked the lower end of Middlepeak Quarry (i.e., the northern end of Stoneycroft Quarry) with the loading area at Cromford Road. It outlasted the more southern of the two narrow gauge lines, still being used in the 1950s, by which time the single line with passing loop had been converted to a double line throughout. When the overhead conveyor was built, however, it was converted for use by lorries. It was photographed on 3rd May, 1982.   *Author*

In 1976, British Rail announced a plan to build new sidings at Wirksworth which would have done away with the remaining internal railway network. It involved the use of a 2,000 ton storage and loading hopper between Cemetery Lane and Cromford Road which would be fed by a conveyor system passing under Cromford Road. The scheme was given planning consent but was not implemented.

In November 1979 it was announced that the plans were to be revived and re-submitted to Derbyshire County Council. To be included, was part of the original plan which had not initially found favour. This was for a new road going from Cromford Road to Wash Green to divert traffic away from the town centre. However, nothing further was heard of the scheme.

An interesting assortment of locomotives has worked between the quarry and the branch. The earliest I have been able to trace may well have arrived shortly after Bowne and Shaw's agreement with the Midland in 1876. This was a Manning, Wardle 0-4-0ST (Works No. 99) which was completed by 30th December, 1863 for its original owners, G. Dawes, Milton Ironworks, Yorkshire. It was known there as No. 5 *Milton* but it is not known whether this number and name were carried after it had been sold to Bowne & Shaw.

On 22nd June, 1891 Bowne & Shaw ordered a Hudswell, Clarke 0-4-0ST (Works No. 357) which left the works on 5th October, 1891 at a cost of £625.

It is not known how long these locomotives were in use, or what happened to them, but on 5th February, 1916 a further Hudswell, Clarke 0-4-0ST was ordered (Works No. 1215). It left the works on 22nd January, 1917 at an approximate cost of £875. Painted green, it bore the name *Gertrude*. In 1950, it was transferred to Harston Quarries (Stewart & Lloyds) where it became No. 1. It was scrapped in September 1953.

Another Hudswell, Clarke 0-4-0ST was ordered on 7th July, 1927, and left the works on 14th October that year as Works No. 1605. It cost approximately £1,025 and was painted black with red lining. In April 1948, it also went Harston Quarries (Stewart & Lloyds) where it became No. 2. It was scrapped in 1952.

These two locomotives were replaced by two 0-4-0ST engines that were brought in from other Stewart & Lloyd's locations. The first, and more interesting, arrived in August 1946 from the Harlaxton Ironstone Mines, Lincolnshire. This was owned by the Holwell Iron Company, which was also part of Stewart & Lloyds. Throughout its life at Wirksworth, it bore witness to its former home by carrying the name *Holwell No. 3*.

Built by Black, Hawthorn at Gateshead in 1873 (Works No. 266) it worked until 1977 and at that time was the second oldest steam locomotive in active service (although 'active' is perhaps an overstatement). It had been rebuilt in 1894, 1901, 1911 and 1935 and spent all but the first few years of its life with either the Holwell company or Bowne & Shaw's. Its original owner was a contractor by the name of Walter Scott and, at that time, it carried the name *Wellington*.

Over the years, several new items were added including a new chimney, mechanical lubricator and cast-iron brake blocks. In 1948 an extension was fitted to the right-hand side of the cab. Otherwise, the locomotive was original including its spring-balance safety valves and handbrake working on the rear wheels only.

Baguley Ind Coope No. 1 is seen here in the Middlepeak exchange sidings on 15th December, 1977. A feature of interest here is the raft of 'Mermaids' on the right.   *R.G. Cash*

A view along the standard gauge link between Stoneycroft Quarry and the Middlepeak loading area, where it crossed Old Lane by a level crossing. Taken in January 1975.   *R.G. Cash*

Left: The standard gauge line from the loading area to Stoneycroft Quarry ran under Middleton Road, and is seen here in 1960 looking towards the quarry. The restricted clearances are demonstrated by the two 'scrape' lines on the wall to the right caused by hopper wagons. *David Ibbotson*

Below: After passing under Middleton Road, the line fanned out onto the floor of the quarry. All this has now been filled in and trees planted on the site as a Millennium project. *David Ibbotson*

A Lilywhite postcard view inside Stoneycroft Quarry during the 1920s, showing how the lines from the tunnel under Middleton Road fanned out across the floor of the quarry.
Tony Holmes/Wirksworth Heritage Centre

A view of Stoneycroft Quarry with the tunnel under Middleton Road on the right taken on 3rd May, 1982. Although long out of use, the standard gauge tracks lasted for some years. *Author*

The Middlepeak loading area in June 1970 with Hibberd 'Simplex' design 0-4-0 on the left, Baguley Ind Coope No. 1 in front of the engine shed, and *Holwell No. 3* also visible in the background. Just visible to the left is a derelict wagon.   *R.G. Cash*

After travelling along the conveyor from Middlepeak Quarry, stone was loaded into the wagons from the hoppers on the left. The locomotive is one of the two Baguley 0-4-0 diesels that were bought from Ind Coope, Burton (almost certainly No. 1). It stands in the loading area at Middlepeak in 1979 with the engine shed on the right. The Cromford & High Peak Railway runs across the skyline, a bridge being visible on the left.   *A.R. Kaye*

Taken from the 'dust dock' in September 1970, and with the photographer's father standing on the platform, the Pooley weighbridge test van appears to be in attendance. To the left is what looks like the match truck for a crane, indicating that there has been a derailment somewhere in the yard - a common occurrence in later years!   *R.G. Cash*

In April 1972, *Uppingham* was pressed into service when there was no diesel available. On the right, forming a wagon sandwich, are the Hibberd 'Simplex' (presumably out of use) and *Holwell No. 3* hiding under a tarpaulin.   *R.G. Cash*

In its later years, it was looked after by Ted Sallis who was Works Engineer at Wirksworth. He moved to Middlepeak in 1954, but had already met *Holwell No. 3* when he overhauled the locomotive at Stanton Iron Works in 1950. It was in full-time use at the quarry until 1966, when it became a stand-by locomotive. In Spring 1973, in its centenary year, *Holwell No. 3*, was restored for the Well Dressings festival, and appeared in steam, running around the loading area.

At the end of 1977, it was sold for preservation to the Stephenson & Hawthorne Locomotive Trust, which was formed in 1971 to preserve Tyneside-built engines. It was soon back at work on the Tanfield Railway in County Durham, and at the time of writing it is on loan to the nearby North of England Open Air Museum at Beamish.

It was partnered at Wirksworth by *Uppingham*, a Peckett 0-4-0ST dating from 1912 (Works No. 1257). *Uppingham* had been transferred in 1948 from Market Overton Quarries in Rutland (another Stewart & Lloyds undertaking), and although not as distinguished as *Holwell No. 3*, it survived to be preserved initially at Butterley, Derbyshire and now at the Rutland Railway Museum, Cottesmore. Eric Green recalls seeing *Uppingham* coming down the incline from the quarry with its fireman sitting on a pick-shaft stuck between the wheel spokes of a wagon 'to slow it down a bit'!

Towards the end of the quarry's active life, a number of diesel locomotives were employed. The first, which arrived in 1966 to replace *Holwell No. 3*, was a 0-4-0 made by Baguley of Burton-upon-Trent with a Paxman Ricardo engine. It was purchased from the Burton brewer Ind Coope, and for a few years continued to wear the livery of that company, green with red/black/yellow lining, 'Ind Coope Ltd' and the 'red hand' trademark on the cabside and No. 1 on the red buffer beams. It was too large to run through to Stoneycroft, so *Uppingham* continued to be steamed a couple of days a week (often on Mondays) until its replacement arrived. The Baguley fell out of use in the late 1970s, and was stored at the end of the exchange sidings as a spare engine. It is doubtful whether it was ever used again, and as late as August 1989 it was still standing abandoned on a siding in the Middlepeak loading area becoming more and more overgrown with foliage; its ultimate fate is not known.

The replacement for *Uppingham*, which had arrived by June 1970, was a very small 'Simplex' locomotive built by F.C. Hibberd. It had a very angular body, built of flat plate, and is believed to have come from Hopton Wood Stone Firms' Middleton branch via Tarmac's Caldon Low quarries in Staffordshire. It dated from 1936, was painted in unlined green, and carried a large plate with 'Derbyshire Stone' in raised letters on the end.

By 1971, both steam engines were dumped on the siding behind the engine shed, *Holwell No. 3* sheeted over, but *Uppingham* open to the elements. During this period, its chimney rusted through, and the cap fell off. Nevertheless, when both diesels failed in Spring 1972, *Uppingham* took over for a couple of weeks, and seemed to manage perfectly well without it.

A third diesel made its appearance at around this time. This was Ind Coope No. 2, which was identical to the other, and is believed to have come from Burton via Cawdor Quarry, Matlock. Over the years, it became increasingly difficult to tell the two engines apart. By June 1976, No. 1 had yellow ends,

Holwell No. 3 at Wirksworth in June 1957, having just brought a train of empties from the exchange sidings into the Middlepeak loading area. The 'home-made' extension can be seen on the far side of the cab.
G. Yeomans

A view of *Uppingham* on the standard gauge internal railway system at Middlepeak Quarry. While under the ownership of Tarmac, both *Uppingham* and *Holwell No. 3* had a map of England and Wales painted on each cylinder casing.
John Kitchen

including the buffer beams, and so had lost its painted number, but it retained the lining on the panels. By 1980, No. 2 was unlined green including the ends, and the cabsides bore a Tarmac motif of interlocking letter 'T's. It had the plant number 525 29 441 and was dumped out of use with the Hibberd.

The fourth diesel locomotive, which was destined to be the last used in the quarry, was a Rolls 'Steelman' 0-6-0 built by Thomas Hill with a Rolls-Royce engine. Bought from British Steel in 1980, this was by far the largest locomotive to be used at Middlepeak, and after withdrawal it is thought to have been sold on for further use elsewhere.

Technical details of all these engines have been omitted here, but appear in *Appendix Three*. Drawings of Bowne & Shaw's private owner wagons are included below and overleaf, but it is not known how many were owned. A photograph of the quarry in the mid-1930s shows hopper wagons lettered 'STANTON', and two correspondents remember seeing 8 ton Stanton wagons (painted red with 'STANTON' in white letters) working on the branch in the 1930s and 1940s after which LMS 16 ton mineral wagons took over.

Middlepeak was the last quarry to operate in the area, and the sole reason for the Wirksworth branch lasting as long as it did. A major project in the late 1960s was to supply a quarter of a million tons of limestone to build the tidal harbour at Port Talbot, and all the stone was taken away by rail, 22 tons in each wagon.

The latter-day facilities at the exchange sidings can easily be viewed from Cromford Road and by walking along Old Lane, which branches off Cromford Road just north of its junction with Middleton Road. Old Lane also give access to what is left of the extension to the Cromford & High Peak Railway. Rock House is still *in situ* in the 'V' of the junction between Cromford Road and Old Lane.

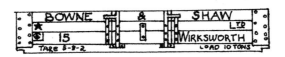

Body: Red oxide
Lettering: White (optional black shading)
Ironwork: Black
Length: 15 ft 0 in.
Width: 7 ft 11 in.
Wheelbase: 9 ft 0 in.

Grease axleboxes
Diagonal strapping inside body

Wagon No. 18 identical except:
　　Tare: 5-7-0
　　3-plank dropside wagon

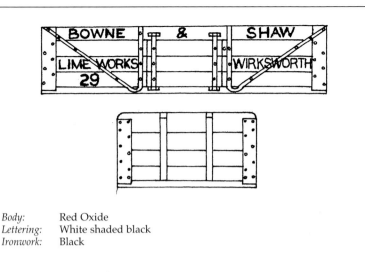

Body: Red Oxide
Lettering: White shaded black
Ironwork: Black

Other 4-plank wagons had more rounded ends:

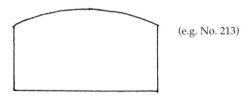

(e.g. No. 213)

Some had dumb-buffers on at least one end

Middlepeak Quarry (Hopton Wood Stone Firms)

Early in the 19th century, the Hopton Stone Firm was founded by the Killer brothers and quickly became known for the quality of its carved stone. Their quarry was served by a branch from the High Peak line at Steeplegrange. Meanwhile, David Wheatcroft had opened Hopton Wood quarry which was served by a ¾ mile branch from the High Peak line at Hopton, the firm being known as Hopton Wood Stone Co. Ltd.

In 1905 Hopton Wood Stone Firms Ltd was formed by the amalgamation of the two firms and by then they had become owners of the northern half of Middlepeak Quarry. This quarry had a connection with the Cromford and High Peak line at Middlepeak Wharf and, as a result, yet another mineral line crossed the Middleton road on the level.

In 1895, returns made under the Quarries Act of that year show Hopton Wood Quarry and Killer's Middleton Quarry separately as does the 1904 *Railway Clearing House Handbook*. In 1907, the Killer's quarry branch was taken over by Hopton Wood Stone Firms but it is not clear when Middlepeak quarry came under this company's ownership.

This tangled web would not concern us here if the connections with the High Peak line had been the only rail links. However, the 1913 Midland Railway distance diagram shows a siding for Hopton Wood Stone Firms at the same place as Bowne & Shaw's sidings. In addition, the MR/LMS registers of private owner wagons show, under reference number 66648, 'Hopton-Wood Stone Firms, Nos. 1-20'. The photograph reproduced overleaf shows No. 2 which was built around 1910 or 1911 so it is clear that the MR was taking away stone from Hopton Wood Stone Firm's Middlepeak Quarry.

The way in which this was achieved appears on the 1922 Ordnance Survey 25 inch map. An aerial ropeway is shown running from Middlepeak Quarry to the formation of the Midland Railway incline just south of Old Lane. Where it meets the incline, it turns south-east, and runs above and across the MR formation to a rectangular hopper building directly opposite the loading dock for Bowne & Shaw's (hence the two sidings being shown at the same mileage on the 1913 diagram). The hopper is most likely hidden behind the large stone crusher shown in the 1932 photograph on page 152, although by this time the aerial ropeway had been removed. The ropeway is not shown on the 1899 map, and on the 1922 edition it is shown as disused. It operated from around 1905, and only lasted for about 15 years. Stone from this quarry continued to be taken away on the Wirksworth branch, and this must have been achieved by bringing stone to the yard at Wirksworth by lorry. The quarry manager for a time was called Storey, and under his régime, productivity was quite high.

In 1935 Hopton Wood Stone Firms became a founder constituent of Derbyshire Stone Ltd, but it is not certain whether this company's wagons were ever seen on the branch.

All in all a fairly confusing story, but one worthy of inclusion if only to allow the reproduction of the superb 10 ton private owner wagon. The builders were Birmingham Carriage & Wagon Co. Ltd and the ends of the wagon are slightly rounded, it has wooden solebars and grease axleboxes are fitted. Livery details are not known for certain, but the main body colour is probably grey. Ironwork and shading to the letters is black, the letters themselves being white, but the lettering is positioned so as to leave room for shading to the right and below. The fact that this shading is not apparent on the photograph points to a dark shade for the diagonal band, and Bachmann have interpreted this as dark red on their 00 gauge model of this wagon.

Colehill Quarry

The history of this quarry is even more muddled than that of Middlepeak, the reason being sheer carelessness in the spelling of the name. On either side of the High Peak line between Steeplegrange and Middleton are two quarries. On the north side and served by that line, is Coal Hills Quarry (owned by Hopton Wood Stone Firms) but on the south side, linked with the extension from Wirksworth is Colehill Quarry. The quarries are quite separate and only the southern quarry is of interest here. Over the years, however, references to these quarries have been indiscriminately spelt with such variations as Coals Hill and

Hopton-Wood Stone Firms Ltd, No. 2, built by the Birmingham Carriage and Wagon Co. Ltd. Note the rounded ends. A fine Bachmann model has been produced based on this photograph.

Historical Model Railway Society

Body: Black
Lettering: White
Length: 16 ft 6 in.
Wheelbase: 9 ft 0 in.

Small lettering reads 'Empty to Matlock'

Colehills. The spellings used in this book are as given on the Ordnance Survey 25 inch maps.

There had been some quarrying in this region in the 19th century, but it was not until 1912 that serious production began. It was started by Alfred Shaw, a local builder and cousin of John Shaw (of Bowne & Shaw). There are actually three quarries in the complex, Colehill, Pensend and Steeplegrange, though only Colehill was linked to the Midland Railway directly. Also involved was Alfred's son, Charlie.

The 1899 Ordnance Survey shows no activity at the site but a Midland Railway 2 chain to 1 inch plan reputedly drawn up in about 1900 shows A. Shaw's siding on the incline and 'Coleshill' Quarry. However, the plan must be a later revision as the siding is not mentioned in the 1904 *RCH Handbook*. There are references here, though, to Shaw & Lovegrove's Longcliffe Limestone Co.; Shaw Bros, Matlock Bath; Shaw Bros, Intake Siding (Steeplehouse); and Shaw's Limestone Siding, Matlock Bridge. The Lovegrove connection is not clear but there was a saddler in Wirksworth by that name who married a Shaw. He became a quarry developer at about the time of World War I and opened Longcliffe Quarry near Brassington.

World War I led to a great expansion of the quarry and, by 1920, over three acres had been excavated. It was thought that there were large deposits of barytes in the quarry and this was the prime reason for its development, as this commodity was needed in the war. Unfortunately, the mineral was not present so only stone was quarried. For many years the Manager was Mr C. Lowndes who is known to have reported the discovery of basins filled with charcoal in the limestone. Presumably, they were of pre-historic origin and may have led to the area being known as 'Cole Hill' (however you care to spell it) meaning 'the hill where the charcoal burners worked'.

Body: Red (Oxide?)
Lettering: White, shaded black

The 1956 *RCH Handbook* shows 'Shaw's, A. Coalhills Quarry', so even this august body was sometimes caught out in its spelling. A change of ownership occurred in about 1960 when W.H. Phillips and Sons, a large haulage contractor in the town, took over the quarry. They leased it, in 1964, to George Wimpey and Co. Ltd who wanted to extract limestone for their M1 motorway contract from Pinxton northwards. Proposed production at this time was 250,000 tons and some 35 acres were being quarried.

Like most of the other quarries in the area, Colehill is now owned by Tarmac Ltd though it is not in production. A measure of the amount of stone quarried is given by the fact that most of the Midland Railway's High Peak extension is now completely quarried away except for the bridge over Old Lane.

The area to the east of Colehill Quarry and the MR incline has now become the site of the National Stone Centre, and a small industrial estate has also been built. The National Stone Centre tells the story of the development of quarrying, methods of extraction and past and present-day techniques, and is well worth a visit for anyone wanting to learn more about this part of the history of Wirksworth. Similarly, the Wirksworth Heritage Centre, just off the Market Square, also includes information about the quarries, and much more about the wider history of the town.

The bridge that carried the Midland Railway incline over Old Lane is still in existence, though little remains of the trackbed on either side. It is pictured here on 24th July 1982.
Author

These were the quarries served directly by the branch. The MR/LMS register of private owner wagons has been mentioned but there is an intriguing entry. Number 100950 refers to Duns and Co., Wirksworth but the name is not clearly written. I have not come across any names which could be badly transcribed as 'Duns'. The nearest I have found is Innes & Co. who, for a time, owned Wirksworth Quarries. Unfortunately, they were a London-based company and, having taken over Wirksworth Quarries, would not be contemporary with that firm as the registration numbers suggest.

Other wagons that might have been seen on the branch include those of William James, a mineral merchant based in Derby, Stewart & Lloyds, sometime owners of Middlepeak Quarry, and Derbyshire County Council, which had its own fleet of wagons for transporting stone. For their help with this difficult aspect of the working of the branch, I would like to thank Chris Crofts and Bill Hudson of the Historical Model Railway Society. In addition, I have been greatly helped by George Cash, who has confirmed what was correct in the first edition, corrected the information that was a little wayward and significantly added to the story for this second edition.

Official figures for the tonnages handled at Wirksworth tend to group limestone in with coal and coke (both inward commodities). However, the production of lime products is so huge that in any recorded figures, coal products are almost insignificant. Figures for minerals are also to be found in the official records and these would include lead, its associated gangue minerals, silicas, and any 'foreign' minerals brought in by rail. The most complete set of records refers to the period 1872 to 1922 and extracts are given in *Appendix Two*. These show just how dramatically production was affected after the arrival of the railway.

From 1965, all statistics for limestone originating from the C&HP were dealt with at Wirksworth. In 1954, 262,346 tons were sent from Wirksworth and this remained fairly constant through to the mid-1960s when the total tonnage (including C&HP figures) amounted to some 500,000 tons per year. Roughly half the total output originated at the Wirksworth quarries and represented about 5,000 tons of limestone being dispatched every week along the branch. This was the only traffic being handled on the line, all limestone being weighed before leaving for Chaddesden Sidings. Mineral wagons over the years rose in capacity from 8 and 10 tons to 16, and at the end, 21 and 25 ton hoppers, typically 40 such in a train load.

Also in the mid-1960s, about 2,000 tons of coal and coke were being brought in by rail each year. Lead does not figure in any recent figures, the last load having left Wirksworth station in 1946.

Chapter Eleven

Signalling, Operation and Rolling Stock

The signalling and operation of the branch is quite interesting and the development of the signalling at Duffield is also described here. When the main line was opened in 1840, it is doubtful whether there was any centralised control. Signalling in those days consisted of railway policemen placed at strategic locations quite literally on point-duty. As mentioned in Chapter Three, a new signal box was built at Duffield at the same time that the branch was opened, and it will be remembered from the correspondence relating to the Board of Trade inspection that the line was to be worked with a train staff. No details of this box have been found though the 1879/83 Ordnance Survey map shows a signal box on the up side of the main line opposite the junction. Signalling consisted of a starter and a distant at each end of the station on the main line and a signal at the junction to control the branch.

Notes from the November 1874 Appendix to the Working Timetable show that trains approaching the junction bound for Belper were to whistle twice and those for Wirksworth were to whistle three times. 'Tariff Wagons and Vans' were sent from Derby to Wirksworth on the 9.45 am from Derby and back to Derby on the 5.30 pm ex-Wirksworth. Loads for engines were also given and these are shown below:

| | Loaded | | Empty |
	Goods	Mineral	
Duffield to Wirksworth	30	24	40
Wirksworth to Duffield	45	45	50

In around 1875, the original Junction signal box was replaced by a new box on the down side of the main line in the 'V' of the junction; this box was to the company's standard design and consisted of two bays. The February 1880 Appendix reveals more about the operation of the branch at that time. The system of working is given as train staff and ticket between Duffield and Wirksworth and on the incline to the exchange sidings at Wirksworth. 'Signal posts' are mentioned at Peckwash Mill (closed each night and on Sundays) and at Duffield Junction; both locations had a 'speaking telegraph'. Hazelwood and Shottle were 'signal posts' as well (probably not actually concentrated in a signal box structure), and the telegraph is also shown at Shottle and Wirksworth stations; there were no intermediate block posts on the branch. A note informs the reader that the branch closed each night and on Sundays, for as yet no Sunday service had been introduced. The Junction box was open continuously. Tariff vans were carried on the 12.00 noon from Derby and the 6.00 pm from Wirksworth and the details of loading of goods trains had been considerably amended as shown below. As with the system of working, Wirksworth station to Bowne & Shaw's exchange sidings (the 'incline') is shown separately.

| | Double-framed Engines | | | Single-framed Engines | | |
| | Loaded | | Empty | Loaded | | Empty |
	Goods	Mineral		Goods	Mineral	
Wirksworth to Bowne & Shaw's	-	-	10	-	-	-
Bowne & Shaw's to Wirksworth*	-	8	-	-	-	-
Duffield to Wirksworth	30	24	40	36	29	48
Wirksworth to Duffield	45	45	50	50	50	50

* 2 wagons spragged and 2 with brakes pinned down.

There is also a special regulation concerning Hazelwood which reads:

No train or engine running towards Duffield must be brought to a stand at the Wirksworth end of the Hazelwood Goods Yard for shunting purposes unless the driver is in possession of the Train Staff.

An official MR notice relating to Duffield Junction states that:

Commencing 7.30 am Sunday August 17th (1884) the old box will be closed and the new box opened. The points farthest from the signal box giving communication between the sidings alongside the Wirksworth branch, and the Wirksworth branch, will be controlled by Annett's Key affixed to the Wirksworth branch train staff. The connection with the down main line at the Ambergate end of the siding alongside that line will continue to be worked in accordance with the instructions (in the) Appendix to the Working Time Table.

This was supplemented by a further notice that 'from August 25th this signal box will be the train staff station for the Duffield end of the Wirksworth Branch'. The following year, at 9.00 am on Monday 18th May, the 'arm distant signal worked by guards and shunters from a stage at the north end of the Down sidings' at Duffield was superseded by a disc signal near the box.

In 1890, staff and ticket working gave way to electric tablet working, the signal boxes at Idridgehay, Wirksworth and Gorsey Bank being opened at this time. The changeover was carried out over a number of weeks. At 10.00 am on 8th September, 1890, coincident with the opening of the signal boxes, the branch became worked by block telegraph, with Gorsey Bank as an intermediate block post. The signal boxes all closed at night, and only Wirksworth was open on a Sunday. Then, at 4.00 pm on Sunday 19th October, train staff and ticket was withdrawn, and train tablet working was introduced. Duffield Junction to Idridgehay was worked by train tablet only, and Idridgehay to Wirksworth by train tablet and ticket (the train tablet taking the place of the staff). Block telegraph working continued, with Idridgehay, Gorsey Bank and Wirksworth being the block posts (although Gorsey Bank was not a tablet station). At the same time, the branch siding at Duffield became controlled by the Duffield-Idridgehay tablet. On 2nd November, the connection between the running line and the goods yard at Wirksworth became signalled, and on the 18th of that month, signals were removed from Hazelwood and Shottle, and the sidings were controlled by the tablet as at Duffield. The previous day, at Wirksworth and Idridgehay, points and signals were connected to the signal boxes, except the points in the yard at Wirksworth and at the entrance to the goods yard at the Duffield end of Idridgehay, which was thereafter controlled by the tablet.

The incline at Wirksworth was to be worked under 'one engine in steam' and had its own staff, square in shape and blue in colour. The station master was appointed to receive the staff from, and deliver it to, the driver. It was noted that for a train fitted with automatic brakes, no more than the equivalent of 2½ vehicles could be coupled behind the rear brake van of a passenger train.

Goods train loadings on the branch had changed again as follows:

	Double-framed Engines			Single-framed Engines		
	Loaded		Empty	Loaded		Empty
	Goods	Mineral		Goods	Mineral	
Wirksworth to Bowne & Shaw's	-	-	12	-	-	12
Bowne & Shaw's to Wirksworth*	-	12	-	-	12	-
Duffield to Wirksworth	32	24	48	38	29	50
Wirksworth to Duffield	50	45	50	50	50	50

* From Bowne & Shaw's three wagons must be spragged.

On 7th May 1892, a bracket signal was brought into use for down trains at Duffield Junction, and on the 20th of the same month, a notice concerning mixed trains showed that this type of train could be worked on the Wirksworth branch, but at no greater speed than 25 mph. The Appendix to the Working Timetable of August 1893 is as before, but with an additional note that speed over the junction, to or from Wirksworth, should not exceed 20 mph.

In 1897, with the introduction of the new up goods line between Milford tunnel and Peckwash Mill, a new box was provided at the north end of Duffield station between the up goods and the up (later down) passenger lines (opened on 28th February that year), and another new box at Milford tunnel (opened on 16th May). The former was known as Duffield Station signal box, and had a 24 lever frame with two levers spare; Milford Tunnel box had 16 levers of which three were spare. An intriguing notice states that at 8.00 am on 24th July, 1898 a new ground signal would be brought into use to control movements onto the Wirksworth branch from the siding alongside the down main line 'now used for tipping purposes'. It is not clear what tipping was going on at this point.

The opening of the new down slow line on 8th September, 1901 meant that now both down lines were on the west side of the island platform, and the up lines were on the other side. This entailed some resignalling of the existing lines, resulting in alterations from that date to the signal boxes at Duffield, both of which were reframed. Duffield Station box received a 32 lever frame (4 spare) and Duffield Junction box a 36 lever frame (7 spare). It is possible, but cannot be confirmed, that the Junction box was extended at this time to accommodate the 36-lever frame. Some records have given the date of the extension as 1910, but there are a number of factors supporting the earlier date. A 36-lever frame is big - possibly too big for a box with two bays (or 'flakes' in MR parlance), and the photograph on page 100 which shows the extended box has been dated as January 1904.

The notice for these 1901 works contains wonderful details about the signalling at the junction, and these are given here in full:

The signals will be:

- A home signal between the up passenger line and up goods line, to regulate the running of trains and engines on the up passenger line; and a home signal alongside the up goods line, to regulate the running of trains and engines on that line.
- The present starting signal for the up passenger line.
- A two-armed bracket distant signal, a two-armed bracket home signal, and a two-armed bracket directing signal alongside the Wirksworth branch, to regulate the running of trains and engines approaching from Wirksworth; the right-hand arms will apply to trains and engines going forward on the up passenger line, and the left-hand arms to trains and engines going on to the up goods line.
- A seven-armed girder signal over the down fast line and down slow line, to regulate the running of trains and engines on the down fast line and down slow line:
  1. Duffield Junction down slow line home signal to siding alongside Wirksworth branch.
  2. Duffield Junction down slow line home signal to Wirksworth Branch.
  3. Duffield Junction down slow line home signal to down slow line.
  4. Duffield Station box down slow line distant signal to down slow line.
  5. Duffield Station box down slow line distant signal to down passenger line.
  6. Duffield Junction down fast line home signal.
  7. Duffield Station box down fast line distant signal.
- A starting signal applicable to trains and engines going towards Wirksworth, on the bracket post of the home signal near the Wirksworth end of the branch platform.
- A ground disc signal to regulate the running of trains and engines from the siding alongside the Wirksworth branch on to the up passenger line and up goods line.
- A ground disc signal to regulate the running of trains and engines from the siding alongside the down slow line on to the Wirksworth branch or into the siding alongside the Wirksworth branch.
- A ground disc signal between the down fast line and down slow line, to give permission for trains and engines to set back from the down slow line on to the up passenger line and up goods line.
- A ground disc signal alongside the down fast line, to give permission for trains and engines to set back from the down fast line on to the up passenger line and up goods line.
- A ground disc signal between the up passenger line and down fast line, to give permission for trains and engines to set back from the up passenger line on to the down fast line, the down slow line, on to the Wirksworth branch, or into the siding alongside the Wirksworth branch.
- A ground disc signal between the up passenger line and up goods line, to give permission for trains and engines to set back from the up goods line on to the down fast line, the down slow line, on to the Wirksworth branch, or into the siding alongside the Wirksworth branch.

The north end of the goods yard was locked by a bolt released from the Station box, and these details were supplemented in a further notice that from 6.00 am on 15th September:

The left-hand arms of the two-armed bracket distant and home signals applicable to trains and engines approaching from Wirksworth and going on to the up goods line will be removed and dispensed with; and the right-hand arms of those signals will regulate the running of all trains and engines approaching from Wirksworth to the two-armed bracket directing signal at the Derby end of the Wirksworth branch platform.

As a reflection of the lighter traffic on the main line on Sundays, Milford Tunnel box did not open; a notice in the June 1904 Appendix reads:

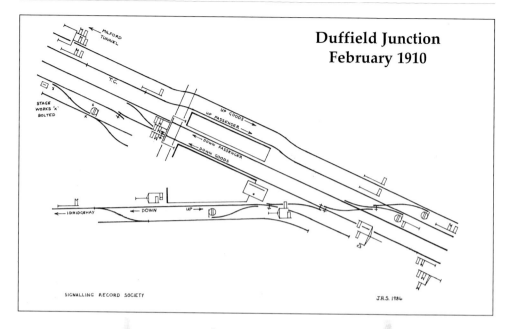

Duffield Junction
February 1910

Of indifferent quality, but delightful nevertheless, this rare view of the signal box at Idridgehay was probably taken at around the time of the Grouping in 1923, judging by the ladies' dress.

Knighton Collection

Duffield, Milford Tunnel Signal Box

The Milford Tunnel Signal Box and the up and down goods line between Duffield Station box and Milford Tunnel are closed from 6.0 a.m. Sundays to 8.0 p.m. Mondays and during this time no train or engine must be run on the up or down goods line between Duffield Station and Milford Tunnel.

A further speed limit of 15 mph was added when running from the down slow to the down passenger line at the Station box. In conjunction with the quadrupling, a new system of whistles was brought in at the junction. All trains on the down fast were to give two whistles, while on the down slow, three whistles signified a Belper train and four were given by Wirksworth trains.

In 1909, possibly in settlement of an industrial dispute, there was a need for an arbitration hearing between the Midland Railway and its employees. Mr William Clower represented the company and Mr Richard Bell, MP, the employees; the Arbitrator [*sic*] was the Earl of Cromer. The gist of the company's argument, insofar as it related to signalmen, was that they did very little in the way of hard work, but just sat around doing nothing between trains! They were thought to have no real responsibility, as the interlocking prevented them making mistakes, and their cabins were appointed to a 'better degree of comfort and sanitation than the men had in their own homes'. For some reason, the unfortunate signalman at Wirksworth was singled out for attention by Mr Clower!

Mr Clower: I have a case here of a man getting 21s. a week with a £1 bonus at Wirksworth, which is on a branch line. The total number of trains throughout the whole day was 18. The greatest number in any one hour was one in one direction and two in another.

The Arbitrator: That is 18 trains in the 24 hours.

Mr Clower: The box is not open continuously. It is in the 13 hours.

The Arbitrator: Only one man is on duty there?

Mr Clower: That is so, only one man for 12 hours. The other hour is covered by a porter signalman.

The Arbitrator: Then he has very little to do.

Mr Clower: That is so.

Later, there was a more general (and rather simplistic) summary of the duties of other signalmen on the system:

The Arbitrator: There is a large number of intermediate signal boxes where they have nothing to do but block working and signals, and no points.

Mr Clower: Merely passing trains through; no sidings, no connections and no junctions? Yes, that is merely to shorten the block system, to prevent delays to traffic.

Altogether, a fascinating insight into the way in which the Midland Railway regarded its employees – at least when it came to determining their wages!

On 16th January, 1910, the Station box at Duffield was removed, and its functions transferred to the Junction box, where a new 38-lever MR tappet frame was installed. In order to accommodate the larger frame, it has been suggested that the box was extended at this time. However, as mentioned on page 186, it is possible that the extension had been added some nine years

Idridgehay
c.1930

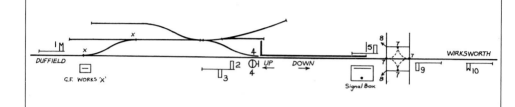

DUFFIELD

G.F. WORKS 'X'

UP ←   DOWN →

Signal Box

WIRKSWORTH

BASED ON THE RECOLLECTIONS OF
MR R. BROWN

6, SPARE

JHS 1982

Wirksworth
c.1930

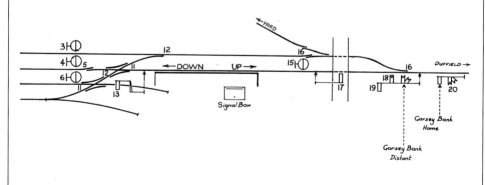

←YARD

←DOWN   UP→

Signal Box

DUFFIELD →

Gorsey Bank
Home

Gorsey Bank
Distant

1, 2, 7, 8, 9, 10, 14 , SPARE

JHS 1982

earlier. There were no spare levers in the new frame, and a track circuit was provided to the north of the station on the up passenger line. Entry to the goods yard was controlled by a ground frame probably released from the Junction box.

The track circuit and ground frame are both shown on the February 1910 signal box diagram on page 188, but to add further confusion, the original from which this drawing was made referred to '36 levers, 2 spare', which was the configuration before the 1910 frame was added! The final form of the Junction box consisting of three standard flakes each measuring 10 ft by 10 ft survived until made obsolete by the introduction of the power box at Derby in 1969.

The Appendix of July 1913 reflects these changes, and only Wirksworth-bound down trains were to whistle, four blasts being the required number. Wirksworth now had a signal box and opening times were given as follows:

	From	To
Wirksworth	6.45 am	9.20 pm
	4.00 pm (Sun)	6.00 pm (Sun)
Idridgehay	6.45 am	9.20 pm
Duffield Junction	Always open	

The incline at Wirksworth was worked as before, but there was now a signalman to deliver and receive the staff. A reflection of the increasing power of locomotives is shown in the following table:

	Up				Down			
	Mineral Class of Engine			*Max. No. of of wagons*	*Mineral Class of Engine*			*Max. No. of wagons*
	1	*2*	*3*	*for one engine*	*1*	*2*	*3*	*for one engine*
Wirksworth and Duffield	45	54	65	65	24	29	35	60

A further note stated that the branch could accept 9 ft 3 in. wide stock, though this is not altogether surprising in view of the fact that it was built for double track and only one line was laid.

In December 1927, there was a proposal for a new box at Wirksworth, the new box to measure 22 ft 1 in. by 11 ft 6 in. compared to the existing box which was 27 ft 6 in. by 9 ft 8 in. Like the existing box, the front of the new box would have been 13 ft 11 in. from the rail. It is not clear what changes this new box would have heralded, but the work was never carried out, and the signalling on the branch was to undergo more drastic changes in the next few years.

The signal boxes at Idridgehay (with its 10 lever frame and gate wheel) and Wirksworth (20 levers) were closed on 8th July, 1934, and from this date, the branch was worked by an unusual (some have said unique) system that combined long section 'one engine in steam' with electric token working over two short sections. The system used depended on whether or not Idridgehay was open or closed, as this was the intermediate token station. Idridgehay was provided with a small ground frame hut operated by a porter-signalman in place of its signal box. This was named 'Idridgehay Goods (West end)', the existing ground frame being called 'Idridgehay Goods (East end)'. A five-lever

Key Token Working—Wirksworth Branch:—

Apparatus is installed to enable Idridgehay token station to be closed at certain times, and during the times this token station is closed the line between Duffield Junction signal box and Wirksworth is worked in accordance with Section VI. of the Rule Book, by long section token. The long section token is lettered "Duffield Junction and Wirksworth." Duffield Junction signal box is the token station, and the signalman there is the person appointed to receive the token from and deliver it to the driver. In addition, the signalman at Idridgehay Station is authorised to deliver the long section token to and receive it from the driver for the purpose of closing or opening. When Idridgehay token station is closed the long section token will be handed to the driver, and when Idridgehay token station opens the long section will be collected from the driver at Idridgehay and a short section token for the Idridgehay-Wirksworth or Idridgehay-Duffield section, as may be required, will be handed to the driver after permission has been obtained in the latter case for the train to enter the advance section.

Drivers of trains from Duffield or Wirksworth proceeding towards Idridgehay with a long section token, may be required to exchange the long section token at Idridgehay, and must be prepared accordingly.

When Idridgehay token station is open and it is necessary to clear the single line to enable a short section token to be obtained at that place for a second train to proceed to Wirksworth, or to enable a short section token to be obtained at Wirksworth for another train to proceed to Idridgehay, the first train must be drawn clear of the single line at Wirksworth and the token passed through the instrument in accordance with the instructions exhibited there.

When long section token working is in operation and a train, which has arrived at Wirksworth from Idridgehay, requires to proceed on to the Wirksworth Incline Branch, the whole of the train must be drawn clear of the single line at Wirksworth Station, and when this has been done the long section token must be handed to the Station Master at Wirksworth, who will take charge of the token until the train requires to return to Idridgehay.

When long section token working is in operation the departure of all trains which leave Wirksworth without the token being passed through the instrument at that place must be telephoned to Idridgehay, and the Station Master at the latter place must advise Duffield Junction when the trains in question leave Idridgehay.

When short section token working is in operation no train must proceed on to the single line between Idridgehay and Wirksworth Station unless the driver is in possession of a token, or he has seen one in the possession of the driver of an engine to which his engine is attached, except as provided in Electric Token Regulations 14B, 14C and 25.

Pouches are provided in which the token is placed before being handed to the driver.

Section obstructed by Accident or by Disabled Train
Engine entering section for examination of Line.
Train or portion of train left on single line.
Working of trains to and from point of obstruction.
Failure of Token Instrument or Token damaged.

During the time short section working is in operation, Electric Token Regulations 14, 14B, 14C, 23, and 25 will apply. The person working the instrument at Wirksworth Station must be regarded as the signalman.

When it is necessary to ascertain if the line is clear an engine must not be allowed to enter the section unless a token has been obtained from the token instrument and is in possession of the driver. The circumstances must be explained to the driver, and he must be instructed to proceed cautiously through the section, prepared to stop short of any obstruction. Where practicable, the engine must be accompanied by a Station Master or other competent person. After sunset or during fog or falling snow, the engine must always be so accompanied.

(b) The person in charge of token station at which the engine enters the section can in these circumstances obtain a token, and the token so obtained must not be placed in the instrument at either end of the section until the person in charge or driver, as the may be, has reported that the line is safe for the passage of trains.

The Sectional Appendix to the Working Timetable, March 1937.

(one spare) ground frame named simply 'Idridgehay' was installed on the platform near the booking office to work the up and down distant, home and starting signals, and the necessary token and signalling equipment was housed within the booking office itself. The crossing gates were to be worked by hand and padlocked across the railway lines when open to road traffic. From this time, only Idridgehay was available to shunt a train to let another past.

At Wirksworth, all signals except the down distant were abolished, and at Gorsey Bank the up distant signal was raised 4 feet on the existing post. Two ground frames were installed at Wirksworth, one near Wash Green bridge called 'Wirksworth Goods (East end)', and one on the platform, 'Wirksworth Goods (West end)', to work the crossover at that point. At Duffield, the down sidings were worked from a ground frame released from the Junction box. The branch siding had its own ground frame controlled by both the long and short section tokens.

A signalling alterations notice issued for 30th June to 13th July, 1934 included details of the new method of working:

> Commencing at 9.0 a.m. on Sunday, July 8th, the electric tablet working between Duffield Junction and Idridgehay and Idridgehay and Wirksworth will be substituted by long and short section token working.

The notice continued to give further details on the working of the branch, some of which are included here:

> When Idridgehay key token station is closed, long section key token working will be in force between Duffield Junction and Wirksworth, and the key token will be lettered 'Duffield Junction and Wirksworth'.
> When Idridgehay key token station is open, short section key token working will be in force between Duffield Junction and Idridgehay and between Idridgehay and Wirksworth.
> The short section key token instruments at Idridgehay and Wirksworth will be fixed in the booking offices at these places.
> The ground frames between Duffield and Wirksworth, now controlled by Tablets will be controlled by the long and short section key tokens.
> The Wirksworth incline staff (square-blue) will be kept in the Booking Office at Wirksworth, and the Station Master will be the person authorised to receive the staff from, and deliver it to the driver.

The rest of the notice was later repeated in the Sectional Appendix to the Working Timetable, March 1937, part of which is shown opposite.

In practice, the first train of the day collected the long section token at Duffield Junction box, and used it at Idridgehay to release the two short section tokens. From then onwards, these two sections could be worked independently until the last up train of the day deposited its short section token at Idridgehay, collected the long section token, and took this back to Duffield. This seemingly complicated system of working had the advantage of allowing a fair degree of flexibility, and allowed long section working over the whole branch when required. This meant that Idridgehay did not have to be open at all times, Sunday being a case in point.

WIRKSWORTH BRANCH

KEY TOKEN WORKING. The single line between Duffield Junction and Wirksworth is worked by token with " No Signalmen " type of token instrument at Wirksworth, and no train must proceed on to the single line between Duffield Junction and Wirksworth unless the Driver is in possession of a token, or he has been shown the token which has been delivered to the Driver of an engine to which his engine is attached except as provided in Electric Token Block Regulations 14, 18 and 25.

Pouches are provided in which the token is placed before being handed to the Driver.

Section obstructed by accident, by disabled train, or by portion of train.

Engine entering section for examination of line.

Working of trains to and from point of obstruction.

Failure of Token Instrument or Token damaged.

Electric Token Regulations 14, 15, 18, 23 and 25 apply. The person working the instrument at Wirksworth must be regarded as the Signalman.

When it is necessary to ascertain if the line is clear an engine must not be allowed to enter the section unless a token has been obtained from the token instrument and is in the possession of the Driver. The circumstances must be explained to the Driver, and he must be instructed to proceed cautiously through the section, prepared to stop short of any obstruction. Where practicable, the engine must be accompanied by a Station Master or other competent person. After sunset or during fog or falling snow, the engine must always be so accompanied.

The Person in charge of the token station at which the engine enters the section can, in these circumstances, obtain a token, and the token so obtained must not be placed in the instrument at either end of the section until that Person in charge or Driver, as the case may be, has reported that the line is safe for the passage of trains.

WIRKSWORTH—MOVEMENTS OF WAGONS FROM WIRKSWORTH QUARRIES TO WIRKSWORTH GOODS YARD. Except as shown below, the firm's employees will obtain permission from the Person in charge in the Goods Yard before the firm's engine enters upon the B.R. lines.

In clear weather, however, if the B.R. engine is not in the Goods Yard when the movement requires to be made, such permission need not be obtained, but the firm's employee will immediately advise the Person in charge should the B.R. engine return to the Goods Yard before the firm's engine has completed its work.

The firm's employee will advise the Person in charge in the Goods Yard when their engine has completed its work.

WIRKSWORTH BRANCH INCLINE. When wagons for despatch from Messrs. Bowne & Shaw's outwards siding have been attached to the train, the Guard or Shunter must attach a tail lamp to the last vehicle which will indicate to the firm's employees that the train is complete. After sunset or during fog or falling snow this tail lamp must be lighted.

The maximum number of wagons to be brought down the incline by a Class 3 or Class 4 Freight tender engine is 36.

The hand-brakes on not less than one-third of the vehicles must be pinned down before the signal to start is given. The Guard must travel on foot alongside the train to Wirksworth Station Yard and be prepared to apply further hand-brakes should the necessity arise.

When Messrs. Bowne & Shaw's Staff position vehicles in the outwards sidings, a sprag is secured in the wheel of the leading vehicle at the lower end of the gradient, and a further sprag in the third or fourth vehicle therefrom.

If vehicles are left in the siding after a train is despatched to Wirksworth Station Yard, the Guard or Shunter in charge must place a sprag securely in the wheel of the first and third vehicles at the lower end of the gradient.

The incline to the Middlepeak exchange sidings was still being worked as an entirely separate section using a square blue staff. Gorsey Bank was not a block post, but did have repeating instruments to receive messages from Wirksworth and Idridgehay; it had an 8 lever MR 6 in. frame and a gate wheel. A small further change was made at Duffield when in May 1939, the 'dwarf shunting signal regulating the running of trains and engines from the down sidings' was abolished. Signal box diagrams for all the boxes are included here, that for Idridgehay being based on the recollections of Reginald Brown, to whom I am most grateful. The development of the layout and signalling around the turn of the century at Duffield, in particular, is extremely confusing. At least one correspondent queried several details after the publication of the first edition, and, with further research, the information presented here considerably updates what I wrote previously. I would not pretend that I have answered all questions and eliminated every conceivable anomaly, but I am most grateful to Pat Larkham and Dave Harris, both of whom have made a study of Midland signalling in this area; I am sure that with further study, more could be written about the developments at Duffield.

Milford Tunnel signal box was closed from 3rd June, 1956, and attention was drawn to the fact that, because of the hours during which the branch was operating, two porter-signalmen were required at Idridgehay to work the shifts. As traffic dwindled, this became increasingly extravagant, so, according to a notice published in December 1956, Idridgehay station was renamed Idridgehay Crossing and closed as a block post. From then on, the short section key token working was withdrawn, and the branch was worked with a key token, coloured red with round ends and lettered 'DUFFIELD JUNCTION-WIRKSWORTH'. The remaining sidings at Shottle and Wirksworth were to be released by the new tokens. In the same month, the up main outer home signal at Duffield and the lower up main outer distant signal for Peckwash Mill Sidings box were renewed 83 yards farther from the box at Duffield Junction, at a point 1,580 yards from the Peckwash Mill Sidings up main home signal. The up main distant was replaced with a colour light signal 12 feet above rail level and 1,068 yards further from the box, making it 2,051 yards from the repositioned up main outer home signal.

The 1960 Appendix shows a speed limit of 20 mph over the junction for Wirksworth trains, the maximum on the main line being 70 mph. Trains were still required to whistle at the site of the 'Old Cattle Arches Bridge', a 'No Signalman' type of token instrument was present at Wirksworth and as before, the incline was traversable only on receipt of the staff. The speed limit on the incline was 20 mph and it is interesting to note that the quarry was still referred to as 'Messrs Bowne and Shaw's'. The maximum number of wagons to be brought down the incline by a class '3' or '4' tender engine was 36. Not less than one-third of the vehicles were to have their brakes pinned down and the guard was required to walk down alongside the train in order to apply more brakes if required. Any vehicles left standing in the exchange sidings were to have sprags placed in the wheels of the leading vehicle and the third or fourth vehicle back. An extra note showed that over bridge No. 16 on the branch (between Idridgehay and Wirksworth) there was a 10 mph speed restriction applying to locomotives Nos. D5000-5049, D5300-5319 and D5700-5719. These locomotives

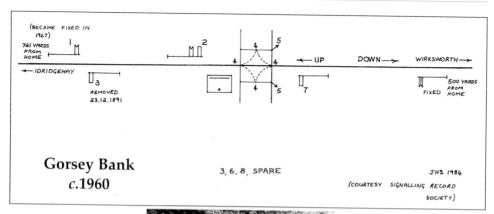

(BECAME FIXED IN 1967)

721 YARDS FROM HOME

IDRIDGEHAY

REMOVED 23.12.1891

UP   DOWN →   WIRKSWORTH →

FIXED   500 YARDS FROM HOME

Gorsey Bank
*c.*1960

3, 6, 8, SPARE

JHS 1984

(COURTESY SIGNALLING RECORD SOCIETY)

Right: Gorsey Bank up distant signal in about 1965.
R.J. Essery Collection

Duffield Junction signal box on 3rd June, 1967. The extension at the platform end can be clearly seen. The windows on the back of the extension are not apparent on the photograph shown on page 100. *G. Yeomans*

Duffield Junction signal box in June 1969. As the extension to the box encroached onto the platform, the catwalk at that end had to be made higher to provide adequate headroom underneath. The vertical boarding on the first floor is narrower on the extension than on the original box, and the ground floor window has been added since the photograph on page 100. *V.R. Anderson*

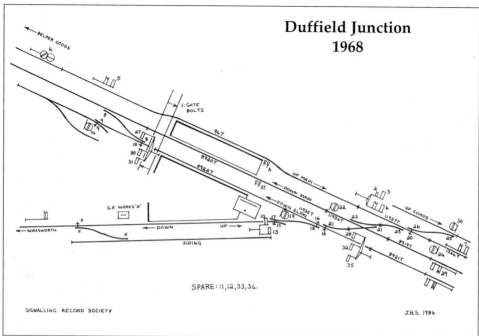

Duffield Junction
1968

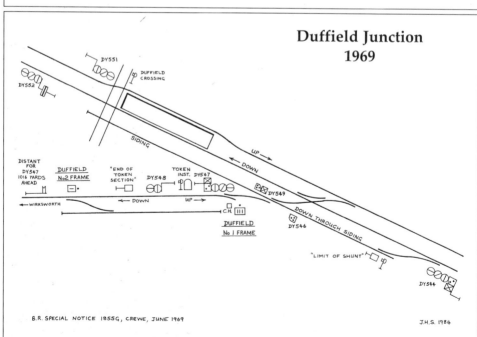

Duffield Junction
1969

Top: A view of Duffield in June 1969, shortly before removal of the buildings and semaphore signals.

V.R. Anderson

Above: Class '20s' Nos. 20192 and 20172 stand at Duffield as the driver of this loaded stone train inserts the token into machine, prior to seeking the signalman's permission to continue to St Mary's yard, Derby in September 1978.

R.E. Ruffell

Right: The token instrument that latterly stood on the branch platform had no fewer than 20 tokens available for working the branch when photographed on 26th May, 1985.

Author

Right: The ground frame at Idridgehay in March 1978. The purpose of the hut behind is not known, but it is probably associated with the conversion to a gateless crossing.
Anthony Straw

Below: A Midland Railway signal and crossing gates at Idridgehay shortly before closure. *A.R. Kaye*

were, respectively, BR/Sulzer Bo-Bo type '2s', Birmingham RC&W/Sulzer Bo-Bo type '2s' and Metro-Vick Co-Bo type '2s' all weighing over 75 tons.

The next major changes occurred at the end of the 1960s in connection with the resignalling of all the lines in the Derby area. On 25th February, 1968, the up goods line through the station at Duffield was abolished leaving quadruple track south of the junction only. On 22nd March, 1969 the remainder of the up goods line was removed, leaving only one line in the up direction between Milford tunnel and Little Eaton Junction. On the same date, the down goods between the station and the tunnel was also abolished and on 14th July, 1969 the Junction box was closed, to be demolished on 8th October the same year. The power signalling scheme at Derby was introduced in three stages, the Wirksworth branch being included in stage three. This entailed a changeover from the old system between 10.00 pm on Saturday 12th July and 6.00 am on Monday 14th July, 1969, during which period all points and signals worked from the old box were disconnected.

After the introduction of the new scheme, tokens for the branch were housed in instruments (released from Derby) on the branch platform at Duffield and near the 'dust-dock' at Wirksworth. Two ground frames were retained at Duffield, one to work the branch siding, and another at the headshunt near the junction.

The Appendix of February 1975 showed two speed limits to be observed by trains bound for Wirksworth: 15 mph to gain access to the down through siding (formerly the down slow) and 20 mph from there to the branch proper. Since all trains had to stop to pick up the token this was all rather academic. On the branch itself, there was a 30 mph limit throughout with a 20 mph maximum on the incline although another note restricts speed to 5 mph down the incline. Also on the incline, the brakes on all wagons were to be pinned down on one side presumably because of the relative inferiority of the brake power on the diesels compared with steam locomotives.

A minor addition to the regulations permitted trains from Wirksworth to work as far as the loop at Gorsey Bank without a brake van at the rear.

Up until now, crossing keepers were still required at Idridgehay and Gorsey Bank but in 1978 BR revealed that they wished to make Idridgehay into an open crossing. This did not please the local residents and protests were raised by the parish council. Their main concern was that tests had shown heavily laden trains failing to stop until several hundred yards past the crossing. In support of this it was alleged that the crossing was used a lot by pedestrians and people on horseback. It was felt, however, that automatic half-barriers would be acceptable.

Despite their objections, the ground frame was closed on 3rd December, 1978, the three-lever frame recovered, and the crossing converted so that only lights governed the passage of trains or road users. Red lights were displayed to the latter, while a white light gave the all-clear to trains, these lights being treadle operated. Gorsey Bank was similarly converted, on 3rd June, 1979, the change having been postponed from 29th April.

To coincide with their introduction, new speed limits were imposed at the crossings:

	Down	*Up*
Idridgehay	15 mph	10mph
Gorsey Bank	15 mph	Stop and alter lights manually

Gorsey Bank Crossing looking towards Wirksworth in June 1967.   *G. Yeomans*

The signal box at Gorsey Bank photographed on 24th July, 1982, shortly before removal to Peak
Rail.   *Author*

At the Wirksworth end of the 'No Signalman Token' section were placed 'Stop and Await Instructions' and 'End of Single Line' boards.

The 1980 Appendix limited up trains to 15 mph through the junction at Duffield. At Wirksworth, trains from the sidings were required to stop beyond Gorsey Bank before the guard was allowed to normalise the ground frame points. It is interesting to note that by the time BR had caught up with the fact that Bowne & Shaw's had become Derbyshire Stone Co., and were referring to the quarry as such, they were already out of date - Tarmac Ltd now being the owners. At this time there were two lines between Wirksworth and Gorsey Bank. The original down running line into the platform was truncated just short of Gorsey Bank, and the up road through the yard was extended to join the running line at this point.

The down slow between Peckwash Mill and Duffield station was taken out of use on 26th April, 1987, to leave the erstwhile up and down fast lines passing each side of the island platform, and in November 1989, just prior to the last sugar-stone working, further rationalisation took place at Wirksworth, with the ground frames and associated catch points at Gorsey Bank and the Incline being secured out of use. The branch was now 'One Train Working' from Duffield to the Wirksworth station ground frame, with the line from there to Tarmac's sidings being worked as sidings. At this time, the branch carried class D.1 (Goods Line) status, and for a while, these were the last changes to affect the working of the line. However, as mentioned in Chapter Six, on 8th February, 2003 the trailing crossover between the up and down main lines at Duffield was removed, and the branch was marooned with the removal of the facing connection from the down main.

Rolling Stock

As might be expected, a variety of motive power could be seen on the line over the years but there were locomotives which could be said to be 'regulars'.

The first known engine after that shown on page 38 is that mentioned in connection with the Idridgehay accident of 1884. This was No. 81, a 2-4-0 tender engine built by the Midland at Derby in 1862. It had 6 ft 2 in. diameter driving wheels and 16½ in. x 24 in. cylinders and was reboilered in March 1879 with a boiler from the 1874-built No. 131. No. 81 was broken up in October 1890.

Mr A.C. Sharpe has been able to furnish me with details of some of the locomotives used and remembers his father telling him that, towards the end of last century, Midland 'singles' made occasional forays to Wirksworth. It is thought that these were probably 2-2-2s as opposed to 4-2-2s. Mr Sharpe's brother recalls that, after 1910, '156' class 2-4-0 No. 5 appeared on the line. This number was only carried from November 1907, and from its date of building in 1867 the locomotive enjoyed a chequered career. In 1879, having until then been numbered 102, it went to the duplicate list as No. 102A. It was rebuilt in 1881, restored to the capital list as No. 118 in 1890, was rebuilt again in 1895 and returned to the duplicate list as 118A in 1897. After its appearance in the branch as No. 5 it was rebuilt for a third time in 1912, reboilered in 1924 and again in 1927 and finally withdrawn in 1928.

WIRKSWORTH BRANCH

Wirksworth Up Siding. A train from Wirksworth Up Siding must not be brought to a stand, to enable the Guard to normalise the ground frame points, until it has passed clear of Gorsey Bank level crossing.

Wirksworth Incline. When vehicles for despatch from Derbyshire Stone Co's outward sidings have been attached to the train, the Guard or Shunter must attach a tail lamp to the last vehicle to indicate to the firm's employees that the train is complete. After sunset or during fog or falling snow this tail lamp must be lighted.

The handbrakes on one side of all the vehicles must be pinned down before the signal to start is given. The speed descending the incline must not exceed **5 m.p.h.**, and the Shunter must walk alongside the train to Wirksworth Station and be prepared to apply further hand-brakes if necessary.

Before departure, the Driver of a train standing in the Exchange Sidings at Wirksworth Incline must hand the staff to the Guard or Shunter to permit the ground frame to be released, the trap points closed and the signal cleared to allow the train to leave the Exchange Sidings.

The clearing of the signal at the ground frame is the authority for the train to proceed from the Exchange sidings to Wirksworth yard, without the train staff and, unless otherwise instructed, the Driver must not depart from the sidings until the Shunter has returned from the ground frame to accompany the train down the incline.

Before operating the ground frame, the shunter must first ensure that no conflicting movement is being or is about to be made. After clearing the signal for a train to depart from the Exchange sidings, a conflicting movement must not be authorised until the train has passed clear of the Wirksworth Incline line.

When Derbyshire Stone Co's Staff place vehicles in the outwards sidings, a sprag is secured in the wheel of the leading vehicle at the lower end and a further sprag in the third or fourth vehicle.

If vehicles are left in the siding after a train is despatched to Wirksworth Station, the Guard or Shunter must place a sprag securely in the wheel of the first and third vehicles at the lower end.

The Sectional Appendix to the Working Timetable, 1980.

The solar panels at Idridgehay that were installed to power the level crossing lights, photographed on 24th July, 1982. *Author*	Idridgehay crossing and the line towards Wirksworth taken from the solar panel gantry on the same day. *Author*

Also in this period, 0-4-4Ts Nos. 1422 and 1423 were seen on the branch and it was from the 1900s onwards that the 0-4-4T locomotives supplanted the 'singles' and worked alongside 2-4-0s on the passenger turns. Nos. 1428 and 1429 have already been mentioned in connection with the fog-signalling trials of 1908, and these two engines saw regular service on the branch. No. 1429 was the locomotive driven by Sir Gilbert Inglefield at some time in the 1920s.

They were built in 1900 by Dübs & Co. (Works No. 3916 and 3917) and until renumbering in 1907 carried the numbers 2628 and 2629. Driving wheels were 5 ft 3½ in. and trailing wheels were 3 ft 0½ in. with 18 in. x 24 in. cylinders. Both were rebuilt in 1927 with Belpaire fireboxes and were motor-fitted. No. 1428 retained its number in LMS days until withdrawn in October 1946. No. 1429 survived until February 1953 having, by then, been renumbered by British Railways as 58090.

Both engines were probably based at Derby from their delivery date but were certainly allocated to that shed at the time of the fog-signalling trials. No 1429 was mentioned as the regular engine for the branch in the December 1947 issue of *Railway Observer*. It went on 'active service' to the Melbourne Military Railway in 1940 along with sister engine No. 1267.

In the late 1920s '4F' 0-6-0s were used and Nos. 4417, 4418 and 4419 are remembered in particular by Mr Sharpe as being very new with large tender numerals. It is probable, therefore, that these locomotives were being run-in. The Hazelwood accident of 1935, however, resulted in their withdrawal from passenger services and the 0-4-4Ts asserted themselves as the staple motive power. Nos. 1408 and 1409 have been recalled as making regular appearances after 1935 and I include here details of several locomotives of this type and the dates when they were allocated to Derby. Any of these may have been seen on the branch and I am grateful to Gerald Nicholls for providing the information from his records. An asterisk denotes motor-fitted engines.

1252*	1940-1948	withdrawn 1950 as 58035
1267	1938-1940	withdrawn 1944
1327	1933	withdrawn 1940
1338	c.1942-1944	withdrawn 1947
1361*	1940-1946	withdrawn 1946
1370	1942-1947	withdrawn 1953 as 58067
1375	1933-1940	withdrawn 1953 as 58070
1408	1933-1935	
	1938-1947	withdrawn 1947
1409	1935	withdrawn 1946
1418	1933-1935	withdrawn 1935
1421	1928-1933	withdrawn 1957 as 58084
1428*	1908-1936	withdrawn 1946
1429*	1908-1948	withdrawn 1953 as 58090

It is interesting that the association of this class with the branch was revived in 1953 when the SLS/MLS railtours were hauled by No. 58077 (formerly No. 1397).

Photographic evidence shows Stanier 2-6-2T No. 112 on the line with a four-coach train in July 1940 but it is not known whether this was a regular sight.

The next major change occurred in 1946 when the then new Ivatt 2-6-2Ts were used on the passenger trains. This was to be a short-lived liaison but Nos. 1205 and 1206 established themselves as the usual motive power. The final week of passenger services brought a surprise in that Johnson 4-4-0 No. 416 was used.

As for the coaching stock, it is unlikely that there was a fixed set for the branch. Mr Sharpe recalls several different arrangements usually of two carriages but strengthened to three or four on Saturdays (when Derby County played at home) and possibly on Fridays for Derby Market. The train usually comprised clerestory bogies in any permutation of non-lavatory and half-width lavatory stock (two adjacent compartments or two compartments with a lavatory between joined by a short corridor). Apart from the passenger milk vans, no six-wheeled stock is remembered.

In the 1930s, elliptical roof stock appeared, often one elliptical with one clerestory and later, two elliptical-roofed coaches. By this time, the formation had been standardised to two non-corridor coaches, usually a brake/third and a first/third composite. Mr R.C. Sinclair remembers these and notes that when strengthened to three coaches on match days this would often be a corridor train. He also recalls that in the war years, the down evening train (and probably others) ran with the brake leading.

Engines used on goods services are less easy to identify, and most references and recollections date from the time of the Grouping. From this time the locomotives used on such trains were invariably Deeley '3F' 0-6-0s or Fowler '4F' 0-6-0s.

Nos. 4585 and 4552 ('4F') have already been mentioned in connection with the oil burning trials and '4F' No. 4252 is known to have been used on stone trains with some regularity; No. 4419 was photographed on a mixed-goods train in 1933. On the penultimate day of passenger working '3F' No. 3496 was noted in Wirksworth yard.

In BR days, a 1951 sighting at Wirksworth was '3F' No. 43763 while a survey of locomotives seen on the Melbourne line between 1954 and 1959 revealed the following:

'3F' class 0-6-0:	43185	43318	43548	43578	
'4F' class 0-6-0:	43879	43881	43925	43987	44042
	44122	44142	44232	44310	44336
	44353	44404	44420	44428	44589

These were noted by Mr G.A. Yeomans and are included here as a guide to locomotives working in the area at this time.

An engine of a different class known to have worked on the branch was 2-6-2 class '2MT' No. 46443. Built at Crewe it entered service in February 1950 and spent 11½ years as station pilot at Derby whence it made forays to most of the local lines on both passenger and freight work. After withdrawal in 1967 (by which time it had moved away from the Derby area) it was bought for preservation by Richard Wilcox.

Mr Dave Foster has been able to furnish me with details of workings on the branch between 1963 and 1965. These were collected during a series of visits to Duffield and are included here, in some detail, so as to show the variety of motive power used during this interesting period.

Date	Engine Nos.	Class	Type	Remarks
6.8.63	44454	4F	0-6-0	limestone train
7.8.63	D8525, D8526	1	Bo-Bo	probably on test
13.8.63	M50426, M50704, M51902, M51648	dmu		probably on test
13.8.63	45274	5	4-6-0	limestone train
13.8.63	75064	4	4-6-0	limestone train
20.8.63	48426	8F	2-8-0	limestone train
25.10.63	90082	WD	2-8-0	limestone train
10.2.64	44888	5	4-6-0	limestone train
10.2.64	92113	9F	2-10-0	
7.4.64	90362	WD	2-8-0	limestone train
7.4.64	48286	8F	2-8-0	empties
20.5.64	48331	8F	2-8-0	limestone train
20.5.64	44690	5	4-6-0	empties
20.5.64	D5246, D5256	2	Bo-Bo	limestone train (a regular pairing on the branch)
29.5.64	90682	WD	2-8-0	
21.7.64	90357	WD	2-8-0	limestone train
28.7.64	48191	8F	2-8-0	limestone train
21.8.64	48017	8F	2-8-0	limestone train
29.10.64	48630	8F	2-8-0	limestone train
29.10.64	44076	4F	0-6-0	limestone train
27.2.65	92231	9F	2-10-0	limestone train
27.2.65	D5241	2	Bo-Bo	limestone train
13.3.65	48698	8F	2-8-0	limestone train
13.3.65	92025	9F	2-10-0	empties/limestone train
28.3.65	D1777, D1795, D1774	4	Co-Co	light engines, painted orange (primer)
13.4.65	78000	2	2-6-0	empties
20.4.65	48128	8F	2-8-0	limestone train
20.4.65	D5247	2	Bo-Bo	limestone train
20.4.65	48538	8F	2-8-0	empties/limestone train
21.4.65	48350	8F	2-8-0	limestone train
21.4.65	90241	WD	2-8-0	limestone train
26.4.65	48359	8F	2-8-0	limestone train
26.4.65	48551	8F	2-8-0	limestone train
29.4.65	48000	8F	2-8-0	limestone train
29.4.65	48604	8F	2-8-0	limestone train
19.5.65	48167	8F	2-8-0	limestone train
19.5.65	48270	8F	2-8-0	limestone train
19.5.65	D7571	2	Bo-Bo	limestone train
26.5.65	D5246	2	Bo-Bo	limestone train
1.6.65	48370	8F	2-8-0	limestone train
14.7.65	D7548	2	Bo-Bo	limestone train
14.7.65	D5255	2	Bo-Bo	limestone train
19.7.65	45346	5	4-6-0	breakdown train to Wirksworth

As might be expected, most of these were local engines from Derby, Toton or Westhouses but, amongst others, Aintree, Newton Heath, Normanton, Rose Grove and Speke Junction are represented in this list. It is known that, around this time, all engines of a power classification greater than class '5' were banned

Proof, if it were needed, that '8Fs' did find their way to Wirksworth despite a theoretical ban on anything above class '5' using the branch. Stanier 2-8-0 No. 48003 in the yard on 1st September, 1965. *H.N. James*

from the branch (with the exception of the Horwich '6P5F' 2-6-0s). In addition, the following were also prohibited:

Stanier 3-cylinder 2-6-4T	NLR class '2F' 0-6-0T
MR Compound 4-4-0	BR Standard class '4' 4-6-0
LT&SR class '3P' 4-4-2T	

In the light of this, some of the entries in Mr Foster's list might seem surprising, but his observations are corroborated by sightings reported by others at the time.

In 1978, maximum loads on the branch were calculated for the following locomotives:

Classes: 20, 24, 25, 31, 37, 40, 44, 45, 46, 47, 50, 2 x 20, 2 x 25 (working in multiple)

Though this does not indicate locomotives that actually worked on the line, it does give an idea of the types of locomotive that could be called upon to haul limestone trains from Wirksworth. The commonest sight in the branch's final years were two class '20s' or '25s' in multiple.

Traffic to Purfleet was undertaken by a company train owned by Tarmac, and provided cement works with their necessary supplies of limestone. Another Tarmac train was used to transport stone to the company's terminal at Hayes and Harlington.

The Lloyd's Siding trains were typically made up of forty 21 ton iron-ore hoppers. Two or three of these sets would be working almost continuously on the merry-go-round principle and were hauled by class '20s' and '25s' working in multiple.

Appendix One

Official Milepost Mileages

	m.	ch.
Duffield Junction	133	0
Duffield Station	133	08
Hazelwood Station	134	77
Shottle Station	136	43
Idridgehay Station	138	05
Idridgehay Signal Box	138	07
Gorsey Bank Level Crossing	140	79
Wirksworth Signal Box	141	35
Wirksworth Station	141	37
Incline Junction	141	39
End of Branch	141	58
Incline Junction	141	39
Wirksworth Lime and Stone Siding	141	54
Bowne and Shaw Stone Siding	141	76
Junction with C&HPR	142	26

And so to the future . . . on 3rd June, 2002, the cutting of the first sod at Wirksworth was re-enacted using the original silver spade and a replica wheelbarrow. Seen here is Neil Ferguson-Lee, a director of WyvernRail (playing the part of Mrs Price Wood) and Cllr Charles Cutting, Chair of Derbyshire County Council, using his left foot to draw attention to the sod.   *Author*

Appendix Two

Traffic and Expenses at Stations 1872 to 1922

	Year	No. of passengers booked	Coal, Coke & Limestone (in and out) (tons)	Mineral Class (in and out) (tons)	Expenses of Station (£)
Duffield	1872	49,658	3,486	2,088	292
	1882	58,648	3,762	933	394
	1892	61,539	7,082	1,577	589
	1893	64,475	6,180	3,556	648
	1902	80,694	5,591	5,926	1,422
	1912	79,979	6,345	6,426	1,422
	1922	66,786	4,281	4,168	3,418
Hazelwood	1872	5,037	1,047	31	64
	1882	6,616	1,517	133	72
	1892	6,118	1,748	233	92
	1893	6,011	1,496	1,271	88
	1902	7,278	2,279	2,806	100
	1912	6,347	2,955	2,983	147
	1922	5,983	3,212	2,636	508
Shottle	1872	6,563	1,436	10	64
	1882	7,799	1,744	356	91
	1892	8,579	2,972	70	87
	1893	8,804	2,365	1,335	88
	1902	10,430	2,838	4,085	104
	1912	10,640	3,140	4,820	104
	1922	11,458	1,341	5,158	367
Idridgehay	1872	9,398	1,807	46	64
	1882	10,586	1,588	42	81
	1892	12,362	1,491	78	139
	1893	12,079	1,402	578	171
	1902	11,254	1,821	1,359	183
	1912	10,481	1,960	2,256	198
	1922	12,286	1,341	1,702	658
Wirksworth	1872	17,619	44,140	715	302
	1882	18,495	131,346	2,772	406
	1892	20,837	115,682	3,205	509
	1893	20,447	115,150	3,779	645
	1902	23,631	123,902	4,506	775
	1912	20,985	120,926	3,674	912
	1922	25,301	84,630	3,899	2,192

Figures are given at 10 year intervals except for 1892/3. These successive years' figures are given to show the meteoric and inexplicable rise in the number of tons of minerals handled. If this was due to a major programme of building in the valley, there should be a corresponding leap in passenger figures but there is not. If it indicates a redefinition of the classification 'mineral', the figure for Wirksworth would be expected to increase in line with the other stations but it does not. This begs the question 'What did happen between 1892 and 1893?' Notice also a leap in the expenses at the stations at the end of this period. Although not immediately apparent from this set of abridged figures, this sudden rise actually occurs at the end of World War I, when returning soldiers came back to work on the line. Also, railwaymen's wages had risen during the war, and the addition of two or three men at each of the stations would have significantly increased the annual expenses for them.

Appendix Three

Details of Locomotives used at Bowne & Shaw's Quarry

Manning, Wardle (class 'B') 0-4-0ST
Outside cylinders: 6 in. x 12 in.
Wheelbase: 4 ft 7 in.
Boiler length: 6 ft 9 in.
Heating Surfaces Tubes: 82 sq. ft
          Firebox: 18 sq. ft
Grate Area: 3 sq. ft

Works No. 99 Built 1863
Driving wheels: 2 ft 6 in.
Boiler diameter: 1 ft 11 in.
Tank capacity: 200 gallons

Total: 100 sq. ft

Original owners: G. Dawes, Milton Ironworks, Yorks. (numbered and named No. 5 *Milton*).

Hudswell, Clarke 0-4-0ST
Ordered by Bowne & Shaw on 22nd June, 1891
Ex-works: 5th October, 1891
Outside cylinders: 9 in. x 15 in.

Works No. 357

Approximate cost: £625
Driving wheels: 2 ft 6 in.

Hudswell, Clarke 0-4-0ST
Ordered by Bowne & Shaw on 5th February, 1916
Ex-works: 22nd January, 1917
Built to a standard design, named *Gertrude* and painted green.
Outside cylinders: 9 in. x 15 in.
Weight: 10 tons 2 cwt 1 qtr

Works No. 1215

Approximate cost: £875

Driving wheels: 2 ft 6½ in.

Transferred to Harston Quarries (Stewart & Lloyds) in January 1950 where it became No. 1.
Scrapped: September 1953.

Hudswell, Clarke 0-4-0ST
Ordered by Bowne & Shaw on 28th July, 1927.
Ex-works: 14th October, 1927
Built to a standard design and painted black with red lining.
Outside cylinders: 9 in. x 15 in.
Weight: 10 tons 15 cwt

Works No. 1605

Approximate cost: £1,025

Driving wheels: 2 ft 9½ in.

Transferred to Harston Quarries (Stewart & Lloyds) in April 1948 where it became No. 2.
Scrapped: 1952.

Black, Hawthorn & Co., Gateshead, 0-4-0ST
Built 1873 for Walter Scott (contractor) and named *Wellington*
Outside cylinders, bore: 12 in.

Works No. 266

Working pressure: 140 psi.

Rebuilt at Holwell, 11/1894, 11/1901, 1/1912 and 12/1934-2/1935.
Transferred from Harlaxton Ironstone Mines, Lincolnshire (Stewart and Lloyds) in August 1946 as *Holwell No. 3*. Sold to Stephenson & Hawthorne Locomotive Trust (Tanfield Railway) for preservation in November 1977, where it was restored as *Wellington*. ●

Peckett and Sons 0-4-0ST
Built 1912 to a standard design for James Pain Ltd, Uppingham Ironstone Quarry
Outside Cylinders, bore: 12 in.

Works No. 1257

Working Pressure: 160 psi

Weight: 32 tons
Rebuilt 6/1931-1/1932 at Holwell. Transferred from Market Overton Quarries, Rutland (Stewart & Lloyds) via Holwell Works in September 1947 as *Uppingham*. Sold for preservation at the Midland Railway Trust, Butterley, 1974. At Market Overton 1979, and later to Rutland Railway Museum, Cottesmore.

In its centenary year, 1973, *Holwell No. 3* was restored, and appeared in steam in the Middlepeak loading area during the Well Dressing festival in the spring of that year.   *Dave Clark*

Baguley (Burton-upon-Trent)   0-4-0 Diesel mechanical
Works No. 3357   *Built:* 1952
Weight: 20 tons   *Engine:* Paxman Ricardo
Power: 150 hp   Painted green
Purchased from Ind Coope & Allsopp, Burton-upon-Trent as their No. 1 in March 1970.
Sold 1990, and preserved at Devon Railway Centre as No. 1 *Boris.*

F.C. Hibberd   4-wheel Diesel mechanical ('Simplex' design)
Works No. 1891   Named *Derbyshire Stone*
Built: 1934   Painted unlined green
New to Calico Printers Association, Whaley Bridge. Sold 1954 to Derbyshire Stone as their
No. 2 and used at Cawdor Quarry, Matlock. To Hopton Wood Stone Firms, Middleton in
1963. Transferred to Caldon Low Quarry, 1967. To Middlepeak in April 1970. Sold
privately in 1993 and taken to Bridgnorth.   *e H n3 c wn7 6R*

Baguley (Burton-upon-Trent)   0-4-0 Diesel mechanical
Works No. 3227   *Built:* 1951
Weight: 20 tons   *Engine:* Paxman Ricardo
Power: 150 hp   Painted green
New to Ind Coope & Allsopp, Burton-upon-Trent as their No. 2 (incorporated some parts
of HL3632). Used at Romford Brewery 1951-55, then to Burton. To Cawdor Quarry, March
1970. To Wirksworth after 1970. Dismantled (unknown date and location) but some parts
to Devon Railway Centre.

Thomas Hill, Rolls 'Steelman'   0-6-0 Diesel mechanical
Works No. 10274   *Built:* 1968
Weight: 52 tons   *Engine:* Rolls-Royce
Power: 450 hp   Painted green
New to Stewart & Lloyds (later British Steel), Corby in January 1969 as their No. 19 (later
No. 38). To Wirksworth in October 1980.

Narrow Gauge Locomotives at Middlepeak Quarry

Ruston & Hornsby S&LM No. 5   4-wheel Diesel mechanical
Works No. 218037   *Built:* February 1943
Power: 33/40 hp   *Engine:* Ruston 3RVO
Not known if new to Wirksworth. Sold to Bórd na Móna, Ireland in 1960 and used at
Littleton, Co. Tipperary as LM177. Refitted with a Gardner 4TW engine.

Ruston & Hornsby   4-wheel Diesel mechanical
Works No. 200494   *Built:* December 1940
Power: 23/30 hp
New to Wellingborough Iron Co. as their No. 5. At Wellingborough it ran on a 2 ft 4 in.
gauge line and worked the Finedon No. 1 mine; it had no cab. Transferred to Bowne &
Shaw in June 1947.

Stored out of use, and photographed in December 1980, are Baguley Ind Coope No. 2 and the Hibberd 'Simplex'. It is unlikely that either of these locomotives was used again, and indeed, it is thought that the Baguley was used very sparingly after its arrival, possibly having been bought for spares.   *R.G. Cash*

Internal rail traffic at Middlepeak was latterly handled by this 0-6-0 Rolls 'Steelman', seen in the exchange sidings on 24th February, 1982.   *Author*

Acknowledgements

So many people have helped with this book that to name them all would fill many pages. To those who have provided photographs, I offer my sincere thanks. They are all named in the preceding pages, so I shall not record their names here. However, I should like to thank them also for the information which they often gave freely in addition to their photographs. To the following who gave help, advice, moral support and valuable material other than the photographic kind I shall always be grateful. If I have missed anyone, my thanks conveyed personally to you at the time are made no less sincere for my omitting you from this list now.

G.J. Aston	Robert Frank	James Morley
Eric Baker	Albert Goodwin	Gerald Nicholls
John Britton	John Hall	Henry Pearce
Reginald Brown	Dave Harris	Brian Radford
Jack Burrell	Roger Holbrook	Edgar Rogers
George Cash	Tony Holmes	R.C. Sinclair
Mike Christiansen	Bill Hudson	Charles Vier
Dave Clark	Pat Larkham	Glynn Waite
Donald Clowes	Nicholas Law	Derek Walker
Chris Crofts	John Marsland	Nick Wheat
George Dow	John Miller	Peter Witts
Neil Ferguson-Lee	Edward Millward	Kathleen Winson
Dave Foster	Tim Moore	

Also my thanks go to the staffs of the Derbyshire County Record Office, Matlock; Derbyshire County Library, Matlock and Derby; The Derby Evening Telegraph; and The National Archives, Kew. Likewise to Ian Kennedy at The Oakwood Press for allowing me free reign to expand on the first edition considerably, and finally to my family who over many, many years have lived as much with Wirksworth as with me.

Bibliography

British Locomotive Catalogue 1825-1923, Bertram Baxter (Moorland Publishing)
The Crich Mineral Railways, 'Dowie' (Tramway Publications)
The Cromford and High Peak Railway, John Marshall (David & Charles)
The Cromford and High Peak Railway, A. Rimmer (Oakwood Press)
Duffield in Appletree, G. Hickling
Forgotten Railways of the East Midlands, P. Howard Anderson (David & Charles)
Hazelwood, Eleanor Mary West
Hazelwood in the Forest of Duffield, Herbert Swift
History of Shottle, Mary Fletcher
Railways in the Peak District, Nicholson and Barnes (Dalesman)
Regional History of Railways of Great Britain Vol. 9 (East Midlands), Robin Leleux (David & Charles)
The Wirksworth Line, Editor: Christopher Charlton (Cromford Church Restoration Committee and The Arkwright Society)
The Wirksworth and Ripley Branches, Laurence Knighton (Midland Railway Society)
Trains Illustrated
Railway Magazine
Railway Observer

Index